# BACKTRACKING
## SPEEDWAY NOSTALGIA FOR FANS OF THE 70s, 80s AND 90s

## VOLUME 1

### Edited by TONY McDONALD

First published in November 2016 by
**Retro Speedway**
**Tel: 01708 734 502**
**www.retro-speedway.com**

Copyright Retro Speedway

All rights reserved.
Without limiting the rights under copyright reserved above, no part of this publication may be reproduced, stored in or introduced into retrieval system, or transmitted, in any form or by any means (electronic, mechanical, photocopying, recording or otherwise) without the prior written permission of the copyright owner of this book.

Designed by Jan Watts
Cover design: William Clayton

Printed by Premier Print Group (London)
Distributed by Retro Speedway
103 Douglas Road, Hornchurch, Essex, RM11 1AW, England
Distribution email: subs@retro-speedway.com

ISBN 978-0-9927427-2-0

# BACKTRACKING

## SPEEDWAY NOSTALGIA FOR FANS OF THE 70s, 80s AND 90s

### VOLUME 1

### Edited by TONY McDONALD

# Acknowledgements

RETRO SPEEDWAY would like to thank the following writers for their editorial contributions: Martin Neal, Rob Peasley, Doug Nicolson, Andrew Skeels and Rob McCaffery.

Most of the photographs in this book are reproduced with the kind permission of John Somerville, who proudly owns by far the largest collection of speedway images in the world. We would encourage to view it online by visiting the John Somerville Collection website at www.skidmarks1928.com

Sadly, a couple of notable doyen photographers who have contributed to this book, and whose many years' dedication to the sport forms part of John's vast collection, are no longer with us. However, we would wish to posthumously thank the late Alf Weedon and Wright Wood, while also crediting their fellow 'snappers' Ken Carpenter, John Hipkiss, Doug Booth, Tony Webb, Steve Magro, Don Ringrow, Mike Patrick and Trevor Meeks.

Our thanks also to designers Jan Watts and William Clayton, as well as our good friends at *Speedway Star,* Richard Clark, Andrew Skeels and Dave Fairbrother.

Cover photographs
Front (clockwise): Anders Michanek (Reading) leading Neil Street (Newport); Ivan Mauger (Belle Vue); Gary Havelock (Bradford); and Shawn Moran (Sheffield).
Back: Christer Lofqvist (Poole).

Dear Alan & Jean

Best wishes
Susie & Tony
Mac

X

# Contents

# Introduction

**B**ACKTRACK **magazine was first published in March 2004 at the Speedway & Grass-track Show in Coventry, where Retro Speedway – our small independent publishing company that Susie and I now run from home – took a stand to promote the launch.**

Since then, and at the time of going to press with this book, we have so far produced 76 issues of the bi-monthly magazine, as well as 30-plus DVDs and numerous other books that all celebrate speedway's last golden era, the 1970s and 80s.

They say 'never look back' but that's precisely what we do. We firmly believe that speedway, like so many other things in our everyday lives, was somehow better 'back in the day'. Even if we could be accused of viewing the past through rose-tinted spectacles, thankfully thousands of our like-minded customers share our passion.

British speedway was in a much healthier, vibrant state in the 70s and 80s than it is today, at the end of 2016, as we watch in dismay and with a sense of foreboding as the sport lurches from one crisis to another.

In the 70s and 80s, generally speaking, the racing was consistently more exciting on well prepared tracks conducive to overtaking. Crowds were certainly much bigger, lucrative sponsors more plentiful and the national media took our sport seriously.

There were a lot more characters around 30-45 years ago, in the pre-PC age (and we don't mean Peter Collins!), when colourful riders had big personalities, were happy to mingle freely with supporters over a few pints in the bar and rode for entrepreneurial full-time promoters who knew how to put on a show.

OK, so let's not pretend that everything in speedway's past was great and trouble-free, nor that there were much less counter-attractions vying for our time and money. Far from it. The sport's history is littered with embarrassing cock-ups, controversies and too many moments and examples of rule-bending that are best forgotten. Worst of all, riders' safety standards were comparatively very poor – it's one aspect we can all agree has definitely changed for the better.

But compared to the era we cover, the sport in Britain is now on its knees and slowly sinking deeper into the mire.

1 Double World Champion Bruce Penhall dominated the cover of our first edition, in March 2004. In later years the American superstar contacted Retro Speedway asking to become a regular Backtrack columnist.
2 Editor Tony Mac travelled to a remote small island in Sweden for an in-depth interview with 1974 World Champ Anders Michanek.
3 Although at first reluctant to re-visit his past glories, the great Ole Olsen eventually invited Backtrack into his home in Denmark for a compelling exclusive interview in 2009 that ran over two issues.
4 The ultra popular Kelly Moran gave his last-ever interview to Backtrack shortly before his sad death in April 2010.

So why not wallow blissfully in nostalgia and take comfort from re-visiting a much happier, more successful period in speedway history?

That's what *Backtrack* is all about. Unashamedly, it's what we do. And I love it.

I am very fortunate to be in the privileged position of being able to sit down with the riders and promoters of yesteryear, some who were my schoolboy heroes and most of whom I had first encountered in my 14 years editing *Speedway Mail,* and listen to their captivating stories from a bygone age. Also, to find out what they have been up to since leaving their racing days behind and what they are doing now.

Forty years on from his greatest day in speedway, Peter Collins gave Backtrack another exclusive interview for issue 76, in which we also looked back in detail at his memorable 1976 World Championship triumph and that sizzling summer as a whole.

In the last 14 years my colleagues and I have had the pleasure of interviewing hundreds of ex-riders and, thanks to Retro Speedway, their candid opinions and memories are preserved in print or on film. In almost all cases, they are only too pleased to talk and warmly welcome the opportunity to reminisce. And because what they achieved and experienced happened many years ago, they can be refreshingly forthright in expressing their views.

I'm lucky, too, to have the backing and support of contributors who are or have become personal friends and I thank them for their output. Our team of writers, Martin Neal, Rob Peasley, Andrew Skeels (*Speedway Star's* deputy editor), Doug Nicolson, respected former promoter Martin Rogers, Richard Bott, and not forgetting our man in the Czech Republic Vitek Formanek, all know their stuff.

And thanks to the cooperation of John Somerville, who owns the biggest and best collection of speedway photographs on the planet and who seems to spend his every waking hour chained to his scanner at home in Bonnie Scotland, we have the greatest images to complement the words.

The commitment of those mentioned is certainly not driven by money – the late, great Malcolm Simmons and John Berry, the best promoter of his time, two regular former columnists and, sadly, both no longer with us, never wanted a penny for their efforts. JB and Simmo are sadly missed but their legacy lives on, through the pages of *Backtrack* and now *Backtracking*.

With most back issues of the magazine now having sold out, we thought it would be a good idea to encapsulate the best of *Backtrack* by reproducing and re-presenting edited versions of the best interviews and features in a series of new books, along with many previously unseen photos. We have a great deal of content to share for your enjoyment (Volume 2 is about to go to print as I write), featuring familiar ex-world champions and other superstars to lesser lights and former juniors who never quite made it. I hope our shared passion for speedway's past comes across in this first volume of *Backtracking* and that you will enjoy joining us on our continual nostalgic journey . . .

*Tony Mac*
*November, 2016*

# 50 MAGICAL MOMENTS OF THE 70s AND 80s

To commemorate our 50th issue we took a chronological look back at British speedway's most magical moments of the *Backtrack* era . . .

**1** The 70s decade dawned with the news that Wembley Lions were returning after an absence from league racing of 13 years.

**2** Ivan Mauger became the first to win three back-to-back World Finals when he broke down East European barriers and overcame communist psychological warfare to win with an emphatic 15 points at Wroclaw in 1970. He still rates this as the toughest of all his six World Championship wins.

**3** The great Ove Fundin capped his last season in the BL by inspiring Sweden to victory in the 1970 World Team Cup Final at Wembley. Pity a section of the crowd had to boo him.

**4** From 1971 the sport entered millions of new homes when ITV introduced meeting highlights from Test matches and other international events as part of their Saturday afternoon *World of Sport* show. After the wrestling, cue studio presenter Dickie Davies handing over to Dave Lanning with his first verbal utterings of 'ducks and drakes', 'high, wide and handsome' and all his other well-worn clichés that we came to love throughout the 70s.

On his way to a record third consecutive world title, Ivan Mauger edges ahead of Jan Mucha and Gennady Kurilenko at the first turn, with his old pal Barry Briggs momentarily squeezed out in Heat 3 of the 1970 World Final.

**5** World Cup Willie had been England's lucky mascot during the 1966 World Cup but the name took on a whole new meaning after Wroclaw '71, when Leicester's Ray Wilson etched his name in speedway folklore by becoming the first Brit to score a maximum in the World Team Cup Final.

**6** League championship wins are always special, but there was something even more meaningful about Eastbourne winning the second division in 1971. Eagles were brimming with a team of home-grown youngsters – dubbed the "Kamikaze Kids" – assembled by Dave Lanning and backed up by veteran rider Reg Trott. Their success and the manner in which it was achieved symbolised what BL2 was originally all about.

**7** Opening meetings traditionally draw large crowds, but there has been little to compare with the 13,000-plus that packed into Foxhall Stadium on Good Friday, 1972, to see Ipswich meet Hackney and herald the start of a golden era for the Witches.

**8** Belle Vue were the powerhouse force of the early 70s and no-one was surprised when the Aces made it a hat-trick of BL first division title wins at the end of 1972.

**9** The 1973 Daily Mirror International Tournament – the Speedway World Cup in all but name – still ranks as one of the best innovations ever conceived by the BSPA. The top seven teams in the world contesting 23 qualifying matches spread over 18 days at 17 different BL1 tracks, leading to semi-finals and a Wembley finale in front of a 30,000-plus crowd. Great stuff.

**10** Who could ever forget the dramatic climax of the aforementioned tournament, when Peter Collins faced Anders Michanek in a sudden-death run-off after England and Sweden had drawn 39-39 at the end of 13 races. Did PC fall or was he pushed? The debate continues.

**11** Another seminal moment at Wembley, also in 1973. After years of brilliant

Eastbourne's Division Two championship-winning team of 1971 entertained enthusiastic Sunday afternoon crowds at Arlington. Standing, left to right: Laurie Sims, Malcolm Ballard, Dave Kennett, Roger Johns, Mac Woolford. Kneeling: Reg Trott, Gordon Kennett. In the background, promoter Dave Lanning making the introductions.

9

service from colonial stars such as Barry Briggs and Ivan Mauger, who had led Great Britain with distinction in the World Team Cup, the BSPA decided the time was right to dispense with these Kiwi giants (Ronnie Moore was reserve in 1971 and '72) and field an all-English side in the final for the first time. The Lions were now roaring.

**12** Part two of the Collins v Michanek duel was even more enthralling, as a huge crowd at Belle Vue watched in awe as they swapped positions on each lap until the Aces' idol just snatched victory from Reading's super Swede to decide the 1973 BL1 KO Cup Final. Absolutely epic. Shame TV cameras weren't there to capture the magic.

**13** March 1974 and the British League welcomed back a legend when Barry Briggs rejoined his first club, Wimbledon. And to coincide with this major coup for the Dons, on the 27th of the month Briggo became the subject of the hugely popular *This is Your Life* show (ITV's most viewed programme that year with an audience of between 12-13 million). Presenter Eamonn Andrews, disguised as a mechanic in overalls, stunned an unsuspecting BB when he unveiled his Big Red Book during pre-season practice at Plough Lane.

**14** At 29 years of age and with a smashed up arm following his bad crash at Newport the previous year, Halifax captain Eric Boocock emerged as the shock winner of the British Final at Coventry.

**15** Booey made history on Sunday, July 14, 1974, by becoming the first rider to be awarded a testimonial meeting in recognition of 10 years' service to one club. They reckon it was the biggest crowd ever seen for a speedway meeting at The Shay.

**16** Another sure sign that England possessed a World Champion in the making came at Wembley in August 1974, when Peter Collins again showed his liking for the Empire Stadium by beating Ole Olsen and Ivan Mauger in a run-off to win the European Final.

**17** To prove that their 1973 triumph had been no fluke or due to home advantage, England (the GB had been dropped by now) went to Katowice, Poland in 1974 and retained the WTC in some style, with Peter Collins and John Louis both going unbeaten. Dave Jessup, who won an epic Heat 10, and Malcolm Simmons completed the victorious quartet.

**18** A bitterly cold and snowy Good Friday morning at King's Lynn on March 28, 1975 became decidedly warmer when a 16-year-old stick insect of a wonderkid called Michael Lee stepped into the limelight for the first time and scored nine points from four rides on his official debut for the Stars against Leicester, including the notable scalp of England skipper Ray Wilson.

**19** Doubling-up between King's Lynn and Boston, young Lee also got an early taste of history in 1975 when the Barracudas became the first second division team to beat top flight opposition in the new Inter-League KO Cup, by seeing off Hackney in the first round.

# Superb Collins the new world speedway king

From KEIR RADNEDGE
in Katowice

PETER COLLINS yesterday put Britain back on top of the speedway world after 14 years when he scorched to victory in the world final in Katowice before a 100,000 crowd.

The 22-year-old Belle Vue flier returned three years after his first world final to break the track record and brilliantly demonstrate what a worthy successor he should prove to Denmark's Ole Olsen.

To add even more lustre to the evening, Poole and England captain Malcolm Simmons, the British champion, finished second—the first time Britain have done so well since 1953. Newport's Australian, Phil Crump, was third.

The last Briton to win this

Malcolm Simmons (left) and Peter Collins after their triumph in Katowice *Daily Mail*

When speedway was big news in the national press. How the Daily Mail and its reporter Keir Radnedge covered the 1976 World Final. Below: Peter Collins in 2016, aboard the Weslake he rode to victory at Katowice 40 years earlier. This bike is on display at the Manchester Museum of Science and Industry.

11

**20** There was added significance to John Louis' superb maximum to win the 1975 British Final at Brandon. It also put the new four-valve Weslake engine on the world speedway map. The shape of things to come.

**21** Ipswich star Louis was in the England team that completed a hat-trick of WTC victories in the 1975 final in Germany. Peter Collins, Malcolm Simmons and Martin Ashby also flew the cross of St George flag with distinction at Norden.

**22** Newcastle dominated the 1976 National League, completing a league and KO Cup double, while their top rider Joe Owen won the NLRC. But Diamonds' glory trail began in that sweltering summer at King's Lynn, where they snatched the inaugural NL Fours title – very apt, too, as it was Newcastle promoter Ian Thomas who conceived the idea of the tournament that endures to this day.

**23** Still in the second tier, Workington have had little to shout about through the years but Comets deserved all the plaudits for consecutive home wins over senior league giants Ipswich and their East Anglian rivals Kings' Lynn in the 1976 ILKOC.

**24** There were two magic moments for Australia in '76. Their shock elimination of England in the WTC qualifier at Ipswich in May was a bigger achievement than their more comfortable success over Poland, Sweden and USSR in the September final at White City.

**25** After 14 years, the wait was finally over. September 5, 1976 and England ruled the world with Peter Collins and Malcolm Simmons standing proud, one and two, on the rostrum at the Katowice World Final. Both mounted on the English Weslake, this was probably the most magical moment of this era.

The triumphant Ipswich squad and management that won the British League and KO Cup double in 1976. Standing, John Berry (promoter), Mike Lanham, Tony Davey, Billy Sanders, Kevin Jolly, Dave Gooderham, Ron Bagley (team manager). Kneeling: Ted Howgego, Andy Hines, Colin Cook. On bike: John Louis.

British speedway celebrated its 50th birthday in 1978. The season curtain-raiser took place at Hackney, where England captains past and present, Jack Parker and Malcolm Simmons, and Johnnie Hoskins took centre stage.

**26** Ipswich shed their country cousins tag by winning their first BL title in 1975 but went one better in 1976, when they achieved the league and KO Cup double. Promoter John Berry and shrewd team manager Ron Bagley shunned the use of guests, moulded together a hungry team of home-grown riders and reaped their just reward.

**27** There was not quite to be a repeat of Peter Collins' World Championship success at Gothenburg in 1977 but his heroics in finishing runner-up to Ivan Mauger with a broken leg and in the most appalling track conditions at Ullevi was a massive achievement under the circumstances. Mike Lee's fourth place at the age of 18 didn't deserve to be overshadowed, though.

**28** England bounced back from their shock World Team Cup elimination in 1976 by making it four WTC wins in five years with another masterly display at Wroclaw in 1977.

**29** King's Lynn grabbed some long overdue limelight in East Anglia as the '77 season came to an end. Reading had one hand on the KO Cup before Mike Lee snatched victory with a superb last bend pass on the final bend of the second leg at Saddlebow Road.

**30** British speedway began its Golden Jubilee season of 1978 with a special individual meeting at Hackney one chilly Sunday in February. The highlight was post-war great Jack Parker riding a modern Weslake in a match-race against current England skipper Malcolm Simmons, mounted on a vintage Douglas.

England's 1980 grand slam winners (minus reserve John Davis) were joined by six times World Champion Ivan Mauger when they visited the ACU to collect their commemorative medals. Left to right: Eric Boocock (joint-team manager), Dave Jessup, Peter Collins, Ivan, Michael Lee, Chris Morton, Ian Thomas (joint-team manager).

**31** When GB/England's domination of the WTC finally came to an end at Landshut, Germany in 1978, their conquerors were Ole Olsen's determined Danes. The 'disaster' headlines that greeted this shock defeat were soon made to look way off the mark, however, as Denmark continued to assert a grip that would become a stranglehold on all the sport's major honours as the 80s unravelled.

**32** How appropriate for the sport's great-grandfather Johnnie S. Hoskins should be awarded the MBE in British speedway's Golden Jubilee year . . . and that his Canterbury Crusaders should cap a memorable year for the sport's greatest showman by winning the 1978 National League.

**33** Spearheaded by Ivan Mauger and with Barry Briggs cajoling and advising from the pits, New Zealand's top riders rode out of

their skins to stun England's finest and win the WTC for the first time at White City in 1979. Having also beaten the USA twice en route to London, no-one could say the Kiwis' success was a fluke or undeserved.

**34** If Mauger took great pleasure from masterminding his country's WTC triumph, the maestro was even more elated to win his sixth individual world title at Katowice in 1979, at the age of 39.

**35** The end of '79 was a great time for veteran campaigners turning back the clock. John Louis, 38, took Bruce Penhall to the brink to clinch the BLRC at Belle Vue in one of the greatest races ever witnessed at Hyde Road.

**36** The only major disappointment for Mauger in '79 was the failure of his Hull team to win the BL championship for the first time. Vikings lost a thrilling October decider at Coventry, who retained the title in front of a crowd of a bumper 20,000-plus crowd at Brandon.

**37** The influx of fun-loving Californians brought much colour and entertainment to the European scene in the late 70s and 80s and never was their skill and showmanship more sharply defined than in the historic England v USA Test series in 1980. The epic 54-54 draw to open the series still rates as one of the best matches ever witnessed at Wimbledon or anywhere else.

**38** In a repeat of '76, Englishmen claimed the top two places in the 1980 World Final at Gothenburg, where Michael Lee and Dave Jessup made it a King's Lynn one-two.

**39** Lee and Jessup were soon joined by Peter Collins, Chris Morton and John Davis in victory at the 1980 WTC final in Wroclaw. With DJ and PC having also annexed the World Pairs, Poland saw the completion of an unprecedented England grand slam for the team and co-managers Ian Thomas and Eric Boocock.

**40** Berwick didn't often feature among the honours, but they deserved great credit for beating Middlesbrough in the 1980 NL KO Cup Final – and they did it the hard way. Homeless after being evicted from Shielfield Park, Bandits had to ride all their matches away. The second leg of the final at Newcastle went down to the last heat before the border club finally won its first major title having been losing cup finalists four times.

**41** How good was the 1981 World Final? The best ever according to many who were there. Maybe. Maybe not. But what set it apart from most others was champion Bruce Penhall's two thrilling on-the-line wins over Ole Olsen and Tommy Knudsen on his way to his

Race for the line . . . Bruce Penhall (outside) just pipped Tommy Knudsen to this enthralling Heat 14 win that effectively decided the 1981 World Final at Wembley.

Who said he was just a gater? Erik Gundersen powering around Americans Shawn Moran (inside) and Lance King on the pits turn at Bradford on his way to the world title in 1985.

Hyde Road was a great loss to the sport when it closed at the end of the 1987 season. But at least the famous Aces were re-housed just up the road in the following spring.

first world crown. The two Danes had to settle for the silver and bronze medals.

**42** The 1982 WTC Final was another all-American hero show as USA captured the title for the first time. But this was a much more sombre occasion. With would-be hosts England already out of the running, the Californians fulfilled their pledge to win in honour of fellow countryman Denny Pyeatt, who had been killed riding for Reading at Hackney earlier in the season.

**43** There were echoes of PC's Ullevi heroics in '77 as his big rival Kenny Carter hobbled around the Coventry pits on crutches, desperate to protect his broken leg, before heroically winning the 1984 British Final despite dodgy track conditions that almost led to a walk-out.

**44** England didn't enjoy much success in the 80s but the day two Partington schoolboy pals and Belle Vue Aces, Peter Collins and Chris Morton, joined forces at Lonigo, Italy to win the 1984 World Pairs Final was a very special moment for both of them.

**45** Bradford might not have been Wembley in terms of aura and prestige, but the racing served up at the 1985 World Final was as good as any final produced during this decade. And renowned trapper Erik Gundersen won his second title the hard way, passing two Americans in one race.

**46** Every now and again, a special young talent emerges who you just know is going to be a big star. And so it proved when 16-year-old reserve Gary Havelock stepped up to lead Middlesbrough to victory in the 1986 NL Fours Finals at Peterborough.

**47** After the sad closure of Hyde Road at the end of 1987, one of the sport's great institutions was re-born the following March as

Barry Thomas in action at Hackney in 1973.

Belle Vue re-located to their new home in the greyhound stadium at Kirky Lane.

**48** As nostalgia junkies, we couldn't let this journey through time pass without mention of the Barry Briggs-inspired Golden Greats series that reunited so many old favourites on the track at Coventry in 1988.

**49** Hackney idol Barry Thomas became the first rider to receive two testimonials in 1989, having spent an incredible 20 years associated with the same club.

**50** Sadly, England's 1989 WTC Final victory at Odsal was totally overshadowed by the life-threatening injuries suffered by Erik Gundersen. What became the 50th magical moment of this era was the day speedway had it confirmed that popular Erik had survived his terrifying crash and would learn to walk again.

# ANDERS
# MICHANEK

**F**OR the best part of the late 60s and early 70s, you would find Anders Michanek's name very near or at the top of the British League averages.

Thirty years ago this month, you would have found him on cloud nine, celebrating his one and only individual World Championship victory in his native Sweden.

Today, if you look hard enough, you can find Anders looking as slim and fit as ever at 61, on a beautiful small island, inhabited by just 300 people, some 80 miles north-east of Stockholm.

That's where I caught up with the man who, without question, was a genuine speedway superstar, a top line points scorer for his main British clubs – Long Eaton, Leicester, Newcastle and Reading.

Even in his briefer spells with Cradley Heath and Ipswich in the late 70s, he showed glimpses of the pure quality that still sees him ranked among the true greats of the sport's last golden era, right up there alongside Ivan Mauger, Ole Olsen and Peter Collins.

What transpired from our first meeting was an illuminating, candid interview with a very humble man who was grateful for his time at the top of the sport.

As Anders sips on a glass of white wine poured by Anki, his wife of the past 10 years, at their secluded, 50-acre farmhouse on the island of Singo, he reflects with quiet contentment, not regret, on a great racing career.

Looking typically cool, calm and collected on parade before the 1974 World Final.

Quiet? Well, he doesn't shout about what he achieved in the sport. There are no visible clues to his years on the track. What mementoes he has are still packed away in boxes. Mercifully, he made a point of keeping his old racejackets, worn with pride for club and country, but he had to reach up into his barn to locate them.

A Weslake, the last bike he rode competitively when he and Bengt Jansson (who lives a short distance away on the mainland) were tempted out of retirement for one last hurrah with second division Rospigarna eight years ago, leans against the side of the shed where Anders keeps his two horses and hens. "Oh, look at the dirt on it, you'd better take the picture from the other side," he says, slightly embarrassed.

Speedway has been good to Anders but this modest man takes nothing for granted and still spends the summer months running his own one-man haulage firm, delivering gravel and digging earth.

**18**

He likes to fish from the little boat he keeps moored just a few minutes from his house.

In the winter, when the local lakes turn to ice, he goes deer hunting with his three dogs.

It's all a million miles from the night of September 6, 1974, when Anders Michanek ruled the speedway world with a 15-point maximum and one of the most comprehensive performances ever witnessed on the sport's biggest night.

"I still remember it as a great night, for sure," he says, eager to soak up the last of the Swedish summer sunshine that bounced off his slender torso. Before I arrived, I tried to imagine what he looked like now and whether I would recognise him from the old pictures from his racing days. Perhaps he'd gone bald, or had piled on the weight. Or both.

After guiding me onto his green and pleasant land by mobile phone, Anders appeared looking like Clint Eastwood – without the stubble. His hair, though now grey, is as thick and vibrant as ever and, physically, he looks much younger than his 61 years.

Anyway, where were we? Yes, back to Gothenburg and the night the Ullevi Stadium drew a record 39,000 crowd for speedway that has never been bettered.

'Mich' broke the track record in four of his five races to finish four points clear of nearest rivals Mauger and fellow Swede Soren Sjosten.

He was head and shoulders above the opposition even though he and his fellow countrymen were banned from riding in the BL that year as the BSPA clamped down on rising commuter costs. Mich now believes that by cutting back on his very hectic routine, he was fresher when it came to the big night. "I was also hungrier than before," he says, having failed to win the World Final at Katowice a year earlier, when he had been the massive pre-meeting favourite.

"You do get a bit fed up doing 60-odd meetings a year, you lose a bit of hunger, so I went to Gothenburg quite confident that I could win it that year."

But, typically, he revealed that the special help he and his five fellow Swedes received prior to the final played a part, too.

With the world title in his sights, Mich races away from Ivan Mauger in Heat 17 at Ullevi.

"The Gothenburg club, and even the Swedish federation, were ever so good. They allowed all six of the Swedish riders in the final to practice at Ullevi the week before, and they asked us if we were happy with the track. I think we spent a couple of days at the track and they asked us how we wanted it prepared.

"I wanted the track to be rough and deep, because I was not a real good speedway rider, more a moto cross rider. I was a bit stronger than most of the boys and when I rode I probably used more muscles than many of the others, although I know that Ivan and Briggo were also strong and could ride bumpy tracks very well.

"So we asked them to make the Ullevi track grippy, which it was – I think I broke the track record four times."

But Anders was in such unstoppable form that night, surely he would have won the crown without favours?

"I think so, because I made beautiful starts that night. I missed it in my first race but after that I was the first away in every one. And at that time you were allowed to touch the tapes without being excluded. I didn't think that was a good thing – the rules are definitely better today – but I did it because we were allowed to. Ole and Ivan were always at it."

Anders revealed a mechanical worry that he feared would cost him the title in his last ride. "I had a guy in Sweden who tuned my engines but he wasn't that good. I would find that my motors would last four or five rides before I ran out of valve springs. I tried valve springs from everywhere – Rolls-Royce, Cosworth, etc – but before my last race in the '74 final I didn't have any compression left in my engine. It was very flat and empty.

Anders and first wife Margarita savour the moment seconds after he was crowned speedway king in 1974. Mich later regretted the toll racing took on their marriage.

Reading's first BL championship in 1973. Back row, left to right: Bob Radford (team manager), Mick Bell, Bobby McNeil, Bernie Leigh. Front: Richard May, Dag Lovaas, mascot, Anders Michanek, Geoff Curtis.

"I did a practice start on my second bike but wasn't happy with it, so I went back to my first bike. It just kept going – I needed only one point from my last ride – but it wouldn't have done another race."

Michanek's legion of fans justifiably claim that he won the title a year later than he should have. In 1973, Anders ruled domestic and international speedway, leading Reading to their first BL title with a career-best 11.36 average and, on his way to the World Final, became Swedish, British-Nordic and European Champion. Surely no-one could touch him at Katowice?

"Everyone said I would win it that year and I believed them. I was too complacent," he admits. "The referee, a German bloke called (Georg) Transpurger, didn't like me and he excluded me. In those days you could break the tape and still not necessarily be excluded. I pulled up in my next ride . . . and then I went to the pub! Well, there was no point in going on, I'd lost it.

"But it was my fault – *why* did I have to break the tapes? I should have waited. And I was also too confident. People had said to me: 'Michanek has only to go down to Poland to collect his gold medal'. I thought myself that it would be easy for me, because everything had gone my way in '73."

Anders attributed some of his on-track brilliance throughout '73 to a better mental approach. "I started to visit a sports psychologist here in Sweden and she got me to train my mind on speedway more, which helped quite a lot. I thought I had been using 100 per cent of my brain for speedway before I went to see her but I probably didn't. I used maybe only 50 per cent.

"I remember going round during races and thinking to myself: 'I wonder what we will have for dinner tonight', or 'tomorrow, I must put my car in for servicing' . . . things like that."

Anders says that becoming World Champion didn't change his life, although he obviously gained many more open meeting bookings in Europe and his earnings were further boosted by regular long-track activity.

Real fears that he would have to miss a second consecutive BL campaign were thankfully allayed when the world fuel crisis eased and he was able to resume his very successful career with Reading at their new Smallmead home in 1975 (like Mich, the Racers had taken a year out while their new stadium was built following the closure of their old Tilehurst track).

Anders had joined Reading when they acquired Newcastle's senior league licence in 1971. He formed a potent twin spearhead with Norwegian Dag Lovaas and, within two years, the Berkshire club became BL champions and KO Cup finalists.

The move to Reading also brought Anders back into close contact with experienced promoter Reg Fearman, a member of the Allied Presentations consortium that ran Long Eaton and Leicester, the teams Anders rode for in 1967 and '68 respectively.

Victory in the British-Nordic Final at Coventry convinced many that Mich would go on to win his first world title in 1973, but it wasn't to be.

"Reg was a tough businessman but I liked him and we had a very good relationship," he says, smiling at rekindled memories of their sparring when it came to striking a deal for the new season.

"Reg phoned me one winter or early spring, asking if I'd come over to ride for him at Reading. I said: 'OK, but what's the deal?' He replied: 'Oh, we'll talk about it when you are here'. Of course, they (promoters) know we want to ride, so they expect us to ride for peanuts.

"Anyway, before the first meeting I actually stayed with Reg at his house in Henley-on-Thames, where he had a terrific sauna and a big swimming pool. Reg suggested we should have a sauna together and, as we went in, I told him we wouldn't come out until we had agreed my deal.

"I said: 'Look, it's easy for you, you don't have to explain how much you have invested in speedway, you just have to say yes or no'.

"As usual, though, he still kept trying to make me understand how hard it was for him and, by the end, we had been in there nearly two hours – I thought Reg was going to die from the heat! He opened the door a little to let in some air, his face was very red, but he wouldn't say 'yes' until he'd nearly died!

"But I liked and respected Reg. Do you know, he used to change his Rolls-Royce every other year!"

Fearman would be the first to agree that Michanek gave full value for money, as an average in excess of 10 points a season – an incredible 11.36 in the championship-winning year and 11.03 when he returned in 1975 – will testify.

"I remember one of the boys, Bernie Leigh, very well," says Anders. "He was not a top rider but he was always so happy and full of fun. We were all happy and the team spirit was good.

"We didn't mix much socially, it wasn't possible with riders like me flying off to the continent at weekends, but I remember one day when we were due to ride at Poole and stayed at Ken Middleditch's place. We found an old trials bike in the garage there and, after setting up a wooden ramp over the concrete flowers beds, we took it in turns to ride up and over and see who could jump farthest.

Mich arrives at Cradley Heath in 1977. He wasn't too keen on his new surroundings, nor abrasive promoter Dan McCormick (below).

"We got faster and braver until one of the boys – I think it was Geoff Curtis – missed the ramp, crashed and I watched in horror as his face hit the ground and his hair was ripped from his scalp. I thought: 'Oh s***!'. None of us wore a helmet – we were dressed only in shorts – and I felt sick at the thought of how badly he must have hurt himself. But as we all ran over to see how he was, he reached out an arm to pick up his hairpiece and then put it back on his head! I honestly didn't know that he wore a wig!

"I thought we would win the league that year because the spirit was so good. If my bike packed up I could use Bernie's and it worked the other way, too."

Although Anders' impressive 11-plus BL average, and runner-up in the World Final (to old rival Olsen) suggests he was as dominant as ever in 1975, he has less happy memories of the year which marked a watershed in his career.

A rare action pic of Mich riding for Ipswich in 1978.

He says: "I cut my foot in two places while riding a trials bike on the beach at North Perth, Australia that winter and came back to Reading in '75 on crutches. It took time to heal and caused me a lot of problems. I had to buy a boot three sizes too big so that I could ride."

At this point we should emphasis what a fitness fanatic Anders was – still is, judging by his slender, six-foot frame. During the winter close seasons in Sweden, he would go into the forest for cross-country skiing, covering six miles every day to stay sharp.

"But in '75 I wasn't fit enough and I couldn't produce what I wanted to. I hurt myself even more by falling off. I wore plastic shields around my thumbs and it wasn't a good season for me."

The high standards Anders set himself became clear when, in a moment of remarkable candour rarely expressed by today's leading sports people, he told me: "When I drove into the Wembley car park for the 1975 World Final, I thought to myself: 'Jeez, Anders, this is a good night, because tomorrow you won't be World Champion any longer'. I didn't enjoy it.

"I won in '74 but I didn't want to win at Wembley the next year. I probably didn't want the pressure of it any more. I felt myself that I was a useless World Champion, that I hadn't lived up to being the sport's No.1. I'd had a bad season, I wasn't anything like as successful as I'd been in '73.

"I felt glad and relieved to get to Wembley that year because I knew it was the end of it. The atmosphere there is great – 70,000-80,000 people – but I didn't want to win the title that year. I didn't feel disappointed to lose it to Olsen. I'd dropped two points in my first ride – to Ole and a Russian guy (Viktor Trofimov) – and I was pleased with my performance on the night, because I hadn't disappointed my supporters too much. I was second and that's good enough.

"I want to be comfortable in whatever I do, and that still applies today when I'm selling earth, digging and making lawns for people. If I do a good job, I'm happy. But if I do a bad job, I know it's not good enough and I don't want any pay."

Does Anders agree that it was harder to win a World Final in the 70s? "I don't know if there were better riders around then but there were definitely more of them. Here in Sweden, there were 600 riders competing around that time. Today, I think it's nearer 200."

Two classic battles between Mich and Peter Collins. Top: The 1973 International Tournament decider, where Anders was excluded for causing PC to slide off on the pits bend at Wembley. Bottom: Another nudge from Mich sends Peter down, this time during the 1975 Spring Classic at Wimbledon.

In 1976, Michanek and Olsen were the two biggest names who missed out on qualifying from the Inter-Continental Final at Wembley, the penultimate round won by Peter Collins who went on to complete a magical year in the final at Katowice.

"I wasn't at all as keen by then," admits Anders, who reveals that the breakdown of his marriage contributed to his early descent from speedway greatness.

Clearly unhappy at the memories invoked, he says: "I had two young girls and a house just outside Stockholm but I was too busy riding to see much of my family. I went to Germany every weekend and was away from Friday dinner time until Monday. Knowing I'd left my family behind again and that my first wife, Margarita, would be upset and that I should have painted the house, I didn't feel good. I had to do it to earn the good money I was getting but it was a big problem.

Top: Anders after winning the 1973 European Championship in Germany, flanked by Ivan Mauger and Vladimir Paznikov.
Bottom: A helping hand from Ole Olsen, even though the Scandinavian superstars were never friends.

Anders at home in 2004 with the racejacket he had worn on the night of his World Championship win 30 years earlier.

"If you are a speedway rider, then your wife needs to be keen on speedway, too, if the marriage is going to last."

Anders and Margarita were divorced in 1985 but he is delighted to receive regular visits from his daughters, Anna and Maria, who are both now in their thirties and living in Stockholm. He remarried Anki, who has three children from her first marriage, 10 years ago. "But she hates speedway, too!" laughs Anders, his trademark smile returning to his face. "No, she's great. We went to a league meeting here at Rospigarna the other week but I don't think she really liked it."

Anders never returned to Reading but he was back, albeit briefly, in British speedway in 1977 when ambitious, flamboyant new Cradley Heath promoter Dan McCormick lured him back to join forces with fellow Swede Bernt Persson.

Anders' return lasted just 11 BL matches in which he still achieved a fine 10-plus average, scored three maximums and, on one extraordinary night at Swindon, romped to 20 points from seven rides (Heathens still lost 41-37!). But he failed to turn up for a Midland Cup match at Leicester in July and, unable to guarantee that continental bookings wouldn't prevent him from missing more Cradley meetings, his contract was terminated.

"I never liked McCormick as a promoter," says Anders. "After every home meeting he said: 'Come on, boys, we're going down the pub' and we could be there until four in the morning. We did it for a couple of weeks until I pointed out to him that, as sportsmen, it was no good for us to be boozing until that time. He was a businessman, not a sportsman.

"I didn't like the Cradley track and the surroundings were dreadful if you arrived there in daylight. But the supporters were good people. In fact, one of them, Brenda Ferkins, still sends me birthday and Christmas cards every year and she's also stayed here with us."

A broken ankle severely hampered Mich's hopes of regaining the world speedway crown when the final returned to Ullevi in 1977 (7th place, 8 points), but he still managed to claim his one and only World Long-track title in Denmark a few weeks later.

He made the last of his 11 individual World Final appearances at Wembley in 1978, scoring seven, before Ipswich offered him a final fling in the BL midway through the following year. "I like John Berry as a person, he was terrific, but I only did a few meetings for them."

After just eight BL matches for Witches (7.33), Anders went home to continue riding for Getingarna in the 80s and prolong his long-track career. He made occasional comeback appearances in Briggo's Golden Greats meetings but he remembers his last competitive speedway meeting as a promotion decider for his local team, Rospigarna, in 1996, aged 53.

The upright Weslake he rode that day is still to be found in his old barn along with the hay, tractor and diggers that are now part and parcel of the immensely likeable Anders Michanek's everyday life.

# Classic battles with PC

**PETER Collins said in issue 3 of *Backtrack* that his greatest, most memorable races were against Anders Michanek, especially in the 1973 season when they met in two dramatic, decisive run-offs.**

The first, at Wembley, was to decide the Daily Mirror-sponsored International Tournament, after England and Sweden had drawn 39-39 in front of the ITV cameras and a 30,000 crowd at Empire Stadium.

At the end of the season, they clashed again after Belle Vue and Reading were tied on aggregate in the KO Cup final, second leg, at Hyde Road.

Now, for the first time, Anders talks in detail about those two great duels with Collins, both of which he lost but, on another day, he could have won.

Years after retiring from racing, Mich showed in these 2004 pictures that he had found different modes of transport. A pushbike and power boat were used to get him round his Swedish island.

"Not many people want to go into a races like these, because you feel uncomfortable carrying the hopes of the whole team. But I liked to do it."

Mich still maintains that he didn't knock Peter off as they entered the pits bend at Wembley. "I don't think I touched him," he says. "I should have done if he hadn't moved and I think I scared him a bit.

"I was sitting behind Peter for two laps or something and then I thought: 'Jeez Anders, this is not good enough, you must do something . . . you must pass him'. I screwed it on, left it open and . . . he fell off. I don't think I touched him . . . well, maybe I moved his leg a little bit?

"I was very worried that I would be excluded and when my light came on I wasn't surprised."

Anders admits he disliked the late Arthur Humphrey, the ACU referee who made the crucial call which handed a home victory to England.

"The Wembley meeting was on Saturday and he was in charge again when I rode in a league match at Reading the next Monday. Humphrey came up to me to talk about the incident at Wembley but I just said: 'It's gone, there's not much to talk about'.

"But he annoyed me when he then said: 'Yes, but I feel sorry for you, so tonight you can have good starts'. He meant that he would release the tapes when I dropped the clutch, which is a dreadful thing for a referee to say.

"I didn't tell him to 'f*** off' but I wanted to. I hated him."

Otherwise, Anders said that he generally got a fair deal from British referees and has no other complaints.

There was no controversy surrounding the next classic Mich versus PC battle at Belle Vue.

"My bike wasn't going very good at Belle Vue, so Bernie Leigh offered me his machine. I couldn't tell whether it was better than mine. I know that a rider can be good on a slow bike and yet useless on a fast one, so it's up to you."

Anders wasn't sure that his epic battle with PC was the best race he has ever been involved in but admits: "I enjoyed it, it was good, but I knew before the race that I couldn't win it.

"I passed Peter going into every corner but he passed me going out of the turn on every lap. And with the finishing line in the middle of the straight, I knew he would get there first. I thought: 'How can I change things?'. Yes, I could have run him down, but that's a bit naughty and I didn't want to do it. So I understood early in the race, on the first or second lap, when I noticed that his bike was quicker, that even if we had done 10 laps I could not have beaten him.

"But I wouldn't say that I would have beaten him if I had ridden my own bike and it was going well. PC was a terrific rider, ever so good."

## Among Swedish legends

**WHERE does Anders Michanek stand in the all-time list of Swedish greats?**
**Ove Fundin, with five individual world titles to his credit, is undoubtedly the King of Sweden.**

"Definitely, Ove has to be top," agrees Anders. "He was so special, I don't know how he could ride because he was so thin and his mind was more on arts and everything except the technical side of speedway.

"We were riding in a Golden Greats meeting together. We were at the hotel, Fundin, Benga Jansson and me, but while Benga and myself wanted to take a look at the track, Ove said he would prefer to go and see the Black Knight appearing at some local castle!

"I would be ever so happy to be ranked in third place among all the Swedes – behind Ove and (six times World Champion) Tony Rickardsson," added Mich. "Tony actually had me sacked when I was the trainer at Rospigarna but I wasn't too bothered. I'm not bitter.

"Even if I don't like the Grand Prix system much, I know that Tony is a very good rider. He's still the best Swede today and, of course, I respect him."

Anders became a World Champion for the first time when he scored 10 points as the Swedes won the Team Cup at Wembley in 1970.

He won the World Pairs title with two different partners over three consecutive seasons – the late Tommy Jansson (1973) and Soren Sjosten (1974 & '75). Would Tommy have been individual World Champion had he lived? "Yes, I think so, definitely," says Anders.

"Once, in a qualifying round at Ullevi, I offered Tommy my bike when he had trouble with his. He won the race but afterwards he said: 'How the hell can you ride a bike like that?' I knew what he meant, because I bent my frame on purpose to give me more drive, but Tommy wasn't used to it."

# Mich on his greatest rivals

**THREE great riders, Ivan Mauger, Ole Olsen and Anders Michanek, dominated the World Championship in the 70s, winning eight of the 10 finals between them in that richly memorable decade.**

Here's what Anders told *Backtrack* about his two main rivals:

### Anders on . . . IVAN

"Ivan was really my idol, a total professional and I looked up to him.

"You talked to him, of course, but you didn't mix with him. I liked him, he was terrific.

"He was definitely more professional about speedway than me. He put his life into the sport.

"For example, when we had practice for a World Final or World Team Cup Final in Poland. You did your laps, changed your gears, cleaned the clutch and did the bikes ready for the meeting the next day. It's six o'clock at night, you're hungry, and so you say to your mechanic: 'Come on, let's put the bike away and go and have dinner and some beers'.

"But Ivan . . . he could be there to nine o'clock in the evening, until it got dark, with no food other than a Mars bar and just a little stove to heat up his tea.

"I did my bike in two hours but Ivan took five hours to do his properly. He wasn't interested in food, beers or girls. He was just speedway, speedway, speedway. I felt sorry for him sometimes!" laughs Anders.

"But I wouldn't change my life for his. One world title is enough for me. I'm happy with that."

### Anders on . . . OLE

"Olsen . . . he was a funny bloke and I didn't really like him. I didn't really know him as a person, so what I mean is I didn't like him as a rider. He would moan if you put dirt in his way or moved him around on the track.

"I earned lot of money thanks to Ole, because I rode against him every other Sunday on either long-track or speedway. The fans loved to see us race each other. If he didn't put me over the fence, then I'd put him over it. I didn't care that we weren't friends.

"I remember once when we were on tour with Ivan and Briggo in Australia. They booked Ole into the same hotel as the rest of us but he never showed up. He stayed at a different hotel somewhere down the road.

"When we saw him, we asked: 'Why don't you come over and join us, we can all have fun together, go water skiing?

"But Ole said: 'No, that's impossible. If I did that, I might become friends with you . . . and then I can't race you'.

Back at Reading with another ex-Racers star, John Davis, for the final meeting at Smallmead in 2008.

"We had good fun without him anyway but I felt sorry for him – and his wife, Ulla, who had to sit alone with him at their motel!

"He was a good rider but he's a Dane – and that says everything!"

### Anders on . . . being ruthless

Anders could look after himself on the track, he was certainly no shrinking violet, but was he really as ruthless as the most successful world champions?

"You must be able to go to work again the next day. You mustn't kill each other, that's not the point of it.

"You had to be tough, definitely, and I'd be surprised if anyone said I wasn't tough. I've heard many different stories about me.

"I told the boys I was training at Rospigarna that the only 'friend' they have on the track when they are racing is the fence. It's the only one who can help you.

"What I mean by that is, if someone wants to pass you down the straight, you can move out to the fence and close the gap. That's the only help you have and it's what I used many times. Why leave only a yard between you and the fence if you are in front? But if someone is already next to you, it's too late, you can't do it."

### Anders on . . . his only regret

Was there one standout incident in his career that Mich had cause to regret?

"There is one, only one," he says, lowering his voice as he recalls a cut-throat Swedish Championship at Gothenburg in 1973, when him and Bernt Persson were fighting it out for the title.

"Bernie and I had both won our first three races and we met in our fourth ride. He was leading and

I thought to myself: 'Jeez, if he wins this race, he will be the Swedish Champion, and I want the title'.

"So in the last corner, I ran over him. It was deliberate, crazy, but I didn't care as it was the only way to stop him.

"I was excluded and Bernie broke his leg – Tommy Johansson won the meeting. I felt so bad afterwards, so sorry, because although I wanted to stop him winning, I didn't want to hurt him in any way.

"The incident made front page news in the Swedish press. I was stupid.

"I saw him in hospital afterwards and said 'sorry'. We are still friends and we talk today, but we had problems with his wife. She hated me."

### Anders on . . . himself

As our delicious meal of fresh salmon and new potatoes at his favourite restaurant nears its end (Anders flatly refused to allow me to pay the bill) and the return trip around the beautiful eastern coastline in Anders' power boat beckons, a final question: How did he see himself as a speedway rider?

"I should say that my talent wasn't all that big and I didn't want to produce more than I could handle, especially at the start. I just became a good rider.

"I'm still a little bit proud of what I did in England – I didn't really go for it, it just happened for me.

"It's true, I wasn't desperate enough to want to keep being World Champion. It was a good time, I liked it, but I should have stopped earlier and saved my marriage.

"There is more to life than going round and round."

## On 2 Minutes With...
## KARL FIALA

**Where did you get your first bike and roughly how much did it cost?**

It was a 350cc BSA B31 that was given to me by a friend of my father. I learnt to ride it at the age of eight. I built my first competitive racing bike, a 200cc Triumph Tiger Cub in an Elstar frame, in 1971. I purchased the frame and engine plates new from Brian Clark, the Peterborough captain who had a shop in St. Ives, Huntingdon. I competed in my first schoolboy grass-track race, aged 15, at Stapleford Tawney, Essex.

**Who helped you most in the early days?**

My friend good friend and mentor Mick Hatfield, who raced grass-track until he had to retire from racing due to an eye injury.

In 1974, aged 18, Colin Pratt invited me to the Hackney training school, where I practiced every Saturday afternoon. It was under Collin's guidance that I signed for Rye House.

In 1976, the Atkinson family, who owned Infradex Ltd, approached me and offered me complete sponsorship. A year later they sponsored the entire Rye House team.

**Best promoter you have ridden for, and why?**

I have only ever ridden for one pair of promoters, Len Silver and Colin Pratt. I knew at the time that they were very experienced and professional in their approach, presentation and preparation of tracks and, above all, were very fair. I also now know that they were/are the BEST in the business.

Len didn't seem bothered when I announced my retirement in February 1981 but once the season had got underway and when it was evident that Rye House were struggling, he did come to see me and made me a very lucrative offer to return. However, my decision had already been made. I have no regrets and still have wonderful memories of my speedway career.

**Favourite track?**

Rye House. Always well prepared, usually with plenty of dirt, which would allow good racing with plenty of opportunities to pass. The supporters were incredible – very loyal – and created a wonderful atmosphere.

**Tracks you never looked forward to visiting?**

The one I found most difficult to master was Crayford, because of its unusually small size and shape, although it was always well prepared.

By John Berry ● Issue 50 (2012)

# 'COVER UP' IS NO SOLUTION TO AGE-OLD PROBLEM

Battling against the elements is nothing new for those who run British speedway, but the wettest April in 100 years has hit hard and led to renewed debate about how best to try and solve an age-old problem. Our Australian-based lead columnist John Berry re-examines the possibility of track covers and considers other factors . . .

**T**HEY tell me the start of the season has been a bit damp over there despite recent drought warnings and hosepipe bans. I don't want to brag but we are still enjoying an Indian summer well into late autumn. Global warming? Well, I am a true sceptic. I blame 0.01 per cent on man affecting weather patterns and 99.9 per cent on the vagaries of Mother Nature.

I know, the summers seem hotter, the winters colder, the rain wetter and the dry dryer. I think the difference between now and before is that we live in a time where there is a massive 'information' industry all trying to make money by outdoing the other media outlets with more and more outrageous

Re-laying drainage and a new track surface at Ipswich in the early 70s.

34

claims and assertions using the most lurid of terms. If we were to have believed the scaremongers of 20 years ago we would already be ankle deep in water even on the top of Ben Nevis, but most of those learned professors who made such claims are now admitting they might have been just a touch pessimistic.

Meantime, we have to live with yet another massive industry inspired by hysterical calls to reduce carbon emissions. Here in Australia coal is now considered a swear word. Everyone is fined enormous amounts for burning it, so we dig it up and ship it to the 'developing countries'. They then burn it, making cheap stuff they sell back to us at a profit while throwing all that nasty carbon dioxide into the air which drifts around the world for all us 'civilised' people to breathe. Funny old world we live in . . .

Anyway, back to the plot.

My editor tells me the UK speedway season has been severely disrupted through inclement weather and wants to revisit the question of rained-off meetings and how they could be avoided by covering track surfaces. It is a subject he and I have debated before but he feels now would be a good time to revisit the question.

It has to be said, he makes a good case for speedway tracks having protective covers to keep the rain at bay. After all, cricket has to cope with the problem and makes a reasonable fist of at least keeping the wicket and surrounds dry and Wimbledon, even before the new roof for the centre court, had covers for all of their courts.

Even Ole Olsen at Vojens, which for all the world appears to have been built under a waterfall, came up with a method of protecting his track for major meetings, so clearly it can be done. What it all boils down to is simply: do the benefits outweigh the difficulties?

So first of all, let's define the problem. I cannot think of another sporting surface that depends on getting the exact amount of water onto it in order to produce good racing. Too little water and (quite apart from covering the spectators with dust) the track has no grip and riders have virtually no chance of passing. Too much and, again, riders cannot find any grip and slide around on the muddy surface. The track needs enough water to soften the sub-surface, allowing tyres to bite into it, but not so much as to cause it to become greasy.

A well prepared track will have a slight crust on top if it has been packed down properly. Light rain will often run off this surface or can be reasonably easily removed. Once the meeting has started and the crust broken, rain quickly causes some area where the shale has been scoured away by the tyre to become greasy, while other areas where the loose shale has gathered become sludgy. Ergo, rain during a meeting is always a real problem.

So a cover would have to be able to be utilised at a stage when the track has had just enough watering but not too much. Therefore it would have to be able to be put into place (and taken down) very quickly. It must also cover the entire surface with cleverly engineered joins so as to avoid leaks, which would produce dangerous soft patches.

Most tracks have enough camber for the water to drain to the inside if the cover was laid on the top but such an arrangement is far from ideal, as the water would most likely collect on the track side of the inner kerb (white line). It would be far better if the cover was raised on the outside of the track (say, about five-feet high), and then pegged to the ground on the infield. There would also need to be some kind of drainage ring leading to a sump to accommodate the run off. Otherwise the water would simply drain back onto the track.

So we would need a substantial framework outside the track to handle the weight of the cover and cope with any strong wind but this framework would need to be quickly removable after the cover had been rolled up. Clearly, one size would not fit all and each track would need the covers and frames to be tailor-made. Tracks would also need to have a team of 20 or so men on hand to erect (and dismantle) the covers in the event of inclement weather. Altogether, we are looking at quite some undertaking.

Now let's look at the costs incurred by a promoter when he has a run of the mill (league meeting or filler event) rained-off. There will perhaps be a rent cost, but by and large if the meeting is restaged, not much is lost there. There will be advertising and promotional losses and wages to be paid, and if the programmes cannot be used again, this is another loss. There might also be some rider travel and/or subsistence costs. My estimate in round figures would be a loss of around £1500 – plus, of course, a loss of profits. Back in the 'Good Old Days' that figure might have been substantial. These days I suspect not so and I wonder if this is why meetings seem to get cancelled earlier and earlier.

I don't think anyone has actually done the stats but my guess would be that, over, say, a 10-year period, a track would lose two/three meetings a year to bad weather but we then have to decide how many of those meeting would have been saved had covers been available. If it rains during a meeting, or indeed is raining at the time a meeting should begin, the odds are it would be abandoned anyway. Several of the recently rained-off meetings have been because continuous bad weather has prevented the track from being prepared. Don't even think about trying to cost out the building of a cover you could work under!

Having spent a good deal of money putting in drainage at Ipswich in 1972, we boasted that provided any rain had ceased by two hours before start time we could get a meeting on. I think we achieved that (except for an infamous WTC round that was cancelled with the track quite raceable and the full house signs posted) and I also recall a violent thunderstorm hitting Foxhall right on start time, flooding everything, but the sun came out and the meeting started just 45 minutes late.

Personally, I do not think the use of covers would save more than an average of one meeting per year for each track.

My guess at installing the hardware and software needed for the kind of cover I envisaged would be around £50,000. Maintenance of the 'software' (the actual cover material) would be ongoing and I would not know how to cost having the erection crew on standby, given that most tracks do not even have a full-time track man.

Even taking into account the use of covers could lift some meetings from 'barely rideable' to providing a good racing surface, I really cannot see how it would make economic sense for every track to install covers. Let's face it, run of the mill speedway meetings are a far cry from the kind of revenue created by Wimbledon or a Lord's Test match but there might well be instances where the use of covers could be justified. If the meeting was big enough, the potential returns high enough and the costs incurred by a rain-off great enough, then there might well be a justification for 'investing' in some kind of temporary track protection. But, here again, how many SGPs have actually fallen foul of the weather? I can only recall two (one indoors!) and both were as a result of poor planning and preparation rather than the weather itself.

Some people seem to think riders are more reluctant to ride in dodgy conditions these days. Others complain of difficulty sourcing good materials and maybe there is a dearth of capable track men. I cannot comment on any of those possibilities but even so, for all of the apparent logic of covering speedway tracks, and even allowing for UK weather patterns, I still cannot accept the idea makes business sense.

What might make more sense is to spend money, but a fraction of the cost of covers, on better track preparation machinery and materials, with perhaps also a speedway version of cricket's supersopper and maybe also, like road-racing, have special wet track tyres to be used whenever the referee rules the track as 'wet'.

Coventry track staff try to get the wet surface rideable before the controversial 1984 British Final, where riders threatened to walk out over track conditions. Improved track maintenance equipment could be key to ensuring more meetings go ahead.

**But I come back to something I have been saying for years: speedway should be searching to produce a synthetic surface which would solve a multitude of track maintenance problems.**

However, like it or not – and many promoters were in the 'or not' category for many years after the first Sky TV deal was done, the advent of league matches being shown live on TV has changed the whole world of speedway, as it does with all sports. The money Sky put into speedway might be a pittance compared to other high profile sports but the revenue paid to the BSPA is not just a thank you for allowing cameras into matches.

In return for their millions TV expects speedway to fit around the armchair viewer's needs rather than the traditional punter. Fixtures are arranged to suit and, in particular, the running of meetings has to fit around TV rather than the other way around. It has been suggested the cost to TV of simply rocking up to a track with its outside broadcast unit costs in the region of £80,000 a meeting. Suddenly the pressure to put on a meeting regardless of conditions escalates dramatically.

Cricket covers don't always save matches. What they do is improve the odds of being able to get some play. How much would it cost to purchase enough covering to lay straight onto a speedway track? My guess would be £5-10k. Such a covering would be far from foolproof, perhaps saving maybe 30-50 percent of matches that would otherwise be lost. Maybe their use might also improve some tracks from 'barely rideable' to 'quite raceable' which, given the shop window nature of the TV coverage, might well be worthwhile.

Maybe the BSPA and Sky might consider a joint-cost arrangement to provide a one-size-fits-all set of covers to be trucked around to each TV meeting, with the BSPA buying the covers and the satellite broadcaster responsible for the trucking?

Maybe the BSPA might assist a promotion to 'invest' in a set of covers and trial them for a season to see what benefits might ensue? If nothing else, such an experiment might score some goodwill points with TV, on which UK speedway is relying on more and more.

# STREET-WISE GENT, FOUR-VALVE PIONEER

The speedway family in all corners of the globe is mourning the sad loss of Neil Street, one of the sport's genuine nice guys who had such a positive influence on countless others. We look back at the life and times of the Australian gent and mechanical maestro who changed the sport forever . . .

**A**S loyal, dedicated and popular servants to speedway go, Neil Street was the yardstick. He was barely out of his teens when he took his first tentative laps around his local track in Melbourne – the beginning of more than half a century's involvement with the sport he loved.

During that time 'Bill', as he was affectionately called, made his name as a rider, manager and, of course, as a maverick engine developer, whose four-valve conversion changed the face of world speedway forever.

It's amazing to think that the young lad who stepped off a boat at Southampton Docks in 1952 with just £25, some tins of food from his mum and a speedway bike to his name would go on to be such an influential figure, continuing in management with Newport into his late 70s.

But Neil, who died peacefully with his family at home in Melbourne at the age of 80 on October 5, 2011, enjoyed a 24-year riding career in the UK with Exeter (1952-55 and 1966-70), Swindon (1957-63) and Newport (1972-76).

Individual success for Neil in his early days with Exeter.

Neil at Newport in 1976, his final season.

**Neil leading Wimbledon's Barry Briggs at Exeter in 1974.**

Capped by his native Australia, Australasia and also once by Britain, it spoke volumes for his class and longevity that he made his penultimate international appearance for the Aussies against the Ivan Mauger-led Rest of the World side in the Daily Mirror International Tournament on July 21, 1975 . . . and was their second highest scorer with 10 points in a 42-36 victory. Two days later, he scored a match-winning three points as Australia defeated Sweden (including Anders Michanek and Tommy Jansson) 41-37 at Poole.

He was 44-years-old at the time.

Neil was in demand as a manager too, taking charge at Weymouth, Poole, Exeter, briefly Swindon and Newport, as well as guiding Australia to World Team Cup glory in 1999 and victory in the rebranded World Cup in 2001 and 2002.

Domestic honours included managing Poole to the National League title in 1989 and 1990, adding the KO Cup in the second of those seasons and the BL crown in 1994.

But he admitted in an interview for *Backtrack* and sister magazine *Classic Speedway* in 2008 that what gave him as much pleasure as anything was helping young riders develop.

"A lot of young riders started out at Weymouth," he said, "guys like Simon Wigg, Simon Cross and Martin Yeates.

"And it was at Poole where I really started to bring young Australian riders over – Mark Lemon, Leigh Adams and Jason Crump were among them.

"They lived with me for the first year or so – they were young lads, so I wanted to keep them on the straight and narrow."

And it was his mission to get the best out of one young Aussie way back in 1970 that led to the development of the Street four-valve conversion.

He met Phil Crump – later to become his son-in-law after marrying daughter Carole – while racing at Mildura during the British close season and took him under his wing.

In the winter of 1974-75 he started looking at ways of getting Crump to go even faster – and his old mate Ivan Tighe came up with the answer.

"Ivan said: 'What about a four-valve conversion?'," Neil explained.

"I said it was a good idea but it would be too expensive. Ivan said he'd pay for it and within half an hour it was all decided.

Still a winner at 44. Neil leading for Australia against Sweden's Tommy Nilsson (inside) and Soren Karlsson during the 1975 Test at Poole, where he went on to become a title-winning manager.

Team manager Neil with Weymouth star Martin Yeates.

"Ivan had a mate who was a draughtsman and could get it all drawn up – and two weeks later we had our first engine built."

Crump used the engine in the Australian Championships at Sydney, where it flew.

"He won every race by a third of a lap," Neil recalled. "As he was finishing, the nearest rider to him was coming round the third bend, and we're talking about a 560-yard circuit. He took two seconds off the track record too."

Neil had an engineering background, so taking the head off a conventional Jawa engine, putting in an overhead camshaft plus a sprocket at the bottom and a chain to drive it, was straightforward stuff to him.

Weslake had been working on a four-valve motor of their own but theirs wasn't ready for the start of the following season and suddenly Neil had, in his own words "about half the market in England."

Inevitably, Weslake responded with their first engine in 1975, as did Jawa who brought out a factory-made double overhead cam four-valve engine in 1977.

With limited resources ("I was 26, still riding speedway and spending 16 hours a day working on engines") and the ability only to convert, rather than build from scratch, the big boys inevitably squeezed him out of the marketplace.

They may have replaced him as market leaders but Neil's vision and determination meant he was the first – and it's a historical status no-one can ever take away.

Neil's last season as a rider was with Newport in 1976, when he was still averaging around five points a match in top flight British League racing at the age of 45.

A year earlier he had been a heat leader for the Wasps, averaging more than seven points a match in the league behind Phil Crump and Reidar Eide and, statistically, among the top 20 riders in the BL, which was a remarkable feat. Of course, as well as Crump, 'Streetie' also benefited from the extra power provided by his conversion creation in the 1975 campaign while most of their rivals were still coming to terms with the four-valve revolution.

**Phil the power: Phil Crump about to race his innovative Street conversion at Newport.**

It was after hanging up his leathers that his management career began to take off and among the riders he played a key role in nurturing was his grandson Jason Crump, World Champion in 2004, 2006 and 2009.

In his 2006 autobiography, *A World Of My Own,* Jason fully acknowledged the vital role his grandfather – along with Neil's wife Mary and their sons Drew (who became an ever-present member of Jason's GP pit crew) and Graham – had played in his path to the top. Reflecting on his days as a promising junior in the late 80s, he wrote: "He didn't get to all that many of my junior meetings but when he did, there was always a word of advice or encouragement. So to have him in my corner in Western Australia, that was something else.

"Bill Street is a wise and worldly man, and he had it tough when he was growing up. What he

Neil with Phil and Jason Crump, the two who benefited most from his expertise, at Swindon in 1993.

doesn't know about speedway bikes, riders and tracks isn't worth knowing.

"The Street family were magnificent to me in that first year (In British racing). I kidded myself that I was handling it all, being independent and responsible and all that, but thinking back, they must have worked overtime to prop me up, to keep me going and steer me in the right direction. I'll be grateful forever."

Of all the many young riders who benefited from Neil Joseph Street's intelligent influence, Jason probably has the most to thank him for. But there are innumerable others who will now be recalling all the sensible help and advice Neil gave them, too.

Well-liked, dedicated and as madly in love with speedway as he was when he first sat on a bike six decades ago, he received a much-deserved testimonial meeting at Broadford, in Melbourne, in 2002 and was awarded the Order of Australian Merit – the Australian equivalent of an MBE – the same year.

## BRIEF ENCOUNTERS WITH… Peter Boston

### Why did you return to the UK?

I worked and saved like mad and then around April 1971, I spent six weeks sailing from Fremantle to Southampton. Ship life was great fun but by the time I arrived in Southampton funds were running low and I was bordering on having an alcohol problem. I walked miles trying to buy a van on my first day in the UK. I came

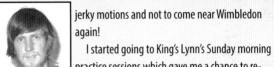

across Freddie Williams' car sales showroom in Wembley. I explained my situation and Fred offered me an old Bedford van for £65. Fred was also team manager of the Wembley Lions and said if I had my leathers with me I could have a ride on their track spare in the second half . . . but my riding gear was in a packing case with my bike clearing customs in Southampton. The fact that the great Freddie Williams was interested in giving me a run lifted my spirits no end.

### How did you progress in British speedway?

I got a copy of the *Speedway Star* to see what meetings were on, then went to the nearest one. I'd then try and find the promoter and see if he would give me a ride in the second-half or after the meeting. I was allowed to practice after the meeting at Wimbledon and off I went with my super-fast action Claremont-style throttle, big layback handlebars for more drive and very sharp engine. I was having fun until down I went. While I was trying to get bike and body out of that tangled mess of wire fencing and cables, the rest of the guys and promoter came at me looking really angry. The promoter looked at the fence, then turned to the riders and said it was stuffed, so that was it for the night. Then he turned to me, told me to go away in short

jerky motions and not to come near Wimbledon again!

I started going to King's Lynn's Sunday morning practice sessions which gave me a chance to re-learn how to ride a speedway bike UK-style. Also I could sleep in the van in the car park and use their shower and toilet.

King's Lynn and Boston promoter Cyril Crane was a bit of character and he saw value in giving this big, tall Aussie called Boston a run as the Boston name had a good connection, plus I was over-riding like mad just trying to get on the pace.

In one second half he put me in the vultures' race – I kissed the fence a couple of times and got away with it but then the fence got me and I ended up in a big heap, very dazed. I got up and tried to remember where I was and what happened. The next thing, Cyril was at my side and in his broad Norfolk accent asked: "You all right, lad? I'll get you back in the rerun if you want?"

Next thing I knew, another Aussie (Bob Humphreys I think) was sorting out my bike and putting me on it for the rerun. I must have won because I got into the second half and made it into the final after similar crashes and reruns organised by Cyril, a man that knew the value of entertainment.

At the same time I was having some success in the second-halves at Hull and when George Davenport got injured, Ian Thomas asked me to travel to an away meeting as No 8.

43

By Tony McDonald ● Issue 60 (2014)

# IN MY LIFE: LIONS AND THE BEATLES

Before he became a best-selling author and the world's only professional Beatles historian, Mark Lewisohn was passionate about speedway and Wembley Lions . . .

IN May 1970 two important events happened that would change a young boy's life. Mark Lewisohn was almost 12-years-old and growing up with his family in Pinner, Middlesex when, on May 8, The Beatles released their last album, *Let It Be.* Who could possibly have realised then quite how they'd endure in the lives of millions worldwide?

Just 22 days later, Wembley Lions roared back into life as league speedway returned to the Empire Stadium after a 14-year absence.

At various stages since then, The Beatles and speedway have been the consuming passions of Mark's social and working life.

He didn't discover the Lions until the August of their first season back in the shale big-time, but remained an avid fan until their closure at the end of the 1971 campaign, before eventually switching his allegiance to White City and Eastbourne.

As a kid, he enjoyed listening to Beatles records. Nowadays, Mark is the acknowledged world authority on Liverpool's Fab Four who have been the subject of seven of his books. These include the bestselling and influential *Recording Sessions, The Complete Beatles Chronicle* and (as co-author) *The Beatles' London.*

The world's only professional Beatles historian, Mark was consultant and researcher for all aspects – TV, DVDs, CDs and book – of the Beatles' own *Anthology* and has been involved in numerous other projects for them, as well as independent works.

His latest tome, *Tune In,* was published last October to critical acclaim – it's the first volume of a biographical trilogy with the overall title *The Beatles: All These Years.*

Mark has interviewed Paul McCartney 15 times and George Harrison twice, so I felt quite honoured when, shortly before flying out to New York with his wife Anita Epstein in early February to begin a promotional tour of the Big Apple that marks the 50th anniversary of the Beatles' first visit to the States, he welcomed me into their home in leafy Berkhamsted, Hertfordshire, to talk about his interest in speedway.

It was Mark's lifelong friend Jeremy Moore, a son of his parents' friends, who introduced him to the sport at Wembley: "The first meeting I saw was the Southern Riders' Championship qualifying round on August 8, 1970. I didn't know what to expect but the people I went with – Jeremy and some of his relations – showed me how to fill in a programme and suddenly this magical evening unfolded.

"I don't remember too much about it, except it was incredibly noisy. We sat on the second bend and Reidar Eide won it with a 15-point maximum. I was tickled by the fact that a speedway rider would be called Reidar but delighted that he was *our* man, a Wembley rider, and from that day on I was a Lions supporter. I saw three or four more meetings before the season ended and very rapidly

PAPERBACK WRITER: Mark Lewisohn, in 2014, with the programme from his first Wembley meeting and a Lions badge.

got sucked into this thing.

"During the 1970-71 close season I put in an order for *Speedway Star & News* with my local newsagent so that by the time the '71 season began I was completely into it. Speedway was all I talked and thought about. I even wrote my own speedway magazine, which I used to type, and my dad photocopied in his office.

"Unlike other teams whose season began in March, Lions' home meetings didn't begin until June, after the football season had finished, and for that reason I was always envious of fans of other clubs. They could go to meetings three months before me – I was too young to go to the Lions' away matches.

"Reidar Eide was my favourite rider, and then one of those 'speedway things' happened, which was all a steep learning curve for me – he was assigned to another team (Poole) for 1971. So suddenly this guy whose name and picture I had on my bedroom wall wasn't a Wembley rider any more. I was also interested in other team sports, mainly football and cricket, and you didn't suddenly see a Liverpool player being given to, say, Stoke.

"In 1971 I didn't miss a home meeting. I used to get to the stadium early with my autograph book, took photographs with my camera, and felt I got to know the riders a little. Bert 'Haggis' Harkins became my new big favourite – it was nice to see a rider wearing glasses, because I was a glasses wearer myself by that point. He was kind of like our Buddy Holly or Hank Marvin!

"I was familiar with the '71 side much more than the one who had worn our colours in '70. There was also Brian Collins, Brian Leonard, Christer Sjosten, Peter Prinsloo and Tony Clarke, who was a bit of a geezer. I seem to recall something famous happened to him around the time of the 1972 World Final . . .

"Ove Fundin had been Lions' marquee signing in 1970 but he'd left by the time I started going. In fact, there was a piece in the programme at my first meeting explaining why he wouldn't be riding for us again.

"Later that season, though, I twice saw Fundin ride at Wembley – in the World Team Cup Final, when I couldn't understand why most of the crowd seemed to be booing a five times World Champion, and in the last meeting, when he rode for the opposition."

What did not come to light at the time is that, apparently, Fundin had an issue concerning his work permit. Typical of Mark's diligent research, just before we met he tracked down Ian Cottrell, son of the late co-promoter Bernard Cottrell, the businessmen who financed Lions' revival, who revealed in an email that there had been problems regarding the Swede's work permit.

"Then, in '71, we had another famous Swedish rider, Gote Nordin, join us," continued Mark. "I was with a Swedish author just a few days ago and, knowing I was doing this interview for *Backtrack*, I wrote down some speedway riders' names from my teenage years on a piece of paper and asked him how they should be pronounced. It turns out that this guy whose name I thought was pronounced Goat Nordin is actually 'Yuur-ter Nordeen'. This might explain why I got no response when I was leaning over the pits wall and trying to get his attention by shouting what sounded like 'Goat! Goat!'. He couldn't possibly have recognised my mispronunciation of his name! I did obtain his autograph on other occasions, though, as well as a photo of him, and I probably said: 'Thanks very much, Goat', which now embarrasses me greatly. All the same, he was a top rider, with a memorably upright style on the bike."

Before we met, Mark raided his cellar and unearthed some retro gems that capture his love of Wembley Speedway. He produces metal pin badges, including one sold on behalf of the Lions supporters' club, and others bearing the names of Tony Clarke, Sverre Harrfeldt and Dave Jessup.

"Sverre was fantastic – he was coming back from what should have been a career-ending injury,

HELLO GOODBYE: The Beatles broke up just as the Lions returned.

SHE LOVES YOU: Young Lions fans with their Swedish idol Gote Nordin.

started the season at reserve, and after a while was picking up 12-point maximums. His gating was out of this world – I still think of him streaking into first-bend leads at Wembley whenever I hear anyone talking about good gating techniques.

"And I always followed Dave Jessup after his Wembley days, because he was a top-class English rider and I was proud that riding for the Lions had been part of his rapid rise."

Mark has a complete set of Wembley home and away programmes, including a rare one from a meeting held at Newport on Friday, April 16, 1971, when – with big-time football still calling the shots at the national stadium until the end of May – Lions borrowed Wasps' Somerton Park track to entertain champions Belle Vue in a British League fixture. Another programme, from Coatbridge in 1969, confirms the source of four Wembley recruits: Eide, Harkins, Brian Collins and Wayne Briggs. Of course, when Lions were revived in 1970 they took over the Coatbridge licence.

Mark also recalls the day he discovered the shock news that after just two short summer seasons back in the top flight, his beloved Wembley would not be continuing in the BL for 1972.

He explains: "In February 1972 I stayed over one night at my friend Jeremy's house in Bushey during half-term week and his dad brought either the London *Evening News* or *Standard* home from work. In it was a piece saying Wembley Lions would not be returning for '72 – they were going to take a year out. It really was devastating and I hadn't seen it coming. Speedway, the Lions in particular, had become central to my life – it had become a passion of mine to follow them.

"The suggestion was that the stadium had so many other events in '72 that the speedway season would have been even more truncated than usual, with insufficient dates to run a full league campaign.

"However, looking back now, that doesn't seem to have been the case, so maybe there was more to Lions' closure than met the eye. I remember co-promoter Trevor Redmond saying he'd be looking for another track where we could race home meetings, before returning to Wembley in 1973 – but neither of those things happened. The Lions never came back.

"I went to a S.O.S. (Save Our Speedway) meeting of the Lions' supporters' club, held at the Norfolk Arms pub in North Wembley. I was 13-and-a-half and had never been in a pub before, so I felt a bit vulnerable going there on my own. The meeting was held in a room off to the side and we were talking about what we could do to save the Lions. But what could we do?

"By then, I already knew from reading *Speedway Star* that tracks closed all the time. I still believed we'd return in '73 but when it became clear that we wouldn't, it was the end of an era for me as well as Wembley Speedway.

"Although I certainly didn't lose interest in speedway, I had nowhere to go. I was too young to attend meetings at other tracks – how could a 13-year-old get to Wimbledon on a Thursday night or Hackney on a Friday? I persuaded my

GETTING BETTER: Dave Jessup began his top flight career with Wembley and became one of England's all-time greats.

GOT TO GET YOU INTO MY LIFE: Roaring ahead for the Lions, popular Bert Harkins winning races in front of large league crowds at the Empire Stadium. Below: The former Scottish No.1 with his original Lions racejacket in 2014. Once a big fan of Bert, Mark Lewisohn now considers him a friend.

dad to take me to Plough Lane once a year and I'd go to the big meetings that were still staged at Wembley – the 1972 World Final and World Team Cup Final the following year. I'd sit in my old seat on the first bend – I used to ask for a ticket in that particular block – but it wasn't the same. It wasn't the Lions.

"By 1974 I was 16 and working in London, so I had money, mobility and the opportunity to go to Wimbledon. By chance, Bert Harkins was riding for the Dons, which was a big part of the appeal for me. But I couldn't bring myself to support Wimbledon as a team. They just didn't float my boat in the way Wembley had. You can't engineer passion – it's either there naturally or not at all.

"But it was fantastic to see Bert riding again – until (in 1975) he had a serious crash and broke his back. *Speedway Star* reported that he was in the orthopaedic hospital at Stanmore – the same hospital my dad had been in six years earlier – and as it was quite close to where I lived, I took a day off work and got the bus to the hospital to see him.

"I'd met Bert at Wembley in '71 but he wouldn't have remembered that and I didn't expect him to. I just wanted to pass a couple of hours for him, to let him know he wasn't alone. I had some spare issues of the *Star* and gave them to him to read, and we chatted about Wembley Lions, which was great for me, though I no longer remember what he said and I didn't record it.

"I didn't meet Bert again for a very long time. I still saw him race, although only until about 1980-81, when I guess he retired. Then I happened to move to Berkhamsted, where he had a motorcycle shop. I didn't go in but I'd see him around town."

Bert and Mark are now firm friends. In fact, it was 'Bertola' who put me in touch with the historian and author.

Wembley and Scotland's former No.1 explains: "A couple of years ago, my wife Edith and I travelled into Euston by train with a stranger sitting opposite. He didn't say a word throughout the journey, including a 20-minute hold-up outside of Euston. Then, as we got up to leave the carriage, he turned to me and said: 'Bert Harkins, you were my favourite rider at Wembley!'

"I was quite surprised and although we didn't have time to continue the conversation, I later found out his name was Mark Lewisohn (check him out on Google), who is the world authority on The Beatles. Reviews of his latest book were in all the national papers."

"It's really nice that I've got to know Bert," says Mark. "When I get a text message on my phone, his name comes up, and I have to pinch myself. Bert Harkins, captain of the Wembley Lions, is texting me. It's great, because our friendship has re-connected me with those lovely teenage memories. Bert was always known for being one of the friendliest and most approachable of riders. He'd always give his time to the fans – and he's still very much that same warm and generous man."

Ownership of his first car enabled Mark to visit west London on Wednesday nights to support White City in their three seasons of BL1 activity between 1976 and 1978.

"I was eager to have a weekly team to support again, so I became a big fan of the City Rebels – but the team never had the support the Lions enjoyed. I was thinking we'd get 30,000 people at home meetings but we only got about 1,500, rattling around inside this huge stadium. The war-cries were a bit pathetic and the racing wasn't as good to watch compared to Wembley, although I barely missed a meeting. When White City packed up, all us supporters knew why. We were surprised it had lasted as long as three seasons.

"The best thing about those three years was winning the league in 1977, which was wonderful, my best year in the sport. I went with friends – other Rebels supporters – to many of the away matches, and I cracked open a bottle of bubbly on the Monmore Green terraces when we clinched the title with a late-season win at Wolverhampton."

When the Rebels' promoters pulled the plug at Wood Lane and Bob Dugard transferred the first

**COME TOGETHER:** White City Rebels line up before the match at Wolverhampton in October 1977 that clinched the BL championship. Left to right: Marek Cieslak, Paul Gachet, Steve Weatherley, Trevor Geer, Dave Kennett, Mike Sampson, Kai Niemi, Lee Dunton (team manager). On bike: Gordon Kennett.

division licence to Eastbourne, where his family had staged second division speedway since 1969, Mark was happy to venture down to Sussex on a regular basis to support the Eagles.

"It was pretty much the White City Rebels side and the meetings were good fun. Home meetings were on Sundays, so we'd drive down in the morning, find a pub for lunch and then go to the speedway in the afternoon. I really enjoyed that.

"Gordon Kennett was my all-time favourite rider – he was our hero at White City for three years before leading Eastbourne from 1979 onwards. I was at Wembley in September 1978 for what was probably the single greatest speedway meeting of my life, when Gordon finished runner-up to Ole Olsen in the World Final. I lost my voice after just a couple of laps of his first ride, Heat 4, when he was out against Olsen and Ivan Mauger – it was an incredibly close race and Gordon was still in with a good chance of winning it until Ivan fell on the pits bend, third lap. He had five good races that night and deserved his second place overall.

"I was also cheering on Dave Jessup, who was back on the Wembley track and could have won the title, or gone very close, but for a push-rod problem that caused his bike to stop while leading in one race.

"Of all the riders I've watched, I never saw anyone with more natural talent on a bike than Kelly Moran, who rode for the Eagles for a couple of seasons. His balance was incredible. You'd long for him to miss the gate – which he usually did – because then he'd have to pick his way through the field to get to the front. I gather now that he led an interesting private life but I didn't know this at the time. He was just brilliant to watch – worth the admission money alone.

"My last season of watching speedway was 1983, the year I became a full-time writer."

Mark had a job in admin at the BBC, and then at the music industry trade journal *Music Week,* before deciding to work for himself.

"Once you're self-employed, no-one pays you to have time off. When you're busy writing articles or books to a deadline, you can't just take the afternoon off to go up to Belle Vue.

"Two other things happened that year: I got a nice new girlfriend . . . and I got fed up with speedway. I'd grown tired of all the petty rules and regulations, the way things kept changing, or didn't change. There was an administrative craziness about speedway that got on my nerves and I'd become cynical about it. So what with one thing and another, after 13 years of going to the speedway, I stopped."

Did The Beatles replace speedway as his main obsession?

"No, The Beatles always came first. I went to speedway from 1970 but I'd been into The Beatles since 1963, when I was five. It's funny how these things dovetail, though – I got into speedway just as The Beatles broke up."

The first book in Mark's new biographical trilogy *All These Years* took 10 years to research and write and runs to a mammoth 1,728 pages – and this only takes the reader up to the end of 1962, just before John, Paul, George and Ringo have their first No.1 single with *Please Please Me.* He estimates that volume two will take about seven years to complete and the same again before the final volume is completed.

There have been at least 500 books on The Beatles, yet none can compare to Mark's widely acclaimed output in terms of research and attention to detail. The fact that he worked for Paul McCartney for 15 years, was commissioned by the Beatles' record company EMI to write *The Complete Beatles Recording Sessions: The Official Story of the Abbey Road Years* and that Paul once described Mark's *The Complete Beatles Chronicle* as "The Beatles' Bible", speaks volumes for his credibility and reputation.

And Mark insists that some 44 years after the world's most famous pop band broke up, he is still uncovering new and previously unpublished material to enthral the hundreds of thousands of connoisseurs who can't wait to devour his next in a long line of best-sellers.

Mark's research and writing is historically contextual and he applies this same process to his thoughts about the impact his beloved Lions' own 'Hello Goodbye' had on speedway.

"Looking back at 1970–71 from a historian's point of view, the fact that racing was taking place in the national stadium on a weekly basis was clearly significant for the sport. The Lions' revival did British speedway a great service, it was a real shot in the arm. Wembley Stadium had an allure all its own, it was served by the Underground and two British Rail lines, and it was Saturday-night racing. Thousands of people went to speedway simply because it was something to do, somewhere to go – it was a Saturday night out in London for couples, for families, for OAPs."

Current day British promoters should look away now, or reach for the Prozac, as Mark recalls Wembley's pulling power.

He says: "It was only later when I realised that other tracks' home crowds might be 1,000, 1,500 or maybe 2,000 people. At Wembley we had 20,000, 25,000, even 30,000 . . . for a league meeting. I once read that 87,000 had packed into the stadium for a Lions' league match in the 1940s, and clearly that wasn't going to happen again – but for 30,000 to see the reopening meeting in 1970 was quite fantastic.

"In 1971 the stadium owners closed the back straight side between the second and third bends, because there was no point opening the whole stadium for 20,000 or 30,000. But it meant that on our side, between the fourth and first bends, the stands were packed and the atmosphere fantastic.

"When the Lions stopped racing, many of the casual spectators never went again. If you plot the decline of British speedway on a graph – if, say, you look at 1972, 1982, 1992, 2002 and 2012 – the trend is a downward one. Of course, there are good years every once in a while, where there might be a bit of a resurgence, but generally it's been steadily downward. With the closure of weekly racing at Wembley, there was nothing to arrest that decline. Wembley's revival and closure were both significant moments in the history of British speedway.

"Imagine the positive effect it would have on speedway in 2014 if there was weekly racing at our national stadium . . . and how far we've come from that, because it doesn't seem to be an option that people consider any more."

*If you want to find out more about Mark Lewisohn, visit www.marklewisohn.com, or follow him on Twitter, @marklewisohn*

# BRIEF ENCOUNTERS WITH... Eddie Ingels

**How did your move to the UK come about?**

George Wynn (an Englishman) was a mechanic for Ivan Mauger and also helped build the famous gold-plated bike. He lived in Anaheim, California, when I moved there in 1982 to race the southern circuit. George took me under his wing, I was able to live with him and he was a mentor, friend and mechanic for me. As he was a good friend of Ian Thomas', he introduced us and set up the contract for the 1984 season racing for Newcastle in the British League.

**What were your first impressions of the UK?**

It was a bit confusing driving on the wrong side of the road. I loved how they had a turf club (greyhound racing) at all the tracks. The weather was a bit dreary but I managed to love the country.

**Did you have an 'English dad' or did you have to fend for yourself?**

Ian Thomas was such a fantastic man. He took very good care of me. He kept me informed of every aspect of racing, and living in the UK, I couldn't have had a better man by my side.

**What did you miss most about home?**

The food! Mexican food, Taco Bell, donuts, root beer . . . hahaha!

**How different were the tracks and racing in the UK and how did you adapt to them?**

They were extremely different. The UK tracks were long, banked and extremely fast. I was able to adapt pretty quickly to my home track at Newcastle. It was a shorter, slicker track and I did fairly well there.

**Did you receive any special treatment because you were American?**

Yes, I feel I did. The supporters, promoters and racers were all kind and the city of Newcastle welcomed me with open arms. The Geordies are a fantastic bunch of people. We lived in Felling, Gateshead, and in our neighbourhood if the kids knew I was home from a race they would stop by and ask for an autograph.

**What was the highlight of your British speedway career?**

Scoring 11 points at Wolverhampton and 15 at Edinburgh; winning the Best Pairs with David Bargh; being a member of the Ivan Mauger Jubilee Series; beating Phil Crump at Swindon (I will never forget that!).

**What was the funniest or strangest thing that happened while in the UK?**

I was married at Brough Park to my still beautiful wife Christina. What happened? I didn't inform Ian Thomas that I had a girlfriend or a son. A few days after I arrived I wanted Christina and my son Ryan with me. Ian asked if we were married and if we wanted to be married, which of course we did. So, he set up our entire wedding on the centre green at Brough Park. Kenny Carter was my best man and the entire Diamonds team were also at the wedding dressed in top hats and tails. An incredible day.

**When did you realise it was time to go home?**

I never wanted to leave the UK, it was my dream to be there. But I didn't make the (minimum 6.00) points average for overseas imports. My mistake was signing for Belle Vue late in the '85 season. They were the league champions but the track was hard for me to adapt to. It was a big mistake on my part and a huge regret.

# GARY
# HAVELOCK

**H**E was World Champion at a time when British speedway desperately needed one, won a host of other international and domestic honours and captained his country for six years.

But as he looks forward to a well-earned farewell meeting to mark a 27-year career that started in 1985, Gary Havelock believes he never gained the respect he deserved from the sport's authorities.

For a time while his career was really taking off, it seemed Havvy was rarely out of the headlines for the wrong reasons.

But, as we talk in his spacious home on a quiet modern estate in Marton, near Middlesbrough, he insists the six-month ban he received for being tested positive for cannabis use in 1989 gave him the kick up the backside he needed and that other apparent indiscretions he was accused of were wrongly pinned on him.

And Havvy, who started his career with home-town club Middlesbrough before spending a decade at Bradford, then moving to Poole, Eastbourne, Peterborough, Arena-Essex and Redcar, says he never did manage to win over the powers that be after being unfairly saddled with a bad boy reputation – the recent, later reversed, decision to stage the Elite Riders' Championship on the same night as his farewell meeting has only emphasised that opinion.

"Did I ever get the respect I deserved from the speedway authorities? No, certainly not," he says, "and the incident which happened a couple of weeks ago with the date of the Elite Riders' Championship pretty much proved that. I said at the time that I thought they had very little respect for me and now I know they don't.

Always spectacular and good to watch, Havvy riding for England against Denmark at Ipswich in 1988.

"Before I won the World Championship times were tough. We were in a recession, crowd figures were down everywhere and all the promoters kept harping on about if only we had a British World Champion we could turn it around. And when I won it, I dedicated the win to British speedway.

"I felt they missed a big chance. They could have maybe hired a PR company to get behind me and push me. But all the PR we were doing in the weeks and months afterwards we arranged ourselves.

"The promoters didn't do a massive amount. I think they just sat back and thought: 'We've got the World Champion, we'll have full stadiums up and down the country now', but it never happened. I'm not bitter at all, though. You can only do as much as you can and I certainly did as much as I could."

Havvy was Britain's first World Champion since Michael Lee 12 years earlier but he strongly suspects that drugs ban was still fresh in the minds of the speedway authorities and that it had turned them against him.

"I definitely think it turned them against me, without a doubt," he reflects. "When I was getting into all sorts of alleged troubles I think there was a strong feeling right from the top that they wanted me out of the sport altogether and it cost me a lot of money in legal fees getting off things I didn't do.

"I made mistakes but everything that seemed to happen anywhere within a 100-mile radius of me got blamed on me."

It's clear from Havvy's body language that it still rankles, although he used it in his favour.

"You take it on the chin, I suppose," he adds. "All the bad stuff that happened certainly made me more determined. I still think I would have been World Champion but whether I would have been world No.1 as early and as young, possibly not.

"You need fuel – everyone does to drive them on – and my fuel was to be able to stick two fingers up at the authorities. I think it certainly fuelled my desire to win."

The suspension which ruled Havvy out of the entire 1989 campaign came as a result of testing positive for cannabis after the 1988 end-of-season British League Riders' Championship at Belle Vue.

But, he says, use of the recreational drug was hardly uncommon among riders at the time and that it could have just as easily been one of his rivals who was caught.

"Without naming any names, back in those days there was an awful lot of speedway riders who were smoking cannabis recreationally," he says. "I don't think anybody would have tried to have smoked cannabis and raced, because you'd have still been at the start-line when everyone else was on the first corner.

**Back in style, Gary locking up at Belle Vue soon after returning from his ban in 1990.**

"I guess I was the unlucky one who got caught. It could have been one of 10, probably. But I'm a big believer that everything happens for a reason and I guess my reason was that the year I missed made me hungrier and gave me an even greater desire.

"The big consensus among riders was that it only stayed in your system for three days but if I remember rightly, I'd been at a party a full week before and smoked it and, hence, found out it can stay in your system longer than any other drug, possibly up to two, three, four months.

"The ironic thing is that if I had taken cocaine or amphetamines or some such much stronger drug, that would have been out of my system after three days and I would never have been caught.

"You can look at it as you will. I did what I did, I was punished and I took my punishment."

That punishment meted out by the Speedway Control Board in January '89 – a four-year ban with three of those suspended – might have been even more severe, as there were calls at the time for a draconian lifetime ban.

Let's remember that Havvy was only 19 at the time.

"If you asked any 18 or 19-year-old about it today, they'd just laugh," insists Havvy. "They'd say: 'It's a bit of pot, who cares?' But back then, society, and certainly the older generation, tended to ringfence drugs as drugs.

"To them I might as well have been a child-molesting heroin addict. Certainly the hierarchy in the Speedway Control Board took a dislike to me.

"I think, and a large percentage of society would agree with me, that a lifetime ban was ridiculous but, unfortunately, the guys who were in charge at the time didn't.

"It was a real threat and I was very worried. It was a difficult time for me and my family but we seemed to get through it one way or another."

Inevitably Havvy found himself the target of the terrace boo boys but by and large he received a good deal of support from within the sport.

"Most of my fellow riders were feeling for me," he says. "The supporters were split. Bradford fans stuck by me, although fans of other teams liked to use it against me, especially when I came back for the first couple of years. I got booed and jeered and had abuse shouted at me but the more stick they gave me on parade, the more determined I was to get one over their team on the track.

"It's receded over the years but every now and then I get someone piping up on social media. But it doesn't bother me, it's water off a duck's back. One thing I have developed from this career is broad shoulders."

And Heaven knows he needed those broad shoulders with a 'Havvy was there, he must have done it' attitude commonplace in the late 80s, when he was linked to a number of controversial incidents.

He was already banned for testing positive when he was hit by a further charge for an incident after the 1989 NL Fours at Peterborough, where he was attending as a spectator.

In a nutshell, Havvy got caught short after the meeting and, with Alwalton virtually deserted, took advantage of a nearby fence. He was charged by the SCB for 'conduct prejudicial to the sport and indecent exposure'. (National Leaguers Mark Courtney and Mark Crang were both given one-year suspended sentences for committing the same offences as Gary at the East of England Showground.)

"It was an empty stadium, everyone had gone home," he protests, "but somebody had seen me. The way that it was put out is that I was running around with my knob out chasing people! But it's a thing that 95 per cent of men have done at some time – if it had been Kelvin Tatum or Simon Wigg, the charge would never have been brought."

At the time, the SCB intended to reactivate all of the suspended part of Havvy's original three-year ban. But he won an appeal, the suspension was reduced to six months and he was cleared to resume racing on May 1, 1990.

Captain Havvy held aloft after Bradford's 1992 KO Cup Final victory against Reading. His Dukes team-mates are (left to right): Sean Wilson, Simon Wigg, Paul Thorp, Antal Kocso. Front: Kelvin Tatum, Stuart Parnaby.

# From drugs ban to Britain's best

**DESPITE spending more than a year on the sidelines because of his extended ban, Gary Havelock looked like he'd never been away when he made his comeback.**

He slotted seamlessly back into the Bradford side, increased his average and won the British semi-final of the World Championship shortly after returning and in 1991 things really started to take off when he won the first of two successive British Finals with a flawless 15-point maximum.

"I'd been riding a motorbike since I was three," he points out, "so I think I could get away with it. I don't remember feeling rusty and I came back with a bit of a bang. I seem to remember doing the British semi-final a matter of days after my ban ended but I'd worked hard in the winter getting fit.

"The funniest thing was that when I first got banned I'd saved up a bit of money from riding and in the year I had out I decided to go and do all the things that 19-year-old kids do – I had a couple of holidays, went to the pub every night, bought myself a boy racer sports car . . .

"So when it came to getting my bikes ready for the following season I didn't have any money left. I had to borrow money from my mum and dad.

"But I think that year I got everything out of my system and did all the things that 19-year-olds do. When I came back I was definitely more focussed."

Bradford stuck by Havvy during his absence and the Dukes management welcomed him back for the 1990 season once his ban had ended.

"They stuck by me, but if they hadn't I think it would have been pretty harsh," he says. "They paid quite a lot of money for me when they signed me from Middlesbrough and if they'd ditched me then, they'd have been ditching an asset. They would have had to sign a rider for £30,000-plus to replace me, so it was a no-brainer really. If the boot had been on the other foot, I'd have stuck by my rider."

Born winner: Gary in his schoolboy grass-track days.

Dad Brian riding for Newcastle in the mid-70s.

Former professional footballer Bobby Ham and brother Allan were the men in charge of the Dukes at the time.

"They were good to ride for," reflects Havvy. "Bobby was an absolute diamond. Alan was the more involved one and I got on with them both pretty well.

"A few little things happened towards the end with Allan – nothing I'd like to go public with, but things I didn't think were really necessary – but on the whole, no problem. They ran a very professional ship.

"Everything about Bradford was fantastic. The pits were the best, the changing rooms were the best, the track was the best and the fans were the best. It was a really cool place to ride, just a shame it was a massive, expansive stadium with 1,500 fans in. It struggled to generate a really good atmosphere – that was the only bad thing about the place."

In fact, Havvy says he's not ridden a track as good anywhere in the world.

His first season with Middlesbrough in 1985.

Gary and reserve Martin Dugard lead the 1992 World Final parade.

"Nowhere has even come close," he insists. "It was really wide, so you had a lot of different lines, it was a really nice shape – the straights and the bends were just the right proportion – but the biggest thing for me was the banking.

"Some tracks have banking but about three-quarters of the way out they have what's called off-camber, where it levels off or goes down, and once you get past that point you're done for – you spin off, go backwards or crash.

"But Bradford was banked all the way to the fence and it was steep. If you stood on the white line on the third and fourth bends, the bottom of the fence was about three or four feet above your head. So you could ride three or four inches from the fence and it intimidated a lot of riders.

"Me and Sean Wilson used to cut our handlebars down by about two inches on either end so that we could squeeze through gaps on the outside when away riders thought they were riding on the fence.

"It was a phenomenal track. The two World Finals they had there (1985 and 1990) were absolute crackers, with racing and passing, and it was like that for pretty much every league meeting."

The team at Bradford during Havvy's 10 years there was always pretty special too, with Simon Wigg and Kelvin Tatum among the star names.

"Wiggy was excellent," recalls Havvy with great fondness. "I spent a bit of time travelling with him and I had a lot of time for him. He taught me a lot professionally – how you should be – and he was a great man. Speedway is a much worse place without him.

"I never really knew Kelvin until he came and he was a good guy to have in the team. I didn't think he would be – he came across as this ex-public schoolboy and I thought he'd only be bothered about himself but he was all right as a team-mate. I had quite a bit of respect for him."

Gary sandwiched in between Jimmy Nilsen and Slawomir Drabik seconds before the crash.

One team-mate he needed no introduction to was Sean Wilson. They had been mates since the age of around seven, from their days starring on the junior grass-track scene.

As well as being colleagues at domestic level, they were also in the same England team – and Havvy, who made more than 70 appearances for his country, remembers their time together in the Test series against Australia Down Under in the winter of 1987-88.

"We were the last official Test team to go out there and we beat them 5-2," remembers Gary, "but it should have been 6-1, because in one of them they cheated.

"We'd brought a load of Barum tyres because they were cheap. You could get Dunlops there but they were really expensive, about £100. So after the practice day for the first Test at Claremont (Perth) we had a chat and suggested a gentlemen's agreement – we'd sell them some Barums at cost price and we'd all use them.

"They agreed and at Claremont the track was grippy, which suited the Barums. It got to the interval and we were well ahead. Next thing, the firework display, due to take place after the meeting, was brought forward to the interval.

"All the lights went out and while they were doing that, a big motorway blade went out and bladed every bit of dirt off the track, and made it rock concrete slick. They came out in the second half with Dunlops on and beat us.

"So for the rest of the tour we bought Dunlops. It was costing us money but we wanted to make sure we won.

"The last Test was at Mildura, where Phil Crump was still king. Sean must have only been 17 but he gated on Crumpie. Without knowing it, Phil was all over him like a rash – wherever Phil went, Sean just happened to go.

*Concerned father Brian (left) after Gary's spill in Heat 8.*

"Phil was waving at him and ramming into him, so after the race Sean took his helmet off in the pits and went over to ask him what was up. And Phil punched him! So that was it, it all kicked off and there was a 30-man brawl in the pits. Someone grabbed someone else and a big line of bikes went down like dominoes.

"Rosco (Alun Rossitter) was cowering in the corner behind the toolboxes but we all got involved. At the end of the meeting we all got loaded up and at Mildura they had a wooden clubhouse. Rosco was saying: 'Come on, let's just go back to the hotel' but I was saying: 'No, let's go to the bar'.

"Rosco said: 'We can't do that, we'll get the s*** kicked out of us', but we weren't going to creep away like chickens and in we marched *en masse*. To be fair, the Aussies were all right – you know what they're like, they like to have a ruck, then shake hands and have a beer afterwards.

"And then there was the infamous hotel room incident in Czechoslovakia," he adds, unable to conceal his frustration at another controversy he had to defend himself against when he was completely innocent. This time he was on England duty in Eastern Europe.

"A certain team-mate of mine in a drunken rage decided to start throwing things out of a 10th storey window. It started with an empty champagne bottle, followed by the telephone, the lamp, the radiogram and then he was halfway across the room with the television when I grabbed him and started wrestling with him, telling him to pack it in.

"Just at that time Graham Reeve, who was just a trainee referee at the time and was out there on a supporters' bus tour, walked in the room and started asking what was going on. I didn't know him from Adam, so we said something along the lines of 'who the f*** are you? F*** off out of our room!'

"I got my team-mate settled down and went off to sleep and the next thing, I was woken up by a Kalashnikov or something similar being poked in my face. Two armed police were there screaming at us and took us down to reception. We had to pay some damages and they let us off."

But that wasn't the end of it and when word got out back home, Havvy was suddenly in hot water with the authorities again.

"It was nothing to do with me, so I said to the guy that if we got a letter saying we had to go to a hearing, he'd have to put his hand up," says Havvy. "I'd been in enough trouble as it was and he said he'd do it.

"We got a letter saying we had to appear at a tribunal, so I rang the guy up and his first words were 'I'm denying everything'. It cost me about £4-5,000 in legal fees to get off something I hadn't even done."

# Boy racer who beat the system

**WHEN your dad's a successful rider and you've ridden a motorbike before you've even had a go at a pushbike, it's inevitable that a career involving two wheels and an engine is going to follow.**

And Gary Havelock was so eager to follow in father Brian's tyretreads that when he applied for his first licence, his birthday had mysteriously moved forward two months . . . which prevented him having to wait until the following season for his first race!

Havvy Snr began his speedway career at Sunderland at the age of 27 in 1973, when Gary was four, and went on to ride for Berwick, Newcastle, Middlesbrough, Workington and Stoke. And Havvy Jnr was often there with him.

"One of my earliest memories is when I was three-years-old and Dad gave me this bright orange mini-motorbike – I was like, 'oh my God!' I hadn't even ridden a pushbike before but I jumped on

Back in leathers to lift the World Championship trophy in Wroclaw.

it straight away and went racing round the garden," remembers Havvy.

"Dad used to take me to the speedway and I'd go round the track before the meeting or at the interval. From the age of three I lived, ate and breathed speedway.

"Over the years I've seen pushy fathers with their kids – it's almost a case of what he wants the kid to do rather than what the kid wants. But although my dad pushed me quite hard, it was what I wanted.

"I started racing junior grass-track at the age of eight and I did that pretty successfully until I was about 14 – I won two British Championships – and then we decided we'd knock it on the head, get a speedway bike and ride demonstrations and practices until I got to 16. Supposedly!

"Dad realised the season would be finished by the time I turned 16, so he applied for my adult licence and put my birthday down as September 4 instead of November 4, so I got a licence illegally for the last two months of the 1984 season and rode in meetings when I was 15. I actually won the Suffolk Junior Open Championship at Mildenhall when I was 15."

In 1985, Gary's dream of becoming a professional speedway rider was realised when he signed for local team Middlesbrough Tigers.

Dad Brian had hung up his leathers and was appointed team manager at Cleveland Park but Mum Marge, having seen her husband come through his career in such a dangerous sport relatively unscathed, now had the worry of seeing her son sign up to dice with the same dangers.

It was an inevitable career choice for the younger Havvy but surely she worried?

"I'm sure she did, you'd have to ask her," says Gary. "She never used to show it, although there was a time when I did junior grass-track, because I was only a slip of a lad I found it hard to hang on when it was bumpy and I was crashing pretty much every week. She must have been worried then because she said to Dad, 'he's going to have to pack it in or he'll hurt himself'.

"But Dad came up with the brainwave of putting a steering damper on, which was like a shock absorber – you fastened one end to the frame and the other end to the side of your handlebars. You

Two weeks after winning the world crown, Gary attends this special family celebration, where he is joined by (left to right) Bonnie Boothroyd, Mum Marge, Dad Brian, wife Jayne and Bradford co-promoters Allan Ham and Eric Boothroyd.

could still turn it but not fast and that seemed to cure it. Soon after that I started winning, and the rest is history."

Gary was an instant hit in his first season of National League racing, finishing with an eye-catching 7.33 average and two paid maximums to his name.

"I had no fears at all," he remembers. "My ambition was to beat as many of the top guys as I could. Dad always used to say: 'Go on, son, make a name for yourself'. The bigger the name, the more I wanted to beat them. I was like that all of my career. It was only after my back injury that doubts would come in."

Despite being the manager's son he was very much there on merit, but not all the old heads in the team were entirely comfortable with the presence of the young whippersnapper.

"I think there were occasions when some of the senior riders were being taken out and I was being put in," he recalls, "because I was scoring points. But I think something was said, because halfway through the season my dad quit. I think the attitude was something like, 'you're costing me money taking me out and putting your lad in', so he told them where to stick it. He just stayed in my pit with me after that."

As anyone who has ever been a 16-year-old knows, of course – you know it all at that age and your parents know nothing. And until Havvy Snr quit, Gary couldn't even get away from his father at work because he was his boss, too!

"We had a lot of arguments when I was between 14 and 18," he admits, "and actually came to blows on a couple of occasions. He had a period when I was 18-19 and he didn't come with me much but I think I was just a young lad slowly turning into a man who wasn't going to be told what to do . . . and Dad still thought I was a kid and was telling me what to do."

By and large, though, they were happy times for the young Havvy and he was particularly pleased to have Mark Courtney as a team-mate in 1986.

Havvy Snr had helped Courtney buy his first bike and he lived with the Havelocks in Yarm between 1979-81, when he raced for Middlesbrough. Gary says: "He was like an older brother to me."

In fact Gary had mechaniced for Courtney on occasions from the age of 14 and learned a lot from him in readiness for his own speedway career.

The season he rode with Courtney turned out to be a very successful one, as he won the British Under-21 title and the Grand Slam at Arena-Essex, after coming from the second row of an eight-man, eight-lap race to win the semi-final. "That has to be one of my greatest ever races," he reflects.

And he'd already been the hero of the hour in 1985, when Middlesbrough won the NL Fours at Peterborough. Havvy was only reserve for the Fours but Mark Fiora was injured early on and he seized his chance to shine, top-scoring in both the semi-finals and final.

"I always seemed to be able to do pressure quite well from an early age," he says. "Some people just fold, but I used to turn it around. If you feel nervous about something, it's an energy."

By the time Havvy joined Bradford in 1987, he'd already ridden in 15 top flight matches for the Dukes as No.8 and scored one paid maximum, so it was inevitable that's where he'd start his full-time British League career.

"At that time all the big World Championship events were almost all on big tracks," he recalls. "Middlesbrough was a tight, technical track, so we decided it would be good experience to be riding a big track every week. With Bradford having reopened as a league venue in 1986, and only being an hour down the road, it was ideal.

"Edinburgh were desperate to sign me in my second year at Middlesbrough and offered me quite a bit more money but I decided to stay with my local track.

"And I was always going to go full-time in the British League in 1987. I'd done pretty much everything I could do in the NL and I needed to be riding against the top riders every week."

Despite finishing with an average of above seven in his first full BL season, Havvy had expected better – and that was because he was on a Weslake while the top boys were GM-powered.

"Weslake wanted to make me a full factory rider and sponsor me with engines," he remembers, "and at the time it seemed like a good move because they were expensive. They were also developing an overhead cam engine, so the thinking was, 'if we developed it and it came good, maybe I could get a long-term sponsorship out of it'.

"But I struggled a bit for speed that season. I remember jumping on Randy Green's GM and thinking 'wow, what am I doing?' The GMs were run by a chain rather than pushrods, so you got more direct power.

"The GM was so much quicker. We decided half way through that year we had made a mistake but I stayed loyal until the end of the season and then bought some GMs for 1988."

Despite breaking his wrist in the '88 British Final, Havvy enjoyed a better time and top-scored for England from reserve in the World Team Cup Final at Long Beach after his team-mates were hit by bike problems.

"It wasn't a good trip for England because we came last," he says, "but it was good for me because I showed them how it should be done."

In hindsight, that night in California was maybe the springboard for the international success Havvy went on to achieve.

# Dreadlock champion suits you
**GARY Havelock's brilliant world title victory at Wroclaw's Olympic Stadium in 1992 was the realisation of a lifelong dream.**

As a young lad Havvy would lie in bed thinking of what it would be like to be the world's No.1 rider and at the age of 23 he realised that ambition in Poland.

Already crowned British and Overseas Champion that season, he dropped just one point in the big one to finish ahead of Per Jonsson and Gert Handberg as he became the first World Final debutant to get his hands on the trophy since Freddie Williams in 1950.

"My whole life, right from a young age, I used to watch videos of Bruce Penhall winning at Wembley and I used to lie in bed at night wondering what it would feel like to go across the line and be World Champion," he explains.

"Having since worked with sports psychologists, it's a thing they call visualisation. You visualise how things are going to be and you do it over and over again. You programme your subconscious mind to get used to that feeling then, when you're in a race, your subconscious mind should take over because things happen in a split second. I was doing that from the age of three or four without realising it.

"I used to think, 'how would I celebrate?' 'Would I do a wheelie?' As it turned out, I just rode across the line because I was stunned. I think I was still stunned on the rostrum at the realisation that a lifetime dream had been fulfilled. I couldn't really believe it.

"As someone who has always been massively patriotic, hearing the national anthem play made me so proud. It was such a special feeling."

Despite his lack of World Final experience Havvy was among the favourites to win in Wroclaw but says he didn't feel any undue pressure.

He recalls: "When I was doing interviews before the meeting people were saying, 'this is your first World Final, are you going there for the experience?' I was saying, 'no! I've beaten every one of those other 15 riders, so in my mind I could do it again'.

"I'd gone there with the full intention of winning. That's one of the reasons I spent four-and-a-half hours having dreadlocks put in my hair. I've always liked to be a bit different."

At one point during the meeting, though, Havvy thought his dream was over. In Heat 8 Jimmy Nilsen knocked Zdenek Tesar off and the Czech's machine cannoned into Havvy, bashing his right knee against his engine. The pain was intense and he thought he'd been seriously injured.

"With upright bikes your knee is pretty much lent against the engine," he says. "The bike hit the fence, came back across the track and slammed into the side of my leg and smashed my knee into the top of the engine. It was pure agony, I thought I'd broken something.

"I coasted round, then laid down for a bit and it started easing off. It was just a dead leg. That was when the heavens opened and the meeting was delayed. A lot of people said at the time it was a good job we had that break so I could get my leg right, but if the two minutes had come on then, I'd have been out for the race. I don't think the delay helped or hindered me in any way."

Gary in 2014 with the Wroclaw '92 programme.

For several months after his triumph, Havvy was in big demand – "your life isn't your own," he reflects – but the financial rewards weren't especially great.

"I got lucky that Sunbrite, who were the national team sponsors, said if an English rider won the World Championship or the World Under-21 Championship, they'd get £10,000," he recalls. "If an English rider won both, they'd get £50,000 to share . . . and Mark Loram lost the Under-21s by about half-a-wheel to Leigh Adams. He still apologises for it!

"The prize money for winning the world title was about £2,950. Back in the day they said winning the world title was worth £250,000 over the next year but I was World Champion at possibly the worst time in speedway history.

"We had no TV deal, so how could you go to major corporate sponsors and say, 'can you sponsor me?' When they said 'what can you do for me?' all you could say was, 'I'll get your picture in *Speedway Star*'. They'd laugh at that.

"I even heard a rumour that the next year Allan Ham had gone to the BSPA's AGM and said he wanted paying for every meeting I was in because I was World Champion and I'd be increasing crowds. I don't know how true this is, but I was told he got paid for every away meeting I rode in 1993. But I didn't get paid anything extra. If that's true, it would leave a very bitter taste in my mouth."

Havvy's win in Wroclaw proved to be his last major international title – so should he have gone on to win more honours?

"All I ever wanted was to be World Champion," he replies. "I never dreamed of winning six or

**67**

seven or two or four. I only ever dreamed of winning one and that's maybe where I went wrong.

"The first year is always difficult. I remember the year after I won it that every time someone beat me in a league meeting they'd go across the line punching the air.

"I think I could possibly have won more, although I was unlucky with injuries. The first year of the GPs (1995) was difficult because we couldn't use laydowns in league meetings over here, so we were at a massive disadvantage.

"I started 1996 really well after we'd had a year developing the laydown, but then I crashed at Poole and broke my back which kept me out for the rest of the season. When it came to the wildcard picks, the last person they were going to put in was me, wasn't it? They never put me back in, which hurt, seeing the kind of people they did call up instead."

# Painful end

**RECOVERING from the horror crash that ended his riding career is a slow and frustrating process for Gary.**

Havvy was captaining Redcar Bears in March 2012 when he went down while leading – a rare occurrence in his long and distinguished career – and Edinburgh's Derek Sneddon, right behind him, had nowhere to go but into him.

Gary broke a staggering 14 bones in the crash and suffered severe nerve damage to his left arm. Even after a seven-hour nerve graft operation he still has no feeling from just above his elbow.

"It's slow and frustrating," he says. "I'm still in a lot of pain. The bones seem to have healed OK but it's the nerves and it drives me up the wall sometimes. I have good days and bad days and still take a lot of medication."

Bearing the scars from his big crash.

But he is, in his own words, "getting on with it". He's driving again after former Bradford team-mate Phil Disney generously gave him an automatic car he had spare and he's able to indulge in his passion for cooking, proudly revealing: "I can peel and chop an onion with one hand almost as fast as I could with two!

"It's not ideal but I've always been a glass-half-full guy. It could have been worse. If I'd been run over six inches the other way it could have been my neck – I could be a quadriplegic now or even dead."

Luckily for Havvy he has the support of a loving family. He met wife Jayne when they were 16 and they still live in their native Teesside with teenage daughters Holly and Erin.

"For the last six, seven, eight years Jayne has stopped coming to meetings," he says, "because she couldn't bear to watch me any more. She was that scared I was going to hurt myself. I guess she was proved to be right.

"But in the early days she came everywhere with me and even when she didn't she was a

Home comfort: Havvy and Jayne, who have been together since they were both 16.

massive support. She used to get it in the neck when I'd come home rambling on about the state of the track or something!"

# Lack of characters

**GARY Havelock has seen a good many changes to the sport since he first took to the track in the mid-80s.**

"Up until the last 10 years it didn't change that much but since then it's changed an awful lot," he says.

"The bikes are going so fast now and the tyres are so rubbish. The top guys are all very professional – they get the right amount of sleep and eat the correct amount of food, train . . . I didn't really ever train. I'd get a bit fit in January, February and at the beginning of March by running and playing football but once the season started the racing kept me fit enough. You could get away with not being a super athlete – you needed to be mentally fit rather than physically fit.

"Obviously when I started we all rode uprights too. Since they changed to laydowns and the way carburation is now, they only really start producing their good power above 12,000rpm, which means you have to keep things singing.

"So young kids today haven't really learned any throttle control because there's only one way to ride a laydown bike and that's fully pinned. Some of these guys don't need a throttle – an on-off switch would do. I wouldn't say laydowns have killed the sport but they've changed the riding style."

Havvy also rues the lack of characters in the modern sport.

"When I was a kid every team had a scrapper in it," he says. "Ours was Geoff Pusey. Every other

**Havvy in his role as Coventry team manager.**

meeting he'd have a nose-to-nose or a shouting match or fisticuffs with somebody. Every track had a telephone on the centre green and if a rider got excluded he'd be taking his helmet off, shouting into it in front of the fans and waving his arms about.

"That's all gone. Riders don't want to get stung with a £300 fine. No-one ever got hurt by it.

"Andrew Silver was a brilliant character, although one night he knocked Richard Hellsen out in the pits with a headbutt. He was partnered with him at Swindon but he always used to get in his way. They'd had words before and one night at Ipswich Andrew had enough and dived under him. And then when he saw him in the pits waving his arms around, he went over and stuck the nut on him."

And then there's the introduction of airfences. Are they really necessary?

"I was riding when they first came in," recalls Havvy. "I don't remember thinking, 'yeah, let's go mental, I'm invincible just because there was an airfence."

With Premier League and National League tracks having to have one in place for this season, it's a far cry from the days of the infamous steel fence at Exeter.

"I remember first going there with Middlesbrough," recalls Havvy. "It was a case of let's go there, lose and get out of the place in one piece!"

But despite it all Havvy's still involved in speedway as team manager at Elite League Coventry and says: "I still enjoy it. When you're a rider it's a 24-hour-a-day thing – you're thinking about getting your bikes ready, booking flights, talking to sponsors and all things like that. It's a lot less involved being a team manager.

"It has much to do with motivation and in every team I rode for except Middlesbrough, I was captain. Speedway is very psychological – a lot of races are won in the head, so I'd like to think that's something I can help with."

## On 2 Minutes With...
## KEITH BLOXSOME

**Where did you get your first bike and how much did it cost?**

My dad was an electrical engineer in Rochdale and one of the guys in the factory had a two-valve Jawa but he hadn't really done anything with it, so we bought it from him for £250, which was a lot in those days. This was 1976 and I was only 15. I used it at training schools but in the winter of 1977-78 I got a four-valve Weslake to use in the National League.

**Who helped you most in the early days?**

I couldn't have got where I did without Dad. Sadly, three months into the season he had a heart attack and died, so I took some time out to grieve.

I didn't drive at that time either. Earlier that season I'd top-scored at Edinburgh and Glasgow, so Glasgow offered me a team place. I passed my driving test, put the bike on the back of the Cortina and off I went.

I spent a lot of time with Rod Hunter and Andy Smith. As for other riders, they either didn't want to help or would give you wrong information.

**Which team-mate did you most enjoy partnering on track?**

That's a tricky one because you always wanted to beat your team-mate and they would do anything they could to beat you. I rode with some good guys, the likes of Charlie McKinna, Martin Dixon, Mel Taylor and Bobby Beaton. Dave Jessup was startlingly fair and quite helpful, too. He was No.1 at King's Lynn, so he'd take the choice of gates in the first race because he'd be up against the other team's No.1, but after that he'd alternative the choice of gate, which wasn't usually the case with top riders.

At Newcastle Bobby Beaton was fair but I'd known him from Belle Vue and Glasgow. Everyone else was as selfish as you like but that's probably what made the team so hard to beat – it was collectively a team of winners.

**Track you never looked forward to visiting?**

Shielfield Park, Berwick. To me it was like a track with four corners, although maybe it was me just riding it badly! But I came to realise that most of the tracks I disliked were ones I didn't go well on early in my career and didn't have the ability to do anything about it. As I progressed in my career it was about which set-up to use.

# GARRY MIDDLETON: FACTS AND FICTION

Nomadic speedway rider, self-publicist, property wheeler-dealer, pilot, born again Christian who was arrested for pushing his beliefs, a most complex and at times troubled character who ended his own life . . . it's time to look closely at and dispel some myths around the former Australian international who became known as 'Cass the Gas' . . .

**G**ARRY Middleton was a larger than life character who craved attention and publicity. **To those who knew him, it will probably come as no surprise that his ability to shock remained with him to the day he died.**

Thanks to six years' of diligent research by Australian-based speedway historian and author Tony Webb, we confirmed in our last issue that Middleton's life ended on November 23, 1994.

What was not known at that point was the actual cause of his death. Tony has since made contact with members of the Middleton family and to finally dispel all rumours about his demise, it can now be revealed that Garry took his own life at the age of 46.

Hackney skipper Garry lifts the KO Cup in 1971

Police found his body slumped in his car beside the Warrigal Highway west of Ipswich, on Queensland's Gold Coast, where he had lived out his last troubled years of a turbulent existence.

It is now 34 years since Garry was last seen on a British speedway track but the legend lives on. After all these years, alongside Kenny Carter, another suicide case, he is still one of the most talked about speedway riders of all-time.

He would have loved that.

Tony Webb set out to try and separate myth from fact about a controversial character he got to know more than 40 years ago. He has chronicled Middleton's story in an illustrated 100-page book, titled *Garry Middleton: Fact v Fiction,* which he has produced with the permission and co-operation of Garry's family.

"I knew Garry through my speedway spares business," said Tony. "During the 70s, I was the resident fuel and spares man at his spiritual home of Hackney and several East Anglian tracks. I visited Garry at his home at Starlings Green, in

With first wife Anne in 1972. The couple were married at High Beech.

Rebel with a cause, Garry in his most productive season with Oxford in 1972.

the village of Clavering in Essex, and he would come over to my shop.

"His mechanic, one of many I must add, was grass-track rider and present day ACU official Steve Brace, who was also a personal friend of mine. I would not claim to understand the inner man of Garry Middleton. Few people did. He was such a complex person and a lot has been written about his character.

"I recall the first time he came into my shop. He was like a kid in a lolly shop, racing around from shelf to shelf. 'I will have one of these' and 'one of those'. The pile of goodies on the shop floor was growing by the minute. Expecting a good sale to boost my cash-flow, I was taken aback when he started to barter an exchange using goods from the boot of his Mercedes. That was Garry.

"What is clear from the many emails I have received is that he was well loved by his fans and large family and a good friend to many people. He may have been a Jeckyl and Hyde character but if you were a mate it was everlasting.

"Over the last few months I have had contact with Middleton family members who were unaware of his life as one of the top speedway riders in the world. By the same token, the fans that loved him for the showman he was, an entertainer, were unaware of his qualities as a family man, his love for his mother and siblings, his faith and business achievement. It cannot be denied there was at times a darker side to his character but the good memories overweigh the negatives. If people got their fingers burnt in dealings with Garry in the business world, then the old adage of 'buyer beware' should have been applied.

"His potential for speedway stardom was unquestionable. He possessed a natural ability and had a sharp mechanical mind. He knew how things worked but did not have the hands-on skills to make it happen.

"I do think his lack of machine preparation and tuning skills held him back. He must have used every engine tuner in the business and had a succession of mechanics and helpers. Most successful riders find a tuner and stick with them, building a relationship, and it's the same with mechanics. It is evident by his many engine failures that often robbed him of the top positions in individual meetings that his preparation was lacking.

"He knew how to work the media, gain sponsorship and was never in awe of the superstars of the day. He possessed a very high IQ, If he had only set his mind to it, he could have been a World

A Birmingham Brummie in 1976.

Champion."

But the fact is, Middleton never won a major individual title. He averaged more than nine points a match in only one of his 10 British League seasons – at Oxford in 1972 – and failed to reach the World Final.

"My guess is that he lost the single-minded attitude and consistency to reach the very top in the sport of speedway," says Tony. "His European excursions opened up more vistas to make money than he could from racing. He liked to have a good deal going and his ventures into business took his focus away from speedway. His dealings with the importation of Mercedes cars, electronic equipment, real estate, training schools and other enterprises took priority. That is my personal view.

"He was also a loner and not always popular with other riders, but if you won his friendship he would do anything for you. As a rider, he was not always a team man – his bonus points were always low, averaging as little as around eight per season, which does not indicate a team commitment.

"However, he displayed leadership qualities when Len Silver shrewdly gave him the Hackney captaincy in 1970, thrusting added responsibility on his young shoulders."

With the exception of the east London club, where Silver seemed able to control the wild colonial boy for three successive seasons, the most productive period in Garry's career, the maximum length of stay with all of his other clubs was just one season.

"How Len achieved this is hard to say, as they were alike in many ways . . . their brushes with officialdom, an entrepreneurial streak and a bent for publicity," Webb added.

# Britain beware

**GARRY was born in Corowa Municipal Hospital, New South Wales, Australia on July 19, 1948. The general impression in England was that he was born with a silver spoon in his mouth, of New Zealand parents who moved to Adelaide where he was schooled and aspired to be a lawyer. According to Webb, this popular story only has an element of truth to it.**

He says: "Garry's father James was a commercial traveller often away on business trips, while his mother Valda was left to bring up the children, which dispels the silver spoon theory. There was a belief in England that he came from a wealthy background, which was partly true, but that was in the family's past. Garry's mum had to walk to the hospital on the day of his birth.

"The Middleton household was a happy home, although money was not plentiful. Every sibling took charge of the immediate younger one. Garry had nine siblings, four of whom are now deceased."

Garry first learned to slide on two wheels aboard a pushbike he rode with his friend Paul Scanlon (for whom he arranged second half rides at Hackney in 1971) on the sandhills in the Adelaide suburb of Royal Park. His greatest influence was his elder brother Jimmy who had an old James 175cc motorcycle that Garry would sneak out from the shed and then ride on the local streets.

He first rode speedway at Rowley Park in the 'Encourage' event on the night of December 26,

1964. The following season, 1965-66, he was still in the novice class, although his form flourished at Rowley Park in 1966-67 and prompted him to try his luck in England.

In early 1967 Garry made a reverse charge call from Australia to the Park Lane hotel in London, where King's Lynn promoter and market gardener Maurice Littlechild was attending a British Mushroom Growers' conference. Garry introduced himself to Maury, asking for the fare to England. His spiel must have been persuasive, because by March he was sailing to Southampton to join King's Lynn Stars and living in accommodation at his new promoter's Waltham Abbey residence.

The 18-year-old Aussie, signed on a two-year contract, was drafted into the team on their northern tour in June – but rode just five BL matches before being dropped to the second-half.

It marked the start of his nomadic, 10-year journey through British speedway . . .

His next move was to Belle Vue but he lasted only six meetings with the Aces. In August he was having second halves at Wimbledon, where he improved and earned himself 11 appearances for the Dons.

Tony Webb says: "Apparently Garry was so desperate to prove himself, he 'bought' second-half rides from other riders and paid them points money. Not that life was easy for Garry. He had taken to sleeping in his car to save money for his equipment."

At the end of that season, King's Lynn suspected they had let a gilt-edged prospect slip through their fingers and tried to claim ownership of his contract. But Wimbledon supremo Ronnie Greene stuck to his guns and retained him for 1968.

Middleton returned to Australia by ship and spent the winter of 1967-68 racing at Rowley Park, Adelaide and the Brooklyn circuit in Melbourne. But before the boat docked, he took the unusual step of writing a letter to *Speedway Star* columnist Angus Kix, thanking him for a supportive article that had appeared in the magazine. Kix supposedly passed Garry's letter to his 'colleague' Danny Carter, who printed it *verbatim* in the *Star* (unsuspecting readers, including Middleton, wouldn't have known that Kix and Carter were, in fact, two of several pseudonyms used by former editor Eric Linden!). Ironically, Linden had incurred Middleton's wrath when he penned an article omitting one R from his Christian name. Garry told him: "Just think of Rolls-Royce, Eric, and you will not forget again."

There was a bizarre moment in March 1969, when he was joined on the return journey to England by Bert Harkins. During a stopover in Hong Kong, Harkins returned to their hotel room to find Garry in front of the mirror repeating the phrase: 'You *will* be World Champion' . . . 'you *will* be World Champion'. A self-hypnosis book lay on the floor.

On his return to Wimbledon in 1969, Middleton discovered to his dismay that he had been transferred under the rider control system to far-flung Newcastle – a Monday track, which would have played havoc with his full calendar of Sunday bookings on the continent that necessitated long hauls by road and ferry. Along with Barry Briggs and Ivan Mauger, Middleton was one of the first British-based speedway riders to cash in on the lucrative long-track and grass-track scene, where he competed regularly in Germany, Austria, Italy, France, Belgium and Holland.

After a mere five matches for the Diamonds he was back in the capital by May – with Hackney. Happy to be back in London, Middleton was eager to project his image. He was dubbed 'Cass the Gas' after the world heavyweight boxing champion Cassius Clay, who had also perfected the art of self-promotion.

As well as a choice of ferries that enabled him to better exploit his overseas popularity and earn more money, he benefited from the use of workshop facilities at Hackney Stadium, run by team mechanic Terry 'Bert' Busch, and help from West Ham rider-cum-engine tuner Don Smith. With ex-Hammer Alf Hagon's spares shop around the corner, Garry was well set up.

Bengt Jansson recalls: "I always got on well with Garry, although I remember one time when I was back home in Sweden and he used my bike for an open meeting at Hackney – it might have been a World Championship qualifying round. He must have been having problems with his bike, so he went into the workshop and pinched mine. I wasn't angry, though. That's what Garry was like."

Middleton gained sponsorship from Rivetts, a sports manufacturer in Leytonstone, and Lewis Leathers of Great Portland Street, London. Veteran rider Wal Phillips helped him with fuel injector systems to boost his two-valve Jawa and introduced Garry to a new sponsor, Peter Elleker, whose daughter he would later marry.

His pursuit of sponsors at a time when the sport had precious few commercial backers had to be applauded. Just a year into his BL career at Wimbledon, he wrote to the Milk Marketing Board seeking backing. Garry said: "It's no good just going to a meeting, riding and coming away. You have to be a personality. It doesn't matter if people don't like you for it – they will still come and watch, if only to see you lose."

Critics may have laughed at him, scoffed at his bold claims, ridiculed his actions and sometimes dismissed him as a crank, but at Hackney he backed up his bold words with consistent results and pushed Colin Pratt hard for the No.1 spot. Because being top man mattered a lot to Garry.

Pratty tells of the night he and Middleton had both scored 11 points for Hawks. "Yeah, but my name will be the only one in the morning papers," boasted Garry, "cos they print the riders' names alphabetically and only the top scorer from each team gets a mention!"

Interviewed for Retro Speedway's DVD, *Memories of Hackney Speedway,* in 2012, Colin said: "Middleton was a big character who had plenty of rabbit even in his early days in England. Me and Bettsy (Terry Betts) used to see quite a bit of him around where we lived in Essex and eventually I bought his house at Clavering.

"I didn't agree with some of the things he did or how he went about it but we got on OK most of the time. "

Middleton's first appearance in the British Final came at West Ham in 1969. It was the closest he ever got to a World Final but he blew his big chance. After four rides Garry had eight points – just one away from a Wembley berth . . . only to be excluded from his last ride for tape-breaking.

But he wouldn't leave it there.

In typically explosive Middleton style, he re-emerged from the pits enraged and roared off in pursuit of the three other riders, Ronnie Moore, Nigel Boocock and Roy Trigg, for four laps while ignoring the marshal frantically waving the black flag.

At first Garry vowed to sue referee Jack Sutton in court. He claimed that not only had the official made an error in allowing the race to be re-run without a reserve coming in to replace him, but he was also wrong to let the tapes up with the excluded rider still on the track.

His protests fell on deaf ears, however, and he missed out on a coveted top six place that went, instead, to shock qualifier Howard Cole. Garry was stranded a point behind the King's Lynn man – on the same tally as Arnie Haley (who had earlier suffered mechanical misfortune) and Eric Boocock, who both finished ahead of him in the run-off to determine who would go to Wembley as reserve.

# A gun in the pits

**JUST four days later and probably still aggrieved about his British Final heartache, he went to Cradley Heath and was at the centre of more aggro. During a hard-fought race with Roy Trigg, Garry fell and was excluded. On his return to the pits he pulled a gun from his toolbox and brandished it at Triggy.**

Thankfully, he didn't pull the trigger and no-one seems to know whether the 'weapon' was genuine or fake.

In his next ride 'Cass' incurred the wrath of home pair Graham Coombes and Mike Gardner, the latter falling and seeking retribution as the riders returned to the pits, with Middleton again excluded. Track staff prevented a fracas, although one Cradley mechanic aimed a kick at the Hackney star and it was about to turn ugly when Len Silver wisely decided to intervene. "We were all horrified and their crowd went mad," said Silver.

In those days riders had to pass through the crowd to get from the pits to the dressing rooms at Dudley Wood, but Silver was taking no chances as the baying mob in green and white gathered with intent. During the interval, Hawks' boss drove Middleton's Mercedes into the pits and ordered Garry – still wearing leathers – to duck down on the floor as he proceeded to drive him out of the stadium under police escort while Public Enemy No.1 hid beneath a blanket in the back of the car. Apparently, Garry and his clothes were later reunited when he met up with team-mates at the Blue Boar services on the M1 motorway!

Colin Pratt said: "A few weeks before the incident at Cradley, I'd gone to Italy with Middleton to race in a meeting at Lonigo. I remember stopping somewhere on the way back so that he could shoot pigeons in a field. It was the same air rifle he pulled out in the pits at Cradley.

"The next time we were riding at Hackney Wick, I mentioned the gun and asked him where he'd put it. He told me he had it in his bag, so I said: 'You'd better give it to me in case you do something stupid and some kids leaning over the fence near the pits get hurt by a pellet in the eye'. In the end, he gave me the rifle and I passed it on to a friend of mine, John 'The Welder', who put a proper brace over the barrel."

Pratt had first encountered Middleton's wild side on track during the 1967-68 British Lions tour of Australia. "I've never seen anyone wind up Terry Betts as much as Middleton did with his on-track antics in a meeting down at Melbourne. Bettsy came back into the pits after one race and wanted to kill him because of the strokes he was pulling.

"He ruffled a few feathers. I saw Maido (Cyril Maidment) go for Middleton one night and on another occasion Briggo came out of the dressing room and was looking to thump him.

"He was a character. When I was recovering from my broken neck in 1970, he used to come and visit me in hospital. He'd sit there and tell me how he'd won more second half finals at Hackney than I had, so I pointed out to him that Len always gave him the easiest race, whereas I had to face visiting number ones in my heat."

"The obsession with Mercedes and other expensive cars was a big part of Garry's business ventures," says Webb. "When I visited his Starlings Green property in England in 1977, the paddock behind the house contained at least 15 Mercedes cars in varying condition. Garry proudly walked around saying: 'This one is for George Hunter' and 'this is for Jimmy McMillan', etc. Whether or not it was just sales talk, I couldn't say, but there were many riders driving Mercedes at the time. Garry himself graduated to a Rolls-Royce – hardly the most suitable mode of transport for a much-travelled speedway rider always on the move!"

In 1971 and to enhance Middleton's powers of self-promotion, he became a regular columnist for *Speedway Star*. A similar column under his name featured in Australia's *Speedway News* magazine in 1974-75. This series ran under the title 'Garry Middleton's Speedway World' in which he was often highly critical of Australian promoters and their involvement in the selection process for international teams. Valid comments, but only Garry was bold enough to go into print in such a forthright manner. His views would confirm his absence from the Test team when his inclusion should have been automatic.

The trouble with those who shout loudest is that their words often carry little weight because no-one listens carefully enough to what is actually being said, or in this case written. In 1972 Middleton wrote in *Speedway Star*: "I would like to see a complete revision in the set-up of the sport – no more specialist machines, inflated expense and impossible spares situations. We should have converted road machines, such as BSAs and Bultacos.

"Then, surely, the average motorcyclist who doesn't come now would do so – it's all a question of giving them something with which to identify. At the same time, manufacturers and the big oil companies could also be interested in giving the sort of support missing at the moment."

Some 40 years on, who can say that he wasn't spot on in his thinking?

# When Middleton accused Mauger

**IN 1971 Garry and fellow *Speedway Star* columnist Ivan Mauger clashed when the brash Aussie sensationally accused the reigning World Champion of using the banned Nitro-methane fuel additive.**

It was my first full season as a fan and I recall being among a large crowd at the prestigious Wills Internationale at Wimbledon on spring Bank Holiday Monday, which was held up for a while thanks to Middleton's sensational protest.

Ivan obviously denied the accusation before calling Garry's bluff. "I'll use your fuel for my last race if you use mine," he suggested.

But Middleton declined his offer and when referee Arthur Humphrey came down to the pits – at Ivan's request – to find out what all the fuss was about, Garry withdrew the allegation. Unfazed by the drama in the pits and false accusations against him, Mauger went on to win the meeting.

Although Nitro was still permitted in domestic speedway in 1971, it had been outlawed from international meetings held under the auspices of the FIM – and the Internationale at Wimbledon was such an FIM-inscribed event.

Ironically, later in that '71 season, Middleton had loaned his Hackney team-mate Barry Thomas a can of Nitro which helped Thommo win the British Junior Championship at Swindon.

Was the Wimbledon controversy a watershed moment in Middleton's racing career? In his *Star* column the following week, under the heading 'I've Reformed', he declared that he was changing his image, ditching the loud and abrasive 'Cassius' persona that brought him so many dubious headlines and would in future heed the advice of his peers, including Mauger.

# Marriage and more mayhem

**A COUPLE of months before the Internationale furore, Garry had married Anne Elleker, the 19-year-old daughter of his sponsor Peter Elleker, from Walworth, South London, whom he had known since 1967. The wedding was held in the Parish church at High Beech, Essex, on March 13, 1971, close to the spot where speedway was first staged in England in 1928.**

Former West Ham rider and European trials champion Don Smith was Garry's best man. Len Silver, Rayleigh favourite Dingle Brown, Wembley promoter Trevor Redmond, King's Lynn skipper Terry Betts, referee Lew Stripp and Garry's first UK benefactor Maury Littlechild were among the invited guests.

Webb recalls: "Garry was at this time living at Busleigh House, Paternoster Hill, Waltham Abbey, a prestigious address in the outer London/Essex stockbroker belt. He and Anne later took up residence at Red Cottage, a historic converted stables in the picture postcard Hertfordshire village of Much Hadham. This was a well-to-do area – the property sold for over a million dollars in 2008."

If anyone thought that marriage would calm him down, a third ride tape exclusion and the chaos that followed it on the opening night of the 1971 season proved otherwise. An outraged Middleton threw down his bike, stormed onto the centre green, grabbed the phone and abused the ref. When that didn't work, he ran up to the official's box, raced back to the centre green phone and then hurled it into the crowd. And in an effort to restrain him, Len Silver fell in the melee and injured his ankle!

Another classic Middleton stunt took place at Wolverhampton, where Ole Olsen was unbeaten, passing people almost for fun. In the second-half and to entertain the crowd, Garry jokingly strapped two broom handles to his handlebars to stop Olsen from passing him. Alas, the match referee did not share his sense of humour and fined him for his antics.

No-one invested more faith and responsibility in Middleton than Silver. As well as appointing him Hawks' captain during the most stable period in his career, he gave Garry control of Hackney's Saturday training school. Tragedy struck, though, during the training session on January 7, 1972, when Kent-based novice Alan Clegg lost his life following a simple-looking fall.

Garry also ran a training school for international riders at Motherwell, while one of his pupils at a winter school he held at Cradley Heath (no gun this time!) was a scrawny, unknown kid called Michael Lee. In fact, Lee's first speedway bike was a two-valve Jawa machine that used to belong to the Hackney skipper, which his father Andy bought from Len Silver in 1972.

Although training schools were another good earner for Middleton, there is no doubt that he took his role of tutor seriously. Lee, who went on to become World Champion in 1980, recalls: "Garry laid into me big-time after I failed to heed his advice and crashed into the fence. He scared me a bit."

Family man: with second wife Diona and daughter Angela.

Middleton joined forces with Silver to promote Hackney Speedway at the Sporting Motorcycle Show held in the Royal Horticultural Halls in Victoria, London early in 1972. He enjoyed some media attention again by turning up with a pet monkey named 'Jenny' which he'd borrowed from Broxbourne Zoo (now Paradise Wildlife Park and the home of the National Speedway Museum). The monkey was introduced as his 'mechanic' for the new season. He did his bit to promote himself, Hackney and speedway in general.

Forty years later, in an interview for the *Memories of Hackney Speedway* DVD, Silver paid tribute to Middleton's crowd-drawing appeal: "Of all the riders that have ever ridden for me," he enthused, "I can honestly say that Garry Middleton is the only one who genuinely put bums on seats. He was such a controversial character, who would argue with referees and fight with other riders and always be in the thick.

"Much as I was told before he joined us that he would be trouble, I have to say he was no trouble to me. He was well-behaved, did all the right things and the only thing he did that used to annoy me was when he'd sit in my office and run up large phone bills to Australia.

"But he was a very good member of our side, very enthusiastic and the crowd loved him. I was very sorry to lose him."

But all good things must come to an end. Garry placed a high valuation on his worth but it was not always a figure that Silver agreed with and just before the '72 season came the parting of the ways. Under the headline 'I Must Go', Middleton stated he had no option but to move on from Hackney.

After initially considering a lucrative offer from the Monowheel Engineering Co. to race short circuit, speedway and long-track in the USA, he declared a preference for Ipswich, who were new to the top flight that year. We can only imagine how long Garry would have lasted at Foxhall under the management of John Berry because the move never happened.

Instead, a deal was struck with new Oxford promoter, TV presenter and publicist Dave Lanning that saw Garry line up for the 1972 campaign as the new-look Rebels No.1. It seemed a match made in Heaven and Middleton, a rebel with a cause, enjoyed his best ever season.

Whereas at Hackney he had ridden in the shadow of Colin Pratt and Swedish stylist Bengt Jansson, at Oxford he became his team's outright No.1 for the first time, recording a career best average of 9.24.

He was, however, still unfulfilled. In August, after an uneasy relationship with the livewire Lanning, Middleton announced his intention to concentrate on business activities and race speedway as a hobby. *Speedway Star* ran the headline 'My Last Season'.

After a winter of speculation, Garry looked set to carry out his retirement plans. He had been taking flying lessons at nearby Stansted Airport and enlisted the help of flight trainer Lynn Hayward who later worked for Garry in his growing business empire.

Hayward, who now lives in America, takes up the story: "Garry was a man in a hurry. When he learned what a long procedure it was to gain a pilot's licence he was dismayed. Somehow I ended up as his personal pilot, mechanic and general gofer – and I still do not know how I got talked into it."

Middleton did in fact gain his commercial pilot's licence in July 1977, after four-and-a-half-years' of study. He never did own an aircraft, though, and, instead, would rent a plane from Luton or Stansted airport.

Despite his flying ambitions and other interests outside the sport, Garry was tempted into joining Coventry in 1973, where he dropped a point on his average and finished the season just behind Nigel Boocock in Bees' scoring ranks. But there was more trouble lurking around the corner.

Coventry chief Charles Ochiltree was furious when, just before the start of the 1974 campaign, Middleton informed him he would not be returning and had decided to focus his racing efforts on the continental long-track scene. He was the first Australian-born rider to compete in the World Long-track Championship qualifying rounds that season.

His BL comeback in 1975 was a disappointment. After nine years away, the prodigal son returned to his first UK team, King's Lynn. By his own admission, his duck in his first meeting was an embarrassment. A brief return to form in June did not last and by August he was dropped and itching to move on again.

Birmingham, newly-elevated from the National League, took a chance on him in 1976 and the following year – his last in Britain – was spent with Leicester. In both seasons those clubs filled the bottom two places in the senior division and the fact that Middleton still attained heat leader status with the Brummies and Lions perhaps said more about the lack of star quality around him than his own performances.

The 1976 season did, however, bring him his only major speedway honour – a World Team Cup winner's medal, as non-riding reserve for Australia at London White City.

His last match in British speedway was at Blackbird Road, Leicester on October 4, 1977, when he scored seven points for Lions against Coventry.

It was reported towards the end of 1977 that he was off to New Zealand to set up an import/export car business but would return to the UK in 1978. This is confirmed by the fact that in late 1977 he imported two late model Mercedes Benz into Sydney, Australia, although prospects of another season of racing in the BL vanished when he sold his property at Starlings Green.

He did appear in two meetings at the Western Springs track in Auckland, New Zealand in December 1977. The second, on December 19, was his last known speedway meeting.

After that spell in NZ he returned to Australia in 1979. Garry was still involved in the motor trade in South Australia but he saw his immediate future elsewhere.

# California dreaming

**A LOVER of the Californian lifestyle, in 1980 he moved to Calver City, west of Los Angeles, and was granted a commercial pilot's licence based on his UK qualifications. For the next few years he had various business ventures in the States, although his only contact with the world of speedway came when LA hosted the 1982 World Final. Somehow Garry managed to talk his way past security and popped up in the pits, much to the amazement of the promoters and others who recognised him.**

"There are three issues in Garry's life that need to be put into perspective," says Tony Webb. "His brush with USA law, his Christian background and his demise. I am well versed in the latter two, so I can make pertinent observations.

"The most disturbing saga of the Garry Middleton story was his arrest by Californian law authorities in the mid-80s over an alternative medication interest. The speedway press abounds with lurid stories, many out of context. I am fortunate to have the full facts which must be told to put the record straight.

"Garry had always been a searcher and believed in alternatives to traditional mainstream medication. In California he met up with a doctor who had discovered an alternative remedy for arthritis and cancer. The law in California is very strict on the components of any alternative medication. The products were widely advertised with the backing of some considerable funding from Garry, marketed and retailed in a professional manner. It was most definitely not selling snake oil off the back of a truck.

"Unfortunately, somewhere along the line, the product was referred to the authorities for testing. The outcome was that the contents of the medication did not fully comply with the very strict state laws. Garry and the doctor were both arrested and charged. A report appeared on Channel 9 TV in Australia and in a national newspaper."

Long after their time together as stars at Hackney, Colin Pratt visited California in 1985 as assistant to England team manager John Berry for the World Team Cup Final. He said: "Me and Briggo heard rumours that Middleton had been entering hospital wards in LA and illegally selling a cure for cancer. Apparently, he'd been arrested and was in prison. We tried to find him but couldn't.

"I went back there three years later for the 1988 World Team Cup Final and Middleton turned up. He walked into the stadium, smartly dressed and was saying 'hello' to everyone as if nothing had happened. I lost contact with him after that."

Webb continued: "Garry subsequently returned to Australia. The authorities never followed it up with extradition orders and the matter just faded away. Garry always stated his faith in the product and in the doctor concerned. His belief was such that Valda, his mother, used the product. If there had been a problem Garry is very unlikely to have approved her use of it.

"Another misrepresentation was his conversion to Christianity. Garry did become a born again Christian. He was a member of a Pentecostal church. As a Christian myself, I know there is always an urge to share your philosophies. Being the character he was, Garry would have gone into his ministry at a hundred miles an hour – it was his nature. I am sure that this area of his life was genuine, though. It was not a cult or an oddball religion. He was a happy-clappy, caring Christian."

By the late-80s he was back in Australia bearing a distinctive American accent and many ideas and plans. He married Diona, a Filipino girl, and they had a daughter, Angela. The family lived together on the Gold Coast. By then Garry had divorced his first wife Anne, although she was always well respected by his family.

There were property investments in Queensland, including a caravan park at Creek Road, Carindale, in Brisbane, which were to create problems in the early 90s.

# Depression and suicide

**GARRY'S health had been a matter of concern to his family for some time. He began suffering bouts of severe depression, which led to a lengthy stay in a Brisbane hospital. No-one knows what put him in this mental state.**

Webb says: "My understanding is that earlier financial problems were overcome when he sold his last investment, the caravan park, for development into housing lots. There were delays with payment – there was an arrangement where funds came in as units were sold – but there was not a long-term problem. Knowing Garry, though, it could have frustrated him.

"The final act came as a terrible shock to his family. Being the fun-loving man that he was, it was never considered that he didn't value the life he had."

There were reports that he had met a violent end in a car crash and rumours of him being the victim of a shooting tragedy, The truth is, Garry simply took a peaceful exit on November 23, 1994, in a manner that had faint echoes of the Billy Sanders tragedy almost a decade earlier. Both of these talented and sometimes volatile Australian internationals ended their lives near the towns of Ipswich . . . Billy in England and Garry in Queensland.

Sadly, Tony Webb and his wife Maggie know the pain of losing a loved one to suicide following the tragic loss of their own son Mark.

"Garry had many reasons to value life – a loving wife and daughter, a large caring family and many interests," says Tony. "The fact is that there can be a medical imbalance that strikes and a decision is made completely out of character. This could have been the situation with Garry."

In the week before Middleton died, doctors had suggested he was – and possibly always had been

Historian and researcher Tony Webb at Middleton's graveside.

– suffering from bipolar disorder, although that was never officially diagnosed.

Garry's funeral at Mount Gravatt in Brisbane's south was attended by a large number of family members. He was interned in a family grave in a beautiful lawn area of the cemetery surrounded by bushland.

"The speedway world was not represented at the funeral for the simple reason he had not maintained contact with anyone in the sport," Tony added.

We have received numerous requests from *Backtrack* readers for us to run an in-depth feature on Garry Middleton. Until Tony Webb had completed his research, there were too many unanswered questions but, thanks to his efforts, most of the facts and myths surrounding this extraordinary character can now be laid to rest.

## BRIEF ENCOUNTERS WITH… Ivan Blacka

### What were the highlights?

I beat Erik Gundersen at Cradley in a Dudley-Wolves Trophy match on June 21, 1980, the season Erik really began to shine in the British League. What pleased me almost as much as beating him was that Erik took the trouble to come up to me after the heat and congratulate me on a fine ride. He was a real gentleman. I found that not all the top men were as gracious in defeat.

In 1981 I won the NL KO Cup and Fours with Edinburgh. The engine troubles that always seemed to follow me around cost me a better average but 7.25 was still good going.

If there was a down side to the season, it was the problems regarding payment, which came to a head when we called a strike! There always seemed to be problems with the riders' payment at Edinburgh and during the 1981 season it came to a head. We hadn't been paid for a number of meetings – I think it was four – and we realised as a group that we needed to make a stand. It happened prior to a National League clash with Mildenhall at Powderhall on July 24.

George Hunter was with us then and he was a wily old campaigner who knew the ropes. He was a great team man

and he said the only way anyone was going to take any notice was if we organised a strike just prior to the meeting that night. I fully supported this action and so did Chris Turner, Roger Lambert and Guy Robson.

Unfortunately, as we discussed the problem in the changing room, we were split into two factions, because Dave Trownson and Neil Collins didn't want to support the action for some reason. The scene was getting very heated and George, as the senior professional, was upset at the lack of support from those two … so much so that he eventually strode over to Collins and smacked him round the head, saying: "Do not be so disrespectful to me!" I think that focussed Neil on how strongly George felt about the matter!

We had no intention of even changing into our racing gear and had put the management in a spot.

The next thing we knew was that clearly some frantic telephoning had been going on and promoter Mike Parker had got into his private helicopter and flown up to the track from his farm near Preston. It was clearly getting serious. Once he arrived, there was a hastily convened meeting and Parker gave his word that he would investigate our lack of payments and would guarantee that all monies owed would be paid.

By John Berry ● Issue 43 (2011)

# LOSING CONTROL

Tackling the major issues that changed the shape of British speedway during the *Backtrack* era. This time JB presents 'A History of Rider Control' . . .

**T**HE most important result of the formation of the British League in 1965 was the escape from the crippling wars between promoters and the formation of a genuine cohesive association where each track took on a series of rights and obligations.

No promoter talked of 'collective responsibility' or 'socialist values' but there can be no doubting the intention of the BSPA members was to present a unity of purpose. Alex Dumas' well known phrase, 'All for one and one for all' summed up the outcome.

By far the biggest expense in running a team and track was, and still is, rider costs. Not just how much the riders are paid, but all the other ancillary costs like local and international travel. In 1965, of course, there was no such thing as transfer fees and rider pay rates were fixed, set each year in discussions between the promoters' association and the Speedway Riders' Association.

In order to get the league started, all the riders' names were put into a very large hat and were then distributed among the tracks so as to arrive at a position where every team was equal in strength –or as near equal as possible.

**SPEEDWAY MAIL** (15ᴾ)

Vol 3 No 42     FRIDAY, JANUARY 16, 1976

## OLSEN TURNS DOWN SWITCH TO VIKINGS

THE saga of world champion Ole Olsen and his unrest continues. Hopefully, by the time this appears in print, everything will have been resolved. But at press time a stalemate had been reached.

At a promoters' meeting last week, Olsen was 'transferred' to Hull in exchange for Jim McMillan and Tommy Johansson. However, the Danish star has appealed against the move. FULL DETAILS INSIDE THIS ISSUE.

DETAILS INSIDE

Ole Olsen was allocated from Wolverhampton to Hull in the winter of 1975-76 but flatly refused to join the Vikings and, instead, held out for a move to Coventry.

Actually, there was no big hat, and riders largely stayed with the teams they had been previously riding for. A few top stars from overseas (almost exclusively Swedes) were invited over to balance out the team strengths and provide extra attraction for the supporters. (Commonwealth riders were regarded as 'British').

Those Swedish riders were required to also race in Sweden, so the cost of flying them backwards and forwards was shared equally among all the promoters rather than simply those tracks who had been 'allocated' a foreigner.

Before the start of each season the management committee (sitting under the title of Rider Control Committee) studied the results from the previous season and moved a few riders around from one club to another (foreign riders, where possible, on the basis it was easier for them to relocate) to balance the teams up again.

What a wonderful system! Promoters could calculate in advance what their rider costings for the season would be and could get on with the job of promoting without having to worry about the team formation side of things. Riders knew what rates they were going to receive in payment and as all tracks paid the same, there was no requirement for them to look elsewhere.

Well, that was the theory anyway, and for a while it worked very well. If a team lost their star man through injury or other riding commitments, it could use a guest or rider replacement. All of this meant teams generally won their home fixtures, which kept their supporters happy and most clubs were more or less in with a shout for the title best part of the season, especially given the cock-eyed fixture list.

But, human nature being what it is, some riders believed they deserved a little more than the standard rate and some promoters believed they would be better off if their team was a little bit more equal than the others. They manipulated the system and rider control, or more correctly, rider allocation, became by far the biggest source of fall-outs and problems between promotions.

It was always destined to be so.

Ipswich took over the West Ham licence in 1972. In doing so, they had an equal right to be provided with a team. West Ham had finished at the bottom of the league in 1971, so, logically, they required bolstering. Depending on your viewpoint, you could look at what Ipswich was provided, which was Olle Nygren, Alan Sage and Alan Bellham (who retired after one meeting), and say they were badly done by.

You could also suggest that John Louis, Tony Davey, Billy Sanders, all Ipswich's own assets, and Sandor Levai and Tommy Johansson were 'allocated', even though those riders were found and recruited by the Ipswich management.

Within three years of joining the big league Ipswich had handed back to the association all five of the riders who could have been described as having been 'provided' by the BSPA. From then on, the Witches were an entirely home-grown team.

By the end of 1974, rider allocation had become a complete farce. The BSPA was operating on a set of rules that could have been shot through at any time by either a rider or a promoter taking legal action. (In fact, one did. It was Graham Drury, who easily won an action against the BSPA, the result of which was kept as quiet as possible).

By now, even those teams that had relied so much on rider allocation since the inception of the British League (like Cradley Heath, Poole, Halifax, Swindon, Wimbledon and Wolverhampton) had got the message that they needed to become 'proactive' in finding their own riders.

At the end of 1975 Ipswich lost Mick Hines to Wimbledon and Coventry had to 'buy' Ole Olsen from Hull, where he had been allocated, in order to prevent him taking legal action against the BSPA. Ipswich let it be known that this was the last time we would accept the forced loss of a rider.

Hmmm. I've heard that again lately. Was I bluffing? To be honest, I don't really know.

Everybody knew rider allocation was effectively dead in the water. All that was needed was a alternative system to ensure equality of teams and to avoid the richer clubs creating 'super teams' as was happening in football. Martin Rogers, Len Silver and myself were invited to sit as a sub-committee and come up with a suitable alternative system.

This sub-committee should maybe have examined in detail how the American professional sports operated a system of 'draft' choices, where the weakest team for the previous season got first call on new recruits to the sport, and the 'salary cap' arrangement whereby teams have a limit to how much they can pay out in player wages overall in any one season.

Instead, they accepted that promoters should take some responsibility in providing their own riders. All that was needed was a scheme to prevent the richer teams from being able to buy up all the available talent. This was what we came up with:

1) At the start of the season no team shall have a combined Calculated Match Average (CMA) of over 52 points.
2) Any team with a CMA of more than 48 points may only change its line-up if the new rider has a CMA lower than the rider he replaces.

A CMA of 52 was more than enough to win the league, so a promoter who had invested wisely in his riders and watched them improve over the years was not forced to change that team until it became excessively powerful. In any case, most promoters would not wish to retain a team with a CMA of over 52 simply because it would be too expensive to run.

A team starting the season with a CMA of 48 had every chance of winning the league with only relatively minor improvements among the team. But a promoter who was more concerned with short-term success could not indulge in 'cheque book' speedway by changing his seven-point third heat leader for a superstar 11-point man.

It was not a perfect solution, primarily because it did not release enough top riders onto the market (because middle order riders were dropping down into the National League instead of moving to another BL track) but at least it did put in place a fail-safe system to stop any promoter more interested in ego than sound business sense from buying up riders and therefore artificially inflating rider costs.

But the concept seemed too complex for the average promoter and within one year the two-tier system was scrapped for a simple 50 point limit. The revised scheme wasn't as good as the original but still workable. There was always going to be an inherent problem with using rider averages to limit team-strengths. The two most obvious were that it was very difficult to assess a suitable average for any rider new to the league and there was always the possibility of riders and/or promoters deliberately manipulating a rider's CMA.

By the 80s both leagues had come up with a bright idea of reducing the overall strength of teams so as – in theory – to reduce rider costs. It was a very short-sighted policy that could only end by pushing up the very costs it was designed to reduce while at the same time reducing standards and increasing the effects of individual rider average anomalies.

For example, in 1998 Ipswich signed Tomasz Gollob on an assessed 7.5 average when the world knew he was worth at least 10.00, so transforming the Ipswich team to runaway champions. Meantime the word was becoming rife that teams were manipulating averages in order to strengthen line-ups after the season had started.

By the end of the 80s the idea of equalising teams by using averages had broken down completely. As fast as the BSPA was trying to block loopholes, promoters were finding ways to circumvent the intention of the policy, both by using those loopholes and by manipulating results.

**Mick Hines (left), with Wimbledon team-mates Larry Ross and Barry Crowson, was effectively forced away from Ipswich to the Dons at the start of 1976.**

Over those two decades there had been virtually a complete change in promoting identities and the whole concept of the rich helping the poor in the overall interests of the sport had been forgotten.

Now I don't for one moment suggest the collapse in stature of the British League was due to rider control by averages. Between then and now we have seen many far more damaging events, like the advent of the SGP and the success of speedway in free Poland.

What I do suggest, though, is that the misuse and abuse of the concept of rider control is a massive symptom of the total collapse of goodwill between promoters.

And it is this breakdown in goodwill and the clash between those promoters who are trying to run businesses and those who appear to be more interested in ego-tripping that has got the sport into the mess it is now in.

# CARL
# BLACKBIRD

**F**OR just a brief while, the entire speedway world appeared to be at the feet of Carl Blackbird. A big money capture for Belle Vue in 1985, Blackbird made people sit up and notice when the Aces visited league champions Oxford on April 4, 1986.

The great Hans Nielsen, who would pick up his first world title later in the season, was almost impregnable around Cowley. To defeat the Main Dane around Oxford once was no mean feat. To do it twice was very impressive indeed.

To beat Hans three times around his own track was completely unheard of.

And yet that's what 21-year-old Carl Blackbird did, his third victory relieving Nielsen of the Golden Helmet.

What's more, the flying Blackbird came from behind on all three occasions.

Carl recalled: "My bikes were going well at Oxford that night. My machinery was going as fast as everyone else's and I could compete.

"I might have even been on an engine borrowed from Eddie Bull – I'd lent one from him to win the British Under-21 Championship at Canterbury in 1985.

"I had as much speed as Hans Nielsen on the night and that made a huge difference. It was a shame I just didn't have the finances to get my bikes as fast as that all of the time."

**Young Tiger Carl raring to go at Mildenhall.**

Born March 26, 1965, Blackbird first tried his hand at speedway at a Mildenhall training school, aged 14.

"My dad (Barry) used to go to King's Lynn as a supporter. He had a bit of go at road-racing. I'd go along to King's Lynn with him and that got me interested.

"They used to run a training school at Mildenhall – I believe it was on a Monday night. My old man picked up a grass-track bike from somewhere. I'd never actually done any grass-track but that's the bike I rode on the speedway track.

"We went to Lynn for quite a few weeks. Bernie Klatt, who ran Mildenhall, was a great guy. I got on well with him and he could see that I was OK on a bike.

"We didn't really have the money to buy a complete machine but Bernie had this old track spare that he let me use. Dad then bought me an old broken down bike. Between Dad and Bernie, they managed to get me up and running.

"I was team mascot around the age of 15 and started doing second halves at Mildenhall as I soon turned 16."

An opportunity to ride for Fen Tigers in the National

In British League action for Ipswich, leading King's Lynn pair Richard Hellsen and Kevin Jolly. Witches' 1984 double-winning team. Back row, left to right: Carl, Nigel Flatman, Chris Shears (promoter), Jeremy Doncaster, Kai Niemi. Front: Richard Knight, Billy Sanders, John Cook.

League would soon beckon.

Carl explains: "Halfway through that year (1981), Andy Warne had to attend tech college and couldn't do the northern tour, so I did the meetings at Middlesbrough and Glasgow.

"I had another few outings in the team during that first year, otherwise it was second halves at Mildenhall. There used to be 14 or 15 of us in the second halves some weeks."

Blackbird was handed a full-time team place halfway through 1982, in place of a struggling Warne.

"I had started to beat Andy on a regular basis in the second halves. He started the year at No.7, but I finished it as one of the reserves."

Mildenhall were a successful side, finishing second in the league in both 1982 and 1983. Only a powerful Newcastle outfit stopped them from getting their hands on major silverware.

"Bernie worked hard to make the club a success," says Carl. "We didn't win the league while I was there but we certainly came close a few times.

"Newcastle had a very strong side, including Joe Owen and Rod Hunter. They were really British League boys but they'd dropped down and they were basically winning everything.

"It was a pretty good team spirit at Mildenhall. I was only a young lad, and quite naive, but I was learning all the time. I really didn't know anything outside what I was doing. To me, it was all fascinating.

"It was a whole different ball game to a regular job. I'd been working, even when I was at school. Once I started speedway, I was doing repairs on cars and a bit of mechanics alongside it. Speedway was completely different to anything like that.

"To be honest, I was quite single-minded. I only really concentrated on my own performances when I was riding; I didn't pay too much interest in what everyone else was doing.

"I tended to turn up for meetings feeling like an individual rider. I guess that may sound a little bit selfish but I don't think I was ever particularly a team man."

Blackbird's steady progress accelerated in 1984 – a year in which he found himself riding almost the entire season for two clubs, Mildenhall in the National League and Ipswich in the British League.

"I was on it in 1984. That was all down to riding for Ipswich in the top flight, with a different class of rider, and it brought me on.

"The opportunity at Ipswich came about thanks to Bernie Klatt. One night, he told me to get my bikes, because they had a second half vacancy at Foxhall. We trundled off to Ipswich, where a handful of tidy National League riders were already challenging for a team berth. I did well. I'm not sure if I won every race but I did enough to impress John Berry.

"I think Andy Hines had a problem with his hip, so there was space for a National League rider to come in and double-up as Ipswich's No.8.

"I was surprised when I was offered it but I thought I'd give it a go. I didn't realise the true extent of how big a deal it was – I was still young and naive.

"I don't think I missed many, if any, Ipswich meetings after I signed. The two clubs sorted it out between them and I remember once riding for both Mildenhall and Ipswich on the same day.

"Jeremy Doncaster became a really good mate of mine and even to this day we're still mates. But I got on with every single rider in that team. Kai Niemi, Billy Sanders and John Cook were all great with me, and each was a class act. It was a winning team and team spirit was huge. Mildenhall had a good team spirit but Ipswich was a winning team spirit. There is a difference there, although I don't think I realised it at the time.

"When we were firing on all cylinders, we were bulletproof. We had Chris Shears as the promoter, while John Berry was a very cool and calculated team manager. He knew what was required and he had a trick or two up his sleeve."

Golden Helmet holder at Belle Vue in 1986.

In 1984, Blackbird won both the BL and the KO Cup with Witches, while Mildenhall again finished second in the National League – this time behind Long Eaton. As a consolation, Fen Tigers won the NL Fours at Peterborough, with Blackbird playing a leading part.

Carl was keen to move up full-time with Ipswich in 1985 but money troubles at Mildenhall resulted in him heading much farther north.

"There was a bit of a situation," explained Carl. "Bernie needed the money from my transfer fee for Mildenhall to stay open. I'd gone to Australia that winter but there was still time to talk over a few things with him.

"I would have loved to have gone to Ipswich but they couldn't pay the money that Bernie needed. Then Stuart Bamforth from Belle Vue came in with such a good offer. Bernie took me up to Hyde Road and showed me around and said: 'What do you think about this?' It was just an amazing place.

"But I was still quite young and I just wanted to go to Ipswich. I already felt settled in there and it was local. But because Ipswich couldn't match Belle Vue's offer (£20,000), I joined the Manchester club."

After starting the 1985 season at Mildenhall, Carl moved to the world famous Belle Vue Aces in May and would spend the next three seasons there.

"I didn't take my percentage of the deal straight away. Mildenhall held on to it for a couple of months, while Bernie got the club back on its feet financially. Eventually I spoke to him and he said: 'Come and get your money'.

"It was a goodwill gesture, because Bernie had always helped me and pointed me in the right direction. At the end of the day, he'd played a part in getting me going in the first place and also fixing me up with both Ipswich and Belle Vue. I had a lot of respect for Bernie."

Sadly the Bernie Klatt story ended in tragedy, when he took his own life later in 1985, due to problems away from the track.

Carl reflects sadly: "I knew there were issues but I was just so busy with the speedway. I knew things weren't quite right. It was so sad the way things ended, and of course it was the same year we lost Billy Sanders.

"I'd stayed with Billy during the winter of '84, along with Jeremy, and we'd had some great laughs.

"Both suicides came as a huge shock. I knew both Bernie and Billy well and was aware of the underlying issues in both cases. Maybe today I'd be able to handle things a bit differently and would try to help them somehow. But I was young and just getting on with life."

A tough start at Belle Vue improved after Carl sailed to the British Under-21 Championship at Canterbury with a 15-point maximum. "I struggled a bit to begin with at Belle Vue. It was a stretch money-wise. My wife Tania and I had bought our first house and we had a baby daughter.

"Eddie Bull lent me an engine for a few meetings and it was just mega. I used that at Canterbury and one or two other meetings but then I had to give it back. I'd have loved to have kept it but, financially, it was out of my league.

"To be honest, that's probably where my career always tended to fall down – the equipment side. I had a family and a mortgage and never had enough money to spend on my bikes. I was always working away from racing to keep my speedway career afloat.

"I guess I wasn't a professional rider, because my bikes weren't the best, but I just didn't have the money to spend on them.

"I didn't have the financial backing or sponsorship. I did the best with what I had, so that was always going to be my downfall."

Carl soon adapted to his new surroundings in the north-west. "The old Belle Vue stadium at Hyde

Carl (second from left) on his Test debut for England against Denmark at Cradley Heath in 1986. His Lions partner is Kenny Carter, with Erik Gundersen and Jan O. Pedersen using their home track knowledge for the Danes.

Road was a magnificent place. I went there feeling very apprehensive but once I settled in, it was great. Chris Morton and Peter Collins, a couple of huge names, were there of course.

"I was made to feel part of the team, by the riders, mechanics and supporters. And I got on very well with Stuart Bamforth."

The 1986 season – PC's last – proved to be a great one for Carl, who finished second behind Morton in the Belle Vue averages on 7.37.

He recalls: "I tended to ride alongside Peter Collins – I was No.4 and he was No 5, or maybe it was vice-versa. He was a great guy to ride with. He was coming to the end of his career but, even so, he could still handle a bike and I learnt a lot from him. More than anything, he made me welcome. I stopped at his and Chris Morton's place a few times.

"I think it might have been Chris who got me to Belle Vue. I'd guested at Cradley Heath for Belle Vue, banged in a second in Heat 1, and Chris told Bammy to go out and sign me."

Carl was called up for his senior Test debut against reigning world champions Denmark in the first match of the 1986 series at Cradley Heath, where he scored three points as Kenny Carter's opening race partner in Sunbrite Lions' 55-53 defeat. Despite zero points returns in each of the next two Tests against the Danes, Carl was recalled for the third, and final, match against the USA at former track Ipswich in August, when he happily contributed five points in a 62-43 win to wrap up a 3-0 series whitewash.

He says: "I rode for England a few times, which was nice, and reached the British Final at Coventry in 1986. But I had horrendous bike problems going into the meeting. I was on the back foot from the beginning at Coventry and just couldn't get going."

Carl's third, and final, season at Belle Vue in 1987 saw his average drop by around two points. He recalls: "Things had changed again. By then, we had two children, we'd moved house and I'd changed jobs. I'd started my own engineering business, so speedway began to get really hard. I was doing a huge amount of driving, work and speedway. I had a couple of injuries but still carried on despite having been knocked about.

"And when talk of Belle Vue closing came along, it hit us all hard. The whole atmosphere changed once everyone knew it was going to shut. It went from a place where you really wanted to be, to somewhere you didn't."

The 1991 Long Eaton Invaders. Left to right: Mark Blackbird, Gary O'Hare, Jan Staechmann (on bike), Peter McNamara, Stuart Parnaby, Kai Niemi. Kneeling: Eric Boocock, Carl Blackbird.

Following the sad closure of Hyde Road at the end of 1987, Carl returned to ride for Ipswich in 1988 and then moved, along with promoter Chris Shears, to Reading in 1989.

"Reading didn't really suit me. It was a gater's paradise and I wasn't a starter, so I was in and out of the reserve berth.

"I was making good money away from the sport by then and my heart was no longer in it. It was touch and go whether I rode that season.

"I remember Mitch Shirra taking me to one side and asking: 'Do you really want to ride?'. And I was honest. I told him I didn't really know.

"I still wasn't that old but the dream to be the best had gone. There was better money to be made elsewhere. The fun element had gone out of speedway for me by then."

Blackbird contemplated retirement during the 1989-90 winter but ended up back in the NL with Edinburgh in 1990.

"Basically, Edinburgh offered me a deal I couldn't refuse. They supplied me with a van and bikes and I thought I'd be stupid to turn this down. I still wasn't sure, though, so they were chucking even more money at me.

"I verbally agreed to ride for Edinburgh but then Poole came on the scene. I spoke to their promoter Mervyn Stewkesbury. They really wanted me and I really wanted to ride for them.

"I hadn't actually signed a contract with Edinburgh but it went to arbitration. It was ruled that I had to ride for Edinburgh and that Poole could have no further contact with me.

"It was a shame, because I think riding for Poole would have been good for me. Although they weren't offering as much money as Edinburgh, I think joining a team as successful as the Pirates would have motivated me more.

"To be honest, I was going through the motions at Edinburgh and waiting for the year to end.

That sounds terrible, I guess, but I was driving up there and still working full-time the next day.

"They were good to me at Edinburgh, though. They were great people but in hindsight, I shouldn't have signed for them."

Carl then spent two-and-a-half years riding for Long Eaton, where he joined Jan Staechmann in a powerful spearhead for the Invaders.

"I was still thinking of packing it in but I really enjoyed Long Eaton. It was a midweek track and fitted in well.

"The promoter Eric Boocock was as good as gold. By then it was in my mind to not do anything silly and get hurt but I was enjoying my speedway.

"I started my third season at Long Eaton in 1993. I was

Carl Blackbird in 2013.

horrendously busy work-wise but Tony Mole, who'd bought the club, persuaded me to start the season and just see how it went.

"But it just wasn't working out. Tony was also the promoter at Oxford and he told me that he had someone there who could look after my bikes. All I had to do was turn up and ride, so I thought that might work.

"I did one meeting for Oxford. I spoke to the guy who was supposed to be helping me out but he was on a different wavelength to me. That's when I decided that was it and I finally quit.

"As much as I had loved the sport and had some good years out of it, I realised it was no longer for me."

## BRIEF ENCOUNTERS WITH… Sam Nikolajsen

**How did your move to the UK come about?**

After I became Danish Junior Champion in 1981 I had a chat with Ole Olsen and we decided that I should try a professional speedway career in England, and that's why I moved to the UK.

**Which clubs did you ride for over here?**

First I rode for Coventry Bees (1982-84) and later Sheffield Tigers (1985) and Wolverhampton Wolves (1986).

**Did you have an 'English dad' or did you have to fend for yourself?**

I was all on my own. I lived in a condo with Peter Ravn and Alf Busk, and later I lived with my girlfriend, Gitte, who became my wife.

**What did you miss most about home?**

In the beginning I missed a lot of the Danish food but I quickly learned how to cook it myself. Now, on the other hand, I miss chicken curry with fried rice!

**What was the funniest thing that happened to you during your time in the UK?**

When Peter Ravn and I lived on the first floor the owner, a nice lady, lived downstairs. We had one of those old washing machines, where you had to use a water hose to put in water from the top of the machine. We forgot all about the water, so our entire floor and her new kitchen were flooded. And this happened twice! Surprisingly, she didn't get upset. She just smiled and said that it would dry.

**When did you realise it was time to go back home?**

I had always told myself that if I wasn't in the top five of the World Championships after three-to-four years in England, it was time to go back home. And I didn't reach that goal, unfortunately. If you keep riding and riding, the distance to a "normal life" gets longer, and I have always been afraid of not having anything to go back to.

**Any regrets?**

No, I would do it again, although maybe this time I'd be a bit more professional.

# BRIAN
# CLARK

**B**RIAN Clark made his debut for second division Peterborough at Ipswich on April 30, 1970. At the time, Panthers were speedway's newest club in their very first season of operation.

Clark's final appearance for the club came at Long Eaton (against Nottingham Outlaws) on October 21, 1979.

He made 329 official appearances for Peterborough, scoring 2304 points, including 30 full or paid maximums.

And remarkably, apart from a few 'doubling-up' appearances as a No.8 in the British League for either Oxford or White City, he never rode for any other club.

Such club loyalty is so rare in modern speedway. It's no wonder when Peterborough started handing out 'legend' status to their former riders a few years ago, that Clark was very high up on the list (he was the second to be awarded, behind another long-term Panther, Mick Poole).

Clark, who also spent two years as Peterborough team manager in 1980 and 1981, recalls how he starting riding for the East of England Showground club.

The Peterborough Panthers of 1973. Left to right: Brian, John Davis, Frank Smith, Alec Ford (team manager), Jack Walker, Roy Carter, Roy Sizmore. On bike: Richard Greer.

**Brian (left) with Tony Featherstone before the 1977 NL Pairs Final. Note the misspelling of his name in the Belle Vue pits.**

He said: "I had done a bit of moto-cross, trials, all sorts of bits and pieces. I had gone to Ipswich a few times to watch speedway. I'd done a few grass-track meetings alongside Andy Ross, and he was going to be captain of the new Peterborough team.

"Andy was a terrific rider. He actually raced ice speedway as well – he was one of the few riders who could live with the Russians on the ice – and it was him who persuaded me to give it a go at Peterborough.

"But that first year was a disaster. We started off with several away meetings before Peterborough opened. If I recall correctly, we went to King's Lynn for a team practice. I took my goggles off because I couldn't see, and ended up with a cut eye. That put me out for two to three months."

Clark made just two appearances for Panthers in 1970, failing to score. In contrast, the 1971 season saw him notch 145 points from 33 appearances, averaging 5.13.

"That was due to lots of practice," he explains. "I practiced every single Sunday during the winter. You do have to put a lot into speedway. In those days, we did quite a lot of the stuff ourselves. We'd go home after a meeting, take the bike apart and then put it back together for the next meeting.

"Speedway is a lot about learning and using your head. My favourite saying was if you could get your wheel spinning one time less than the person next to you on the track, then you'd get the better speed and beat them.

"That certainly applied at Peterborough, which was always a fast track. It did give us an advantage and could be a benefit at times. It was a good track for overtaking.

"I also practiced a lot at Rye House, a very tight track. That paid off, because in 1975 I won the Herts Gold Cup individual meeting there."

It didn't take Clark long to rise up the Peterborough ranks, becoming the club's No.1 for the 1975 and 1976 seasons. He represented Panthers at the league riders' championship at Wimbledon in both these seasons, scoring 10 points to finish joint-fourth in 1976.

One nemesis that Clark did have was Jack Millen, a colourful character from New Zealand whose nicknames included 'Crazy Jack' and 'Millen The Villain'.

Brian recalls: "I had quite a few mishaps with him. I remember one time at Stoke, he put me right through the fence. I was excluded for two minutes because they had to cut me out of the fence.

"We met again in the second-half. I couldn't get him on the first corner but I got him on the second, where he went over the top of the fence. The crowd were jeering me but Jack got up and climbed on the back of my bike and we went back to the pits together.

"Jack was hard, but he could take it. He was one of those people where it didn't matter what he did to you or you did to him, it was never a big deal. He could be dirty but if someone did it back, he didn't complain. Once it got to the end of the meeting, it was over.

"He was actually a really nice bloke."

Millen died in a road accident in early 1978.

Danny Dunton, the boss at Peterborough, was also co-promoter (along with Bob Dugard) at first division Oxford until 1975, and then at White City from 1976 after the Rebels moved to the capital.

Clark was the No.8 at both clubs but this would lead to the crash in August 1976 that eventually contributed to his retirement.

"I had an accident at Swindon while racing for White City," he remembers. "I was trying to go around the outside of Bob Kilby and got my foot stuck in his back wheel. We locked together and I landed on my head.

"My knee took most of the damage, though. Danny Dunton arranged for me to go for private treatment but even so, the knee never fully recovered."

Had Clark ever been tempted to move up to the British League full-time? "I did consider going to Cradley at one point – it was around 1976. But at the end of the day, I preferred National League. I wouldn't have enjoyed first division as much.

"At Peterborough, all the riders were having a good time. You'd go to the away meetings together – we quite often had tours of two to three away meetings on successive nights. We were laughing and joking and telling stories. We were all great friends. I still often see the likes of Richard Greer, Roy Carter and Frank Smith.

"We were doing something we enjoyed doing – it was a bonus we got paid for it. At the end of the month, you'd get a nice cheque. British League would have been more of a business and less fun."

In 1977, Clark captained Panthers to their first piece of silverware – the National League Fours, won in front of their own fans at Alwalton. Ironically, Brian didn't enjoy the best of afternoons but with Ian Clark (no relation), Kevin Hawkins and Andy Hines in fine form, Panthers finished three points in front of nearest challengers Canterbury.

Clark says: "That was very nice to win that. It was great for the club to win something."

Peterborough finished in the top six four times between 1972 and 1978 but had to wait until 1992 to celebrate their first league championship.

"Danny had a different philosophy to most other promoters. Well, at least he did when it came to Peterborough. He didn't actually want to win the league. But he wanted to be in the top three or, at worst, in the top six.

"If we had won the league, he felt the supporters would expect the same the following year, so it would raise expectations to the point where we couldn't match it. He wanted a successful team, but not too successful."

Brian celebrated his testimonial at Peterborough on October 5, 1979. He was only the second National League rider to be granted this honour, following in the tyre-tracks of Peter Reading, who was awarded a testimonial at Middlesbrough in 1977.

He fondly recalls: "That was a good day. We had Michael Lee there – he was still young but

**Brian (outside) and namesake Ian Clark on a 5-1 at Newcastle in 1978.**

already one of the best riders in the world. It was a great line-up and attracted a good crowd for me."

Other riders in the meeting included 1978 World No.2 Gordon Kennett (a team-mate of Clark's at Oxford and White City), John Louis, John Davis, Dave Jessup and Kai Niemi.

At the end of the 1979 season, Clark called it quits. His scoring had gradually decreased over the 1977-'79 seasons.

"The knee was causing problems," he admits. "I knew at some point I'd have to stop. I thought it was a good time – I'd just had my testimonial – and I was no longer scoring the points I once had."

However, Clark's involvement at Peterborough was far from over, as he moved from one side of the fence to the other.

He explains: "Danny thought I'd done a good job as the team captain and believed I could do a good job as team manager as well.

"But being team manager was extremely frustrating. When you get frustrated on a bike, you can take it out on the track. But as team manager, there was no way of letting off steam. I found it very difficult.

"It was the unfairness of it all that really got to me. When you're racing, you tend to shrug your shoulders and get on with it. But as a team manager, you notice everything.

"There were always riders being excluded at the tapes, when someone else caused the problem, or someone being taken wide and forced out of the race. I was just standing there getting angrier and angrier and there was nothing I could really do about it."

Another aspect of team managing that Clark didn't enjoy was having to make tactical substitutes.

"I didn't like taking riders out of races," he admits. "I knew from experience that you could run a last, and then go out and win three races.

"I didn't like dropping a rider from a race – I knew it could knock their confidence. Especially if you were taking a young rider out of Heat 8, a race they had a better chance of scoring in.

"Of course, you had to make the change and bring in the heat leader as a tactical substitute, because otherwise you weren't doing your job properly. But I wanted to encourage people. As a captain, you'd be buoying them up, checking the gear, encouraging them to change things.

"As team manager, one moment you're encouraging them, but the next you were virtually saying to someone that you didn't think they were good enough to be in a race."

Clark stepped down at team manager after the 1981 season. "I did it for two years, and then gave it up. I realised it wasn't for me."

By Rob Peasley ● Issue 58 (2013)

# TURBULENT TIMES BRING END TO SECOND HALVES AND JUNIOR LEAGUES

We weigh up the pros and cons of two controversial decisions taken by promoters, at different times, that brought an end to the traditional second half event and junior leagues . . .

Sheffield's Sean Wilson, seen here at 16-years-old in 1986, was one of the first kids to break through the junior ranks into the top grade.

**T**HE winter of 1984-85 was a highly turbulent one for British speedway and in particular the British League.

The sport's top tier lost five teams – Newcastle, Exeter, Eastbourne, Poole and, most shockingly of all, the once mighty Wimbledon Dons. Wimbledon riding in the second tier National League seemed almost unthinkable but it became reality.

Top flight speedway was in turmoil, with the BL reduced to just 11 teams, by far its smallest membership since the league's formation in 1965.

Due to the drama that unfolded over that winter of discontent, a momentous decision by British League promoters received far less attention than it normally would. They chose to scrap the traditional second half. The rider-of-the-night event or scratch race final, call it what you will, was no more.

It wasn't a move completely without precedence. In 1982 and '83, National League promoters had extended their matches to 16 heats, with the second half reduced to a handful of junior races.

It hadn't proved completely popular, because in 1984 the NL returned to 13 heats and traditional second halves.

BL track bosses went a step further in 1985. They didn't extend the heat format.

Six months after being Hackney's mascot, Mark Loram entered his debut season as a British League rookie. As this shot from that 1987 season clearly illustrates, he was still not fully grown, but quickly developed into a fine talent and in 2000 became World Champion.

Instead, they actually replaced races featuring the superstars with those involving novices. Races that had featured Erik Gundersen, Hans Nielsen and Shawn Moran now featured the likes of Nigel Leaver, Paul Atkins and Tony Forward.

It was a brave move, and almost certainly one that was partially driven by finance – the shrinking BL could simply not afford to lose any more teams. It was one way of cutting the cloth without affecting the main league match.

It was also a decision that has often attracted criticism . . . but was it one that actually gave British speedway a temporary shot in the arm?

Some of the sport's longer-term supporters may disagree. Then again, maybe the demise of the old second half was overdue.

By 1984, first division stars just did not take second haves seriously. They either simply used it to test machinery, went through the motions, or didn't bother with it at all.

Already their diaries were filling with continental commitments. Grass-track or long-track meetings on a Sunday were far more lucrative than a British second half. As soon as Heat 13 was over, bikes were put away into vans and the riders were off.

Once upon a time, the second half final had been a highlight of the evening, often featuring the three home heat leaders and the visiting No.1. By 1984, this was rarely the case.

Several tracks had already taken part in a British Junior League in 1984, which was staged in conjunction with the traditional second half. For 1985, this would be extended. There would now be a junior match after every British League or League Cup fixture, encompassing all 11 BL clubs. Junior leagues had always had voluntary membership. In 1985, it became compulsory for BL clubs.

It also meant the junior meetings would now feature the same two clubs as the first half of the meeting, giving hardcore fans an extra match to watch. In contrast, those who liked the star names simply left the stadium, or headed for the bars, after Heat 13.

There was much to commend about the British Junior League, though. First and foremost, it gave plenty of track time to youngsters.

Under the old second half format, a young rider sometimes only took a single ride. If he didn't do well in that, it could be the end of his night.

The early season British Junior League Cup in 1985 featured four-man teams racing over six races, which meant each rider had three rides. For league matches later in the season (which took place over seven races), a fifth rider, who had two programmed rides, was added to the mix.

And not only did these young men get regular rides around their own home circuit, they also gained vital experience on all the away tracks in the British League.

Suddenly a whole new crop of junior riders sprung up. Among those who competed in the 1985 British Junior League were: Ray Morton, Andy Phillips, Rob Fortune, Jamie Habbin, Jon Surman, David Clarke, Mike Bacon and John Bostin.

Some of them had been riding in second halves for a few years, while others were new to the sport. The new-look second halves provided the public with some lively, meaningful entertainment.

And the league was well organised. True, there was the odd unfulfilled fixture, when the weather intervened before the junior match and there wasn't a suitable second half for the youngsters to return.

But on the whole, both league tables and averages were well-maintained, and some fans really got into the junior action.

Of course, there were a few moans and groans at the passing of the traditional second half, and a concession for 1986 was a Gold Sash race preceding the junior racing, featuring the top two riders from each side.

Coventry's riders were the first to rebel, refusing to take part in the Gold Sash races on away tracks, and so it fell into disarray. It was a reminder of one of the reasons the old second halves had been scrapped in the first place; indifference from many of the star names.

Meanwhile, one thing missing that had existed in the traditional second half was the chance for juniors to test themselves against more experienced opposition. The old second halves often threw the juniors together with the seniors, producing the odd shock result.

That issue would be partially addressed by a very bold decision by BL promoters in 1986 – the No.7 for each senior team would be a rider from the British Junior League.

With relations between the BL and NL becoming increasingly strained, the British League would not have to rely on the National League for young talent. It would produce its own.

It was sink-or-swim for the junior riders. There's no doubt that it was a huge step. The British League was a 'Super League' in 1986, far

Carl Stonehewer, Belle Vue junior who became a GP star.

stronger than the Elite League of today because it contained nearly all of the world's top riders.

Sean Wilson, who replaced Peter McNamara as Sheffield's compulsory junior partway through the season, made it through, but some others floundered as their confidence took a knock.

Perhaps not surprisingly, the compulsory junior rider lasted for only two seasons (1986 and '87), although not before a 16-year-old Mark Loram had spent a season as Hackney's impressive junior in 1987. It could be argued that a young talent with Loram's obvious ability and promise would have eventually made it to the top anyway. But the fact is, Kestrels' boss Dave Pavitt plunged his precocious discovery in at the deep end *because* of the compulsory junior ruling. Had it not be in force, who knows, Mark might have taken longer to come to the boil.

In the meantime, the British Junior League continued and went from strength to strength, as more supporters discovered its delights, featuring young riders who simply never knew when they were beaten. It almost built up a fan base of its own.

Sometimes a humdrum first half could be followed by a corking junior match. There was always a great unpredictability about the racing and meetings being won with a final heat 5-0 were not unknown.

The BJL underwent several name changes – from its original title to the British League Division Two (BL2 for short) and then the Reserve League.

With BL matches extended to 15 races in 1988, the length of junior matches was reduced to five races, although it soon went back up to six for 1989.

And the odd rider continued to make it big.

Arguably, Joe Screen was not a product of the league, since he was always earmarked for the senior Belle Vue BL team. However, Screen's team-mate Carl Stonehewer (along with Screen, a Grand Prix star of the future) was a different matter. Stonehewer worked his way up the junior ranks and into the Aces' main side.

In the meantime, the National League also had junior leagues.

It wasn't possible to have the same all-encompassing junior league as the BL simply because of geography. It wasn't sensible to have junior riders travelling from Edinburgh and Glasgow to Exeter.

The junior leagues were regionalised, and second halves were a mix-and-match affair, sometimes still containing seniors in the second half if there wasn't a junior match. Although the NL reverted to 16 heats in 1988, which more-or-less spelt the end of Rider-of-the-Night competitions in the second half for good.

The mending of broken bridges between the BL and NL during the 1990-'91 winter did little to effect the junior leagues, which carried on in the same fashion in 1991 and '92.

Anyone doubting that the league was still producing riders only needed to look at the Ipswich junior side which swept to the league title in 1992 – Ben Howe, Savalas Clouting, Shaun Tacey and Lawrence Hare would all graduate to top flight speedway in the coming years.

Then came something of a shock.

# Where damage was done

**THE junior leagues were scrapped after the 1992 season. The initial reason given was that the 1993 league format would feature 18 heats and eight riders. And due to the rules governing the two reserves, this in itself would provide opportunities and would allow youngsters to move to the next step.**

But the 18-heat format lasted just a season. In 1994, any protection given to the reserves had gone, and foreign reserves, even in Division Two, started to appear.

It's true that a third division was introduced in 1994 but this tended to feature the British riders who had, until then, appeared in the second tier (which was now becoming more-and-more clogged up with foreign riders). The third division was never a youth development league in the same way that the second half leagues had been.

The scrapping of the junior leagues after 1992 was a big disaster. It's here that real damage to British speedway was caused – far more than the decision to scrap the traditional second half in the British League following the 1984 season.

Suddenly young novices were scrabbling around for the odd second half race. There was no longer any form of regular second half racing. Situations arose where riders would travel to get a couple of informal second half races at the end of a meeting, only for those races to be culled and the riders return home without any action.

Key opportunities for youngsters were no longer there.

There's also, of course, the question of value-for-money for supporters. Junior races are extra races for those paying their hard-earned cash through the turnstiles. Up until 1992, it was rare for there to be less than 20 races in the programme.

These days, some Elite League clubs charge up to £17 for just 15 races. The addition of junior races gave supporters a bit extra, at little more cost to the promoter.

In recent years, there has been an attempt to revive second half junior matches but not all clubs participate and meetings can sometimes be few and far between for riders.

The decision made at the end of 1992 to scrap the junior leagues was the one that caused a lot of damage down the line.

Second halves and junior leagues had their own pros and cons – but both were a lot better than nothing at all.

# ROLL OF HONOUR

**BRITISH JUNIOR LEAGUE WINNERS**
1984    Ipswich
1985    King's Lynn
1986    Coventry
1987    Sheffield
1988    Bradford
1989    Belle Vue
1990    Wolverhampton
1991    Cradley Heath
1992    Ipswich

**BRITISH JUNIOR LEAGUE KO CUP WINNERS**
1986    Sheffield
1987    Bradford
1988    Cradley Heath
1989    Belle Vue
1990    Wolverhampton
1991    King's Lynn
1992    Ipswich

Nigel Leaver was thrust into the big-time at Cradley.

**NATIONAL JUNIOR LEAGUE WINNERS**
1986    Middlesbrough (Northern), Birmingham (Central), Wimbledon (Southern)
1987    Middlesbrough (Northern), Mildenhall (Central), Arena-Essex (Southern)
1988    Poole
1989    Hackney
1990    Middlesbrough (Northern), Stoke (Central), Poole (Southern)
1991    Middlesbrough (Northern), Sheffield (Central), Arena-Essex (Southern)
1992    Middlesbrough (Northern), Exeter (Southern)
(Decided on a percentage basis in 1988 and 1989)

**CLASS OF '86**
**Compulsory junior riders in the 1986 British League**
Belle Vue – Declan Eccles (4.28) & Lee Edwards (1.06)
Bradford – Michael Graves (3.88)
Coventry – David Clarke (3.50)
Cradley Heath – Paul Fry (3.23) & Paul Taylor (2.06)
Ipswich – Robbie Fuller (4.17)
King's Lynn – Ray Morton (4.21) & Adrian Stevens (2.28)
Oxford – Jon Surman (2.44)
Reading – Gary Tagg (1.35) & Billy Pinder (1.27)
Sheffield – Sean Wilson (5.83) & Peter McNamara (3.27)
Swindon – Rob Fortune (3.16)
Wolverhampton – Andy Phillips (2.97)

# IVAN
# MAUGER

**I**T takes only two simple words to describe nine times World Champion Ivan Mauger – The Greatest. There can be no argument, the evidence is overwhelming.

He is the only rider in history to win the individual World Championship six times. He won the World Team Cup for Great Britain (three times) and his own country New Zealand (once) and World Pairs gold for the Kiwis (twice) with Bob Andrews and Ronnie Moore.

And then there were three World Long-track Championships.

His last FIM gold medal, for winning the last of six speedway crowns at Katowice in 1979, was achieved at the remarkable age of 40.

At club level, he won the Provincial League championship with Newcastle and inspired Belle Vue to three consecutive British League titles. He captained Exeter to their first ever championship and narrowly missed repeating the feat with unfashionable Hull.

Ivan had very strong rivals for the right to be recognised as the sport's undisputed No.1. Ronnie Moore and Barry Briggs, the legendary Kiwis who paved the way for their younger countryman to follow them to Wimbledon for his first taste of British racing in the late 50s, and Sweden's Ove Fundin, are also right up there in that elite group of all-time speedway greats of the post-war era.

And in the period when Ivan himself was most dominant – throughout the second half of the 60s and the duration of the 70s – we also saw the brilliance of Ole Olsen and Peter Collins, who both learned much from the maestro in their early racing days. Not forgetting Anders Michanek and a dozen or so formidable Poles and Russians. Michael Lee was another who emerged in the late 70s to challenge Mauger's supremacy.

In the early-to-mid-80s, when Ivan's astonishingly successful career was nearing its end, Denmark's Erik Gundersen and Hans Nielsen took it in turns to rule the roost.

Mauger faced, and beat, them all.

Then we come to super-Swede Tony Rickardsson, the nearest modern day equivalent to Mauger and the only other rider with six individual crowns to his name. Although as Ivan himself points out, it's not fair to compare riders from different eras who have accumulated their success in two quite different 'World Championship' systems.

Ivan respects what Rickardsson achieved but he always known the value of his worth and you can't argue with him when he insists: "If you look at all the major World Championship qualifying rounds – British Final, Inter-Continental and European Finals – and also take into account World Pairs and World Team Cup Finals, they just about always included all the top riders, and I was very rarely outside the top three scorers. So if I'd had the luxury of only having to be consistent, without necessarily winning most meetings, I would have won the World Championship 10 times if the GP format had been in place in my time." After a slight pause, he adds: "And so too would Fundin."

In Ivan's later World Championship years, he had to begin the campaign by competing in qualifying rounds in New Zealand in January, through to Australasian Finals in February, when only the top two or four from both countries progressed to the summer European rounds.

Take all of this on board, write down all the titles he amassed in his illustrious career and at the

Three greats with 12 individual speedway World Championships between them, Ivan Mauger, Barry Briggs and Ronnie Moore find time to chat during an open meeting in 1972. Below: Reunited in more recent times at the annual World Speedway Riders' Association dinner.

end of a very long sheet of paper, if your biro hasn't run dry of ink, you will reach the inevitable conclusion that Mauger's record, spanning the best part of two decades, is incomparable.

He is the greatest. No arguments.

In fact, in a poll conducted by *Speedway Star* and the now defunct *Vintage Speedway Magazine,* asking readers to name their 'Millennium Man', the best rider of the 20th century, Ivan Gerald Mauger, from Christchurch, New Zealand, came out on top.

When he reflects on the significance of that award today, he speaks with the same enthusiasm you would expect from him when discussing one of his celebrated world title triumphs. "I'm very proud to have been named the best speedway rider of the last millennium," he says, "especially as I would estimate that about 70 per cent of the people who voted for me were the very same fans who would have booed me at tracks all over Britain years ago. So it means a lot to me that I won their respect, when the achievements of someone like Hans Nielsen would have been much fresher in their minds."

So where to interview speedway's first millionaire? After a flurry of calls to and from Ivan's British mobile phone, during his recent two-week visit to Britain, we finally agreed to meet up where it all began for him in this country. Well, not quite Wimbledon Speedway . . . but the White Lion pub, which is just across the road from the old Plough Lane pits, where, as a 17-year-old kid in 1957, The Greatest began taking small steps along his long and turbulent road to fame and fortune.

Now 65-years-old, Ivan is still fit and healthy, and shows all his trademark professionalism by arriving early. He greets me on a note of minor irritation, though: "Ronnie Moore, Ron How, Cyril Brine and the rest of the Wimbledon boys were always on at me to join them for a drink in this pub after home meetings every week but I never did. They said it was always full of people and a really fun place to go. I've just popped my head inside, for the first time in my life, and it's the grottiest place I've ever been into!"

Who needs company when you are sitting with world's greatest-ever speedway rider, in a quiet, little corner of the bar where none of the smattering of locals who wander in during the mid-afternoon session show the slightest recognition of the sporting legend in their midst. Ivan, doing his best to suppress a cold, sips on a pint of English bitter.

Let's literally begin at the start. Who taught you how to gate?

"No-one helped me at all," he says. "I run training academies all round the world now but when I was young there were no such places where you could learn. People didn't help, the top riders never helped anyone – it was just a way of life back then. I learned through getting bloody good hidings every so often. That teaches you. I also learned from watching other riders, including their mistakes. I tried different techniques but they didn't always work.

"When I arrived here as a kid, Peter Moore had a reputation as a fast starter, while Jack Young was recognised in Australia as a very good gater. I started to beat Youngie after a little while but he'd still say to me: 'Aah, but you can't beat me out of the start'. But I became so determined that after a while I did beat him from the gate a few times – and I'd 'pat' myself on the back all the way down the back straight!"

As well as being renowned as one of the fastest starters in the business, Mauger was also a notorious 'roller', in the days when riders were permitted to bend the tapes to breaking point without being excluded. He was the master of psychological warfare, renowned for his mind games and often won many of his races at the start line, against opponents who crumbled under pressure. But it begs the question: would he have been quite as effective had he been forced to sit still at the start, as they all must do today?

"One of the best things that has happened to speedway in the last 20-odd years is the rule where

**Looks like Ivan (gate 2) and his former protege Ole Olsen (gate 3) are having their own starting competition in this clash during this 1980 meeting at Sydney Showground.**

riders are automatically excluded if they touch the tapes," he says. "Some of my old rivals might think this is a bit rich coming from me, because I used to push the tapes whenever I could, and whenever I felt I needed to, but the thing is that for about 10 years, all through the 70s when I raced in Germany and other European countries most Sundays, they already had their own domestic rules in place to outlaw tape-touching. So I could push the tapes three, four or five nights a week in England and make most of my starts but I'd go to Europe and ride speedway, long-track or grass-track on Sundays, when I couldn't touch the tape without being excluded, and I still made most of my starts.

"In my time in speedway there have been about a dozen different starting systems around the world . . . but the same guys still made starts. They can change the system tomorrow but the same riders who made starts last year would make them this year. And they can change from 34mm carburettors to 24mm and the same guys who won last year will win this year. Governing bodies all over the world figure that if they change the system, they can change the winner. But they can't change the human factor. They can't stop a winner, or the winner's brain.

"The rule that prevents riders from touching the tapes is a good one. I was in my last season at Exeter (1984) when that rule came in, and I got excluded just once all that year for tape-touching . . . and still made most of my starts. People like Hans Nielsen and Erik Gundersen were very good starters, and they used to be all over the tapes as well, but as soon as that rule came in they actually made a higher percentage of starts, because the element of risk changed in their favour and they were very good starters in any case."

It must be true to say that there were more top riders capable of winning the World Final during Mauger's time at the top compared to those with genuine World Championship aspirations under the current GP series format?

"There were probably more genuine world class riders then than there are today but there are a lot of very good international standard riders around now," says Ivan. "The leading link front forks and soft compound tyres have helped a lot of those riders – it's not so much the laydown engines

The master of mind games meditating before a West Ham v Belle Vue match in 1971, with Tommy Roper, Olle Nygren and Peter Bradshaw in the background.

that have been a factor. The DOHC Jawas, with straight front forks and hard compound tyres, were monsters to ride but if you had put leading link forks on them and soft compound rear tyres, that alone would have turned them into a Rolls-Royce.

"There are a lot more, and better, 20-year-old riders around now than when I rode. But the guys ranked higher than them, the genuine world class performers . . . yes, I think there were more around in my day.

"There are fewer guys now with a chance of winning the World Championship."

Briggo and Ole Olsen were consistently Mauger's two biggest rivals and his fiercest opponents over the longest period, but can he single out one rider who was especially difficult to beat?

"It's a difficult one for me to answer, because I rode for such a long time that I faced different riders from different eras – I came across them all and rode against every World Champion from Jack Young (1952) to Gary Havelock (1992). They were all hard to beat.

"Briggo was great for years, Ole was a hard rival for a shorter period. But I could just as easily say Jack Young. You can only really ask this question of somebody who has ridden at world class level for only 10 years, who could answer it immediately. But it would be unfair of me to give you a name. And besides, to be perfectly honest, I rode against a lot of riders who were all great at different times and for different reasons.

"I also raced in about 24 or 25 countries, so I had hard rivals in different countries. Take Mildura. I don't care who you were, no-one was going to beat Phil Crump there. The best thing you could do before you got there was to say to yourself, 'if you race him four times, make sure you put a bloody big effort in to beating him once and then you've gotta relax', otherwise you'd just de-tune yourself worrying about it. Crumpie could beat anybody on the planet at Mildura."

Ivan clearly relished putting one over on the Aussies in the battle for glory and Sydney Showground, in particular, was a venue where he enjoyed proving his critics wrong on more than one occasion.

Recalling the 1977 Australasian Final – a cut-throat early stage of the long World Championship trail – at the famous, but now defunct Showground, he says: "Crumpie had been dominate there with his double overhead cam four-valve Streetie engines and only the top four qualified for the next round – at a time when New Zealand had Barry and myself, Larry (Ross) and Mitch Shirra, and Aussie had half a dozen good ones as well. People this side of the world don't realise how hard those meetings were, with only two or sometimes four qualifying places to the Inter-Continental Final. It also made for a long World Championship year, from January to September.

"All the boys were on four-valvers by then and I was using the same long-track Jawa four-valver on which I won the World Long-track Final in '76 and we'd been having carburettor trouble around the uniquely big, fast, very narrow Sydney track. With its 12ft high concrete wall on the corners, it made Exeter's steel wall seem like an air fence!

"I had previously only been back to Sydney once since 1962, when I drove over from Adelaide with Jack Young in his van, with our bikes in the back – a 20-hour trip and we went straight to the track, where I finished second in the New South Wales Championship. I thought that was pretty good after a 20-hour road trip and having never seen the place before. My only other appearance there was when I returned as World Champion and had match-races against Jimmy Airey and John Langfield.

"Anyway, come the '77 Australasian Final, all the knowledgeable Sydney speedway reporters wrote: 'None of these NZ riders will be any good . . . it's going to be four Aussies who go to the Inter-Continental Final in England'. They said I was too old and that I was never any good at Sydney Showground in any case.

"Phil Crump was riding his good 'Streetie', (John) Boulger was on his Wessie and all three of us ended up on 14 points – and then I passed Crumpie on the last corner to win the title in a run-off.

"Another great memory for me was also in Oz, at the 1981 Australasian Final, where the same Sydney reporters wrote me off before the meeting, saying; 'Ivan Mauger is now far too old'. But I won that with a 15 point maximum. They were two very satisfying victories because I wanted to stuff the guys who wrote those big headlines in the Sydney papers."

Homecoming hero: Ivan and his wife Raye enter the Exeter track as fans gather in the main stand to greet the Falcons' skipper soon after he'd won his fifth world title in 1977.

With Exeter promoter Wally Mawdsley and Scott Autrey, the American Ivan nurtured through his early years in Britain.

Winning races and championships in the darkest corners of the former communist eastern bloc countries was another massive challenge that Mauger conquered. He says: "I'd go to the likes of Poland and Russia and there were so many riders from those places, who you may never think about but who could always give you a very hard time. We had the European Final at Leningrad one year and I won it with two Russians second and third. They beat all the other good guys from the West.

"There were six Polish riders in the 1970 World Final at Wroclaw but there were probably another dozen sitting in the stands, who had been eliminated from the competition, equally capable of scoring double figures on their day."

He says that winning the 1970 final, the first to be held behind the Iron Curtain, to complete an historic hat-trick of title victories, was the most satisfying of his individual six World Final victories. You would be wrong, though, if you assumed that the most satisfying moments of Ivan's career were confined to the winning of one of his 15 speedway or long-track gold medals. "When people ask about my racing career, the first thing they think I'm going to talk about is my World Championship wins – everyone knows about those.

"But not everybody knows that we won the league at Exeter in 1974 despite being probably the fifth or sixth best team on paper. We would have done the same thing at Hull in 1979, where we won a lot of away matches by 40-38. We had no right to be challenging Coventry for the league championship that season but we would have won the title if half our team hadn't failed to turn up for our match at Wimbledon.

"The riders concerned were told about that, in no uncertain terms, a few days later, at our next home meeting. And I can assure you they were also told about it a second time, after we lost the championship decider at Coventry.

"When you ask what my most satisfying moments were, that involves lots of things and many races. Going into the final heat of league matches, four points down and winning 40-38, gave me a great feeling. I've won so many matches with my teams when we've scored a 5-1 in the last race and won the match by two points.

"Sometimes that's taken quite a bit of working out, a lot of hard riding and a lot of trust in your race partner, which is why so many of those match-winning races brought me a tremendous amount of satisfaction.

"Of the last-race partners I had most success with, Scott Autrey stands out for what we did together for Exeter."

Mauger had the single-minded dedication to drive himself to the top, especially after his early setbacks at Wimbledon before becoming a Provincial League star for Newcastle in the early 60s. But he didn't just have determination and desire for himself. He remains one of the greatest captains, arguably the best ever, and much more influential than most. A genuine leader who would conjure shock performances and results from the most unlikely quarters. For him captaincy was never a case of going through the motions.

"I was never a captain who just tossed the coin and chose either gate one or two," he continues. "At each of the clubs I was at, I had a big say with the promoters and the team management in who rode for us and who we got rid of, and it's fair to say that I fell out with a fair proportion of the existing team at all my tracks.

"Newcastle were really lowly in the Provincial League when I joined them in 1963 but we won the title the following year. Belle Vue were used to finishing somewhere between 16th and 10th in

Another win, this time over Ole Olsen and John Boulger in the 1974 Brandonapolis at Coventry.

the four BL seasons before I went there in 1969. We had a bit of a sweep out and went on to finish second in the British League in my first season, then won it three years in a row and also collected the Knockout Cup two seasons in succession.

"I joined Exeter after the 1973 season had already started, by when they were bottom of the league and already several points adrift of the sides above them. We climbed in to the top eight that year but it was the same there – I fell out with a few of them and we had a bit of a sweep out. But we won the title the following year. We weren't the best team in the division by a long way. But we had the best team spirit.

"Contrary to a lot of beliefs about number one riders always having the best starting positions, you only have to talk to any one of my old team-mates to find out that I would put the team first. As I was looked upon as our best starter, if we went into the last race needing a 5-1 to win, I'd protect my partner against the other team's top rider by taking the worst gate."

With Mauger working closely in tandem with the team manager, the team's No.1 rider would occasionally find himself wearing the unfamiliar 2 or 4 racejacket – a tactical ploy that would give his team additional strength in one or two key races.

"It's not really an accident that all my teams were so successful. We swapped team positions around and did all sorts of things to improve our chances of winning. I had a definite input as to what was best for the team: who rode with whom, who started off a particular gate and so on, and what we had to do to win a match.

"When I signed for Belle Vue, Exeter and Hull I joined them on the full understanding that I would be allowed to have such a big influence over the team. Ian Thomas will tell you how we talked for a day-and-a-half over at my place – he visited me twice before I signed for Hull – and only about an hour was spent talking about money.

"I'd been to Hull before as a visiting rider and the place was just a disgrace, from one end to the other. The team was also very poor at the time. But we changed the pits around, switched the pairings, earmarked one or two riders we wanted – and some we didn't fancy – and we did that early in the piece, so that Ian could use me as a lever to get in the riders we wanted.

"The only place where I didn't have a big effect on the team make up was Newcastle but I'd been there only five minutes before I had a meeting with promoter Mike Parker and Eddie Glennon and told them: 'Listen, there's some dead wood here and if you want the team to win, this is what you're going to have to do'. The immediate reaction was: 'Well, so and so won't like this and so and so won't want that'. So my attitude was: 'If they don't want change, then we won't have success, simple as that'.

"I didn't want to join a team and just ride around as the number one, toss the coin and all that sort of stuff, which is what a lot of captains do."

As I said, Ivan has never underestimated himself – and why should he? He has an unrivalled collection of medals to prove just how successful he was. Even when asked if he had any riding weaknesses, possibly one or two that went undetected by others, he is left scratching his head.

"No, not really. One year (1969) with Belle Vue, I dropped nine points in the league all season. Three of them when my throttle cable broke while leading. Of the other six points I conceded, Clive Featherby beat me in Heat 1 at Hyde Road a week after he'd also beaten me at his home track, King's Lynn. Two meetings in a row without a maximum was the longest I went that season without going through the card, although I must have dropped four other points throughout the year. Another year, I didn't drop a point at Exeter all season. In 26 matches I scored 17 maximums.

"Of course, every human being has weaknesses, but my weaknesses were when I didn't quite feel like winning on certain nights. I didn't dislike any tracks, whether they were big, small, wet, deep

Bruce Penhall won the first of his two world title in 1981 but the Californian had no answer to Ivan in this 1981 duel on Hull's visit to Cradley Heath.

or slick."

Brits have a reputation for disliking winners, particularly phenomenally successful champions like Mauger. It's a curious part of our culture to support the underdog. Some fans went to speedway in Mauger's day simply to boo him – his mere presence at a meeting guaranteed a bumper attendance. But, while he had few British fans beyond the clubs he rode for, as Ivan points out, he was both liked and respected by his peers.

"While I wasn't very popular with the fans and a lot of rival promoters and team managers, I actually had a lot of good friends among the riders. There aren't any riders who I have fallen out with over the years – I had a good relationship with them all and still keep in touch with many all over the world."

While fellow riders possibly had reason to thank the groundbreaking Mauger for taking the sport forward, from a technical and financial aspect, not all of the promoters running the sport at the time were quite so enamoured with the man they regarded as 'trouble'.

Ivan recalls: "I did get a lot of resistance from promoters when I was new to the scene, because they didn't like change. Actually, a lot of promoters today still don't like change.

"Here's a story about Charles Ochiltree, who was a very professional promoter at Coventry. For as long as I can remember going to Brandon – from the time when I first went there with Briggo and Ronnie (Moore) and did their fuel and oil and stuff – the pits and the dressing rooms were always immaculate.

"In the early 70s Peter Oakes and I got a Duckhams sponsorship and it stated in my contract with them that for second halves I would wear a personalised Duckhams racejacket and use a fork cover with their logo.

"We did this at Coventry when Belle Vue were there one night and I can distinctly remember getting ready to push off for my heat in the second half when Charles, standing in front of my bike, said: 'I can't permit you to go on my racetrack with your sponsor's name showing like that'. I told him what I thought and just went right on ahead and rode anyway. Sponsorship then was a dirty word.

Trendsetter Ivan upset promoters with his personalised sponsor's racejacket.

"About three years later, when he was president of the BSPA, I read a big story in *Speedway Star* where Charles was quoted as saying: 'This sport cannot progress without sponsors'. I phoned him that day and we had a bit of a laugh when I reminded him about the Duckhams incident!

"Charles and Ronnie Greene, who ran Wimbledon when I arrived here as a 17-year-old, were the two promoters I respected most. They ran their respective tracks very well and were a bit like Kym Bonython in Adelaide. The infield tracks marshals and rakers were always immaculate and would march onto the track in step with each other to a tune. It was orderly, and the grass was nicely mowed and the pits were great. Those two stand out for me and the sport could do with more Charles Ochiltrees and Ronnie Greenes around today."

Ivan left me clutching a copy of John Berry's acclaimed book, *Confessions of a Speedway Promoter*. He said of our star columnist: "People say that John Berry was outspoken but what's 'outspoken'? It means saying what needs to be said, and he often said things that other people didn't like to hear . . . but they still needed to be said. I don't think any team can be successful without the boss having any sort of control over the whole lot and John Berry obviously had that at Ipswich in the 70s.

"I was grateful to Mike Parker for bringing me and my family back to England, at Newcastle in '63. But Mike was also one who wanted to have the final say in everything and we fell out over a few things – not money, he never owed me a cent – it was always over our policies and ideals, which were different."

# Racing at Exeter was 'fun'

**AFTER five very successful seasons as Exeter captain and No.1, during which he won the fifth of his six world titles, Mauger is better qualified than most to cast judgement on the notoriously fast and dangerous Devon track (if only in terms of sheer speed reached on the massive circuit).**

He told *Backtrack:* "The criticism it used to receive from riders was completely unjust. As I said before, a track's a track. Exeter was a bit like Sydney Showground – great fun to ride round. At the end of a meeting there, if you had done really well and ridden exactly how you'd wanted to, it left you with a great feeling as you drove away from the stadium.

"Whereas you could go to other tracks, score a maximum, but not have a lot of fun. You'd just go through the routine of winning four races, then the second half, and go home.

"At Exeter, I had contests within myself. If I was riding very well, I'd go up around the banked part of turns three and four and let my back wheel hit the fence – it would give me a ricochet and fire me down the home straight. I used to practice doing that because, occasionally, if I was second or third in a race, and went up and got that ricochet on turn four, I knew I would have enough speed to pass guys on the inside by the start line. They were not expecting it.

"Instead, they expected you to creep round the outside. It would take me about a lap-and-a-half to build up to but I'd pass a lot of guys by riding the line of gate one or two down the front straight – after my back wheel had deliberately clouted the fence. When we first used mufflers, I tended to bend them on the fence!

"Yes, Exeter was a really good, fun place to race at."

# New Zealand's greatest day

**ONE of the proudest days in Ivan's life – never mind his speedway career – was Sunday, September 16, 1979 – the afternoon his beloved New Zealand finally became world team champions.**

In front of a sparse White City crowd, reduced in numbers by the shock elimination of the host nation in the UK qualifier the previous May, the Kiwis shone like never before at this level, beating Ole Olsen's Denmark by four points, with Czechoslovakia and Poland out of sight.

Victory in west London was also a triumph for Kiwi strategy and team spirit, as Ivan explains: "Larry Ross (10), Mitch Shirra (10) and myself (nine) were going quite good on the day, so we just said to Cribby (Bruce Cribb): 'You've got to get at least third place in every race, or four points in the meeting - total', and he did exactly the job we asked of him, scoring five crucial points."

Of course, while this was a sensational result for New Zealand speedway, winning World Cup gold was nothing new to Ivan, who had led Great Britain to success in the same competition in 1968 (Wembley), 1971 (Wroclaw, Poland) and 1972 (Olching, Germany) before the British authorities turned to their own fast emerging talent and discarded their colonials cousins without even a backward glance.

One of Ivan's proudest days. It's a wet, murky Sunday afternoon in May 1979 and New Zealand have just dumped England out of the World Team Cup at Reading. Left to right: Trevor Redmond, Mitch Shirra, Roger Abel, Bruce Cribb, Barry Briggs, Larry Ross. Ivan is kneeling with the Maori shield.

It clearly still rankles with Mauger, who says: "For years we had to ride for Great Britain, when Ronnie (Moore), Barry (Briggs) and me could have won the thing by ourselves, without the help of the English riders. We could also have won the World Pairs four years in a row.

"We were never allowed to ride in the World Team Cup as New Zealand then but as soon as Ronnie got injured and Barry retired (the first time), and England had PC and other youngsters coming through, all of a sudden they turned round and said they didn't need us any more. They decided: 'We're calling ourselves England now'.

"I got dropped about two weeks before the WTC final at Wembley (1973), when GB – or England – were sitters to win it, because they didn't need me by then."

With new wonder kid Collins romping to a maximum, 'Great Britain' (they wore the Union Jack body colour, despite it being an all-English squad) won easily.

But Mauger was not finished with the ultimate team prize in the sport.

"A few years later, when my country finally gained FIM status, the authorities said: 'Great news, Ivan, you can ride as New Zealand now'. And I told them to get stuffed! Who was I going to ride with?"

But Mauger did reverse his decision not to appear for his country in the WTC – and to spectacular effect.

He recalls: "One of the most rewarding things for me came in 1979, when we went to Reading for a World Team Cup qualifier in really wet conditions, and knocked England out of the competition. It was almost as satisfying as winning the final itself later that year.

"We thought to ourselves: 'You can all get stuffed now!'."

# World Finals won and lost

**DID what happened in the run-off with Jerzy Szczakiel at Katowice in 1973 make that your most disappointing World Fiinal ever?**

"No, not at all. I made a mistake. It was the same mistake that Jason Crump made against Rune Holta in the 2003 Grand Prix decider. You are in a position to be World Champion but you are not in a position to shut the throttle off. Jason was about a yard ahead and took Rune's front wheel away, so Rune went down and Jason was excluded. I was a yard behind Szczakiel and hit the back of his bike. I was on a long-track engine, so I was getting a lot of grip around the outside."

After Ole Olsen barged his way past on the inside of their last race to set up a decisive run-off between Poland's man of the moment and Mauger, Szczakiel got a flier from the outside and raced into an early lead. Mauger was going considerably faster, however, and it seemed only a matter of time before he passed him . . . until they approached the pits bend for the second time.

Ivan continues the story: "I planned to pass Szczakiel at the far end on the next lap around but I caught him quicker than I had anticipated. I was taking about a lap-and-a-half to build up but there was a gigantic hole there and when he heard me coming up the inside, he moved to the inside. It was a bit slick there and I had no option but to run into him."

Referee Georg Transpurger didn't even stop the run-off. While Mauger lay prostrate, just yards from the pit gate, Szczakiel completed his shock victory unopposed for two more laps, his rear wheel passing within inches of the stricken Kiwi's legs. The ref was working to the letter of the rulebook but, thankfully, safety standards have improved for the better!

**But Ivan doesn't lose sleep over his Katowice catastrophe of 1973. Instead, his biggest blow came at the same Chorzow circuit three years later. He says: "PC won it in '76 – he was brilliant then – Simmo got second and Crumpie third . . . all on four valve engines. Collins and**

Simmons were on those Nourish Weslakes, with the 83 106 cams and twin carbs, while Crumpie was on the first – and I always thought the best – Street conversion.

"What people forget, because everyone was waiting so long for an English World Champion, is that I was on a two-valve Jawa that day and therefore had a tremendous power and speed disadvantage. I was a Jawa factory rider then and they did not finish their DOHC four-valvers until a few days later – in time for the World Long-track Final at Marianske Lazne in Checho the following week.

"At Katowice, I was 30 yards in front down the back straight in my second ride when my jet block – the little block in the middle of my carburettor – broke. That not only put me from potentially first to second in the meeting, it took me down from first to fourth overall. Remember, Crumpie was behind me before I stopped in that race," says Ivan.

Returning to the Katowice pits before his disastrous run-off crash in 1973.

"There were only two World Championships that I figure I really lost – 1976, when I still had to beat PC in the last race (Ivan did so but Collins needed only to settle for second place to clinch the title). But I would have gone into Heat 20 one point in front, and at that time I definitely could have stood the pressure of that situation more than Peter.

"The other one that got away was when clutch trouble in the World Long-track Final at Muhldorf in 1978 cost me the title."

**Of your six winning World Finals, would you agree that Gothenburg '77 was the one in which you enjoyed most good fortune?**

"Yes, I had some things go for me that night," he admits, "but I won other world finals despite a lot of things going against me."

Peter Collins, who finished second to Mauger in monsoon-like conditions at Ullevi, claimed in a previous issue of *Backtrack* that 18-year-old Michael Lee should have been declared the winner of the controversial Heat 18, because he was the only ride at the tapes ready to start the rerun of the race when the two minute time allowance elapsed. Mauger and Ole Olsen were still cleaning the mud off themselves and their machines after Australia's John Boulger had been excluded for falling while setting a reckless pace in the first attempt to run the race.

Ivan now admits now that perhaps it was a gamble on both his and Olsen's part not to be on track and ready to race in the allotted time – but it was a calculated gamble that paid rich dividends for the Kiwi.

"Both Ole and I knew the referee Tore Kittilsen well. He was too weak to cause a controversy. I heard the buzzer go for the rerun and didn't think he was going to exclude anyone, although I'm not sure I wasn't out on the track in time anyway. As an international competitor in any sport, you have to know the personalities of the referees.

**Unruffled Ivan on parade at Wroclaw with Gennady Kurilenko and Briggo before the 1970 World Final.**

"I wasn't terribly concerned about John Boulger riding where he did. He was riding too far out and what amazed me was that Ole was on the outside of him. The track was so wet and the outside was turning to slush.

"Ole and I were both on the DOHC Jawas and at the end of long straights like they have at Gothenburg, the front wheel sledges for a fraction going into the corners. In very wet conditions the front wheel slides a little bit more than you want it to and it's an unreal feeling, especially if you are trying to go the extra mile, that extra 25 per cent.

"So being out where he was, I couldn't imagine how Ole was going to stay on his bike. I couldn't imagine how Boulger was going to stay on his bike either! They were both very good riders but I couldn't understand why they were on that part of the track in those conditions. I only needed to be around the inside of them . . .

"At least when it came to the second rerun, with Ole, Michael and myself, all of us good starters, none of us wanted to take the risk that Boulger had."

With perfect throttle control, Ivan sped from the tapes to win from Lee and clinch his fifth world title.

But would he now concede that the '77 final should have been postponed, or abandoned, as the rain lashed down and conditions deteriorated from treacherous to near unrideable?

"People wouldn't ride in weather like that today," he agrees, "and it would have been called off if an English referee had been in charge. Let's put it this way, European referees used to please the people who gave them a nice, big dinner the night before. There was a sort of cliqué among the European referees and they weren't that interested in the riders.

"I rode in lots of meetings in Europe that should have been cancelled but you get on with it. At Gothenburg in '77, I said to my crew – Norrie (Allen) and Gordon (Stobbs) – 'let's get the other helmets, goggles, tear-offs, etc, out of the transporter and all the other wet weather gear ready, because this is going to happen. It might not happen until midnight but it's definitely going to happen. So let's get everything ready and geared-up to race in the wet'.

"These things are important at the time but now, with the passing of years, they don't seem important at all. I think PC was a bit lucky in 1976 and he thinks I was a bit lucky in 1977. There's probably a bit of truth in both our opinions but it doesn't matter much now whatever way around it was – we both got a title each in those two years."

**Why have you always maintained that the 1970 final was your hardest to win?**

"Yes, it was. And not only that, the 1970 World Final was definitely the hardest single, solitary speedway meeting that's ever been held. There were about six of us from western Europe who could have won and another six from eastern Europe – the Poles and Russians – capable of winning at Wroclaw.

"It was so open and if you look at the film of that final, there were lots of races where all four riders crossed the finish line within a few yards of each other. Positions were changing all the time.

"People have got their head in the sand a bit over the '81 World Final at Wembley. It was great because Bruce Penhall won two brilliant races (against Ole Olsen and Tommy Knudsen) on the last corner. But if you imagine that he won those two races from the gate, would people still be saying it's the greatest World Final ever? No, they're really saying it from a nostalgic point of view, because it was the last World Final held at Wembley and Bruce was brilliant on the night.

"There were also political advantages to be had at Wroclaw that year. The Poles filmed us having breakfast and doing pretty much everything, so we only talked tactics in my van – not in the hotel rooms, because we didn't trust anyone. Everything was geared towards a Polish rider winning it, and the Russians were favoured as well.

"I had a team of people helping me that day: Peter Oakes, Chris MacDonald, Gordon Stobbs and Wilfried Drygala. It was a hot day and I parked our van under a pillar beneath the grandstand. But the Polish organisers wanted us positioned out in the sunlight and they forcibly moved my bikes out of the shade.

"The referee would keep sounding the two-minute buzzer for the western-based riders, just to get us sitting out in the sun longer than our rivals from the east. Meanwhile, I'd walk past the Poles and see them sitting in the shade with ice packs and damp towels on the back of their neck. They didn't even have their racejackets on while we were being told to get ready to race.

"So when they put us on two minutes, I just said to my guys: 'Stuff it, we'll wait until they are all ready to go'. We set up a chain of signals in the pits, so I'd wait until the last possible minute before going out to race. I wouldn't move off my chair until the other riders were out there and sitting on their bikes. It bloody annoyed them but that's the way we had to do things back then.

"A lot of things went into winning that World Final. And I think I won the respect of the Polish people by winning it. They were very respectful after I won, bringing Raye down to the pits to see me. After I won that day, setting the precedent of completing a World Championship hat-trick and the first rider to win the title in eastern Europe, I got a good reception from the Polish people. I think it was a resignation of acceptance on their part.

"I am still proud to have won during that period, as there were about five or six World Finals in a row where we all had two-valve Jawas. We had the same chains, clutch plates, back tyre, piston, valves and valve springs. Cosmetically, the western riders' bikes looked nicer, with perhaps a bright painted mudguard or an aluminium fuel tank, whereas the easterners had the standard dull, blue Jawa mudguards and tank. But otherwise we had the same jets, carbs, magnetos and steel front wheels. No-one had a yard more speed than anybody else."

Ivan on his last visit to Britain in 2011, with former long-time mechanic Gordon Stobbs.

# Who gives a damn?

**DID Ivan care that he was never very popular with most supporters beyond those who followed the clubs he represented?**

"No, it never bothered me too much. I set out as a little kid to be World Champion. I never, ever set out to be popular. Some of my rivals always dreamed – and you've got to have dreams, otherwise you'll never be successful – of winning the World Championship, scoring a maximum and breaking the track record.

"I always dreamed about being World Champion. I wasn't worried whether I scored a maximum in front of 100,000 people, or if it was shown on television throughout the world. That's why, when I went to World Finals and there were 100,000 people present and it was shown on TV around the world, I was never fazed by it. I never got nervous or let it bother me. I had my mind power switched on.

"I could have gone to a World Final in a field – it still would have meant as much to me."

Nonetheless, while the end has always seemed to justify the means for a fiercely driven man with a single-minded dedication to be No.1, Ivan admits that topping the fans' poll as speedway's Millennium Man – he won 12,200-plus votes, some 5,000 more than nearest rival Hans Nielsen – gave him immense satisfaction.

"I was very proud to win votes from fans in all corners of England, which means that people in Poole and Swindon, Cradley and Coventry might not have liked me as a rider, but they obviously voted for me.

"Ronnie Moore was probably the only universally popular World Champion in my time while Peter Collins was also well liked. I can't think of any other who somebody hasn't disliked for one reason or other, though Mark Loram would probably be the only modern exception."

But when Mauger left any speedway track with the fans' boos ringing in his ears (usually with the winners' spoils tucked under his arm), he knew he could always count on the total backing of the people closest to him.

"I had Raye, our family and our little dog – we always had a little dog and still do – and I'd go home from meetings, where people had been booing me, but with my family and dog around me, I'd wake up the next morning and feel that everything was fine. I thought: 'Who cares whether people were booing me last night?'

Unlike many hugely successful sports people, Ivan admits he wished he had won more: "There were lots of disappointments – I'm satisfied with what I achieved in speedway apart from the '76 final but I've always loved the long-track and losing that '78 World Final was probably my biggest ever disappointment.

"Then again, that's what makes the successes all the more satisfying."

*This edited extract is from Ivan Mauger's last major interview with a British magazine. Sadly, in 2016, his daughter Julie confirmed what many of us already knew – that her father was suffering from a form of Alzheimer's and was no longer able to make public appearances.*

** *The White Horse pub in Wimbledon, where this interview took place, is no more and has since been converted into a shop.*

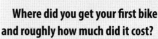 

## On 2 Minutes With…
### JULIAN PARR

**Where did you get your first bike and roughly how much did it cost?**

I got it from Eric Boocock but I'm not sure how much it cost because I didn't pay for it. My stepfather, Mick, took me to watch speedway at Bradford when I was about 11 and I carried on going because it was only seven or eight miles from where we lived in Huddersfield. When I was 16 I wanted to have a go at riding myself, so Mick bought me a bike. We had a pub in Huddersfield and I think that financed it.

Booey had a spares shop in Osset – we didn't have spares vans at tracks like they do now – and he built a bike up for me out of bits. It was an overhead cam Jawa. I didn't start on a two-valve because Booey's attitude was that you needed a bike that was fit to race. He lent me a set of leathers, too, in case it didn't work out for me. He was team manager at Belle Vue at the time and ran a training school. I went there and asked him what to do, so he said: "At the end of the straight turn left."

But I picked it up quickly and after about three or four months I was in the Scunthorpe team (for the 1981 season).

**Best promoter you've ridden for and why?**

Ronnie Russell at Rye House. I had three years at Rye House (1985-87) and Ronnie took over before the start of my second season there. His man-management was good and he was friendly too – not high and mighty like some of them who could be a bit toffee-nosed.

**Favourite track?**

Scunthorpe (Ashby Ville) was my home track and I went really well there. I was the track record holder and I had a nine-and-a-half point average round there in 1984. I liked Milton Keynes and Rye House, too. The first time I went to Rye I think I scored nowt but the next time I scored 13.

**Worst crash/injuries?**

I broke my ankle in 1984. I was doubling-up for Sheffield and as we were coming out of the second bend, Neil Evitts, who was in front of me, lost control and reared. He hit the fence and went over it but his bike rebounded back and caught me. I spent three weeks in hospital before I discharged myself and went to see Carlo Biagi. I've still got screws in the ankle today.

# ALUN
# ROSSITER

NO-one can say Alun Rossiter hasn't put in the hard yards on his way to becoming Great Britain team manager. Quite literally.

Hard miles might be a more accurate description. Around 80,000 of them a year to be precise.

Rossiter, about whom the phrase larger-than-life could have been invented, combines his duties as co-promoter of home town club Swindon with a day job as a lorry driver. "I still drive a truck for a living," he says. "They say average mileage for a car per year is about 12,000 but with my lorry driving and the speedway, I reckon I do about 80,000."

On top of that, this year he will have the small matter of the national team to contend with as well.

Alun Rossiter, GB speedway manager. Who would have thought it? Not bad for a Wiltshire lad who began his working life on the railways.

He wasn't there for long because his emerging talents on a speedway bike took him down an entirely different career path. From Robins' mascot to national team manager, in fact. Yes, it's been quite a journey for the 48-year-old, who lives in Swindon with wife Julie and their four kids,

Young fan Alun Rossiter, in his Swindon replica leathers and racejacket, sits with his hero Bob Kilby as the Robins pose before a match at West Ham in 1970. The others are (left to right): Clive Hitch, Pete Munday, Barry Duke, Barry Briggs, John Bishop and Mike Keen.

Grace (12), Charlee (9), Ben (6) and Ruby (six months).

"Basically, I started off moto-crossing," he said. "I finished second in the British Championship to a guy who went on to become quite successful, Tim Wheeler, but I was waiting for a new bike to come out to be competitive when I needed to go up a class. But it didn't come out, so I moved over to grass-track instead.

"I can remember the big grass meetings, like the Bulmer's one at Hereford, when Crumpie (Phil Crump) and PC (Peter Collins) would be riding, and grass-track was kind of in line with speedway and we started going to Swindon.

"I became the Swindon mascot from when I was about four-years-old to when I was 12, so I must have been one of the longest serving mascots around.

"That all came about through Bob Kilby. Mum and Dad worked on the railways, so we used to get free travel on the trains and would go

Happy days with Exeter, Alun's first club, in 1983.

With Weymouth team-mate Martin Yeates in 1984.

125

all over the country following the Robins. This was in the days when Swindon would ride at places like Hampden Park on a Friday night. "I remember we went up there on the train and came back the next day. We were standing by the pits at Hampden Park and Bob invited me in. Jimmy McMillan was there. Bob said: 'You deserve something for coming all this way to watch us', so he said to Mum and Dad, 'bring him down the pits at Swindon tomorrow night'.

"So it all started from that. Each week, Bob would take me out on his bike on the parade and that sort of went on for a bit. Bob was my biggest hero, even with people like Briggo and Martin Ashby in the team.

"Eventually, I started going to Lew Coffin's training schools at Weymouth. 'He's one of my boys', he would say – but everyone was one of Lew's boys!

"Weymouth was the place to go in those days and we would be there every Saturday morning. At Swindon, though, we had the very successful junior team, the Sprockets. I didn't break into the team straight away because there were riders like Terry Broadbank, Steve Bishop and Kevin Smart. I was sort of on the fringe to begin with but then I broke into the team.

"I wouldn't say I was a natural because I had to work at it. But I started to get more regular rides and I remember getting the phone call, end of '82 it was, from Ron Byford. He said that Peter Oakes had been on the phone asking if I would guest for Exeter at Crayford. That was my debut.

"I was working full-time on the railways, so I had to get a pass out to take a day's holiday. Swindon was a big railway town at the time and my granddad had got me a job there – he was chairman of the local NUR. I started off as a junior storeman but I went on to be a forklift driver.

"Dad had to drive me to Crayford and I think I scored three, paid four, or something like that, which wasn't bad bearing in mind I'd never ridden there before or even seen it." (Checking the records, it was actually two, paid four, in a 49-47 defeat, which was quite an effort from the short-handed Falcons who were able to track only five riders: Keith Millard (20), Bob Coles (11) and Andy Campbell (9) scored 40 between them.)

Rosco must have impressed at the tiny London Road circuit, for Exeter offered him a National League contract ahead of the 1983 campaign.

"I got my chance for real with Exeter the following season but that wasn't all sweetness and roses because I kept breaking down," he recalls.

"I was having a lot of trouble with vehicles and I wasn't getting there until seven o'clock. I couldn't do anything right and Oakesy was threatening me, saying, 'if you don't get things sorted, you're out' sort of thing. There was a bit of pressure on me but I suppose if you went through my scores, I didn't actually do too badly.

"Bob Coles was a big help when I first went there. He was like a big kid. He still is now, to be fair, even at his age!

"There was Robert Maxfield, too, he was quite helpful to me, and riders like Keith Millard and Steve Bishop were in the team at the time. Bish had been in the Sprockets team. He was better than me but I kind of caught him up.

"I didn't mind Exeter. Everybody had this fear of it and it was a standing joke, wasn't it, how many people would break down on the M5.

"The back straight there was classic. You'd have the jumps and you'd take off and just get the front wheel down in time to go into the third and fourth bends.

"If you didn't go there regularly, I suppose it would have been quite scary but it didn't faze me. It's very sad that it's gone now.

"Some of my happiest times were at Exeter. Colin Hill was an absolute dream as promoter. Every week you'd get paid in cash, which he'd put in an old Truprint packet. I think it was cheaper for

**In the big-time with Coventry in 1986.**                    **Home-town boy. A returning Robin in 1987.**

him than buying envelopes! He'd cash up after the meeting and then he'd come in the bar, where the riders would be sat waiting, and every time he paid you on the nail." Rossiter spent only the one season at the County Ground (1983) before moving along the south coast to Weymouth for 1984.

"We'd just won the KO Cup, it was the first time Exeter had won anything in a number of years, but then I went from Exeter to Weymouth, where I became captain and No.1," he said.

"It turned out to be their last year. Mervyn Stewkesbury was great as promoter and the track there was great. Harry Davis, John's dad, built it."

By 1985, however, the big league was beckoning. A full-time berth with Swindon yielded a 3.69 average from 36 ever-present matches but, surprisingly perhaps, Rossiter was on the move again within 12 months, this time to Coventry.

"I didn't have a bad season at Swindon but I got farmed out to Coventry in 1986," he recalls. "I always remember going up there to meet Charles Ochiltree in his office. I took my boss with me to help do the deal because he was keen on speedway but the deal Charles offered me was more than we wanted anyway, so I just said to my boss: 'Shut your mouth!'

"It was just so different at Coventry. The CO really stepped it up a notch. Everyone called him 'Mr. Ochiltree' but I used to call him 'Mr. C'. I'd always walk straight in the office as well. Everyone else had to knock and wait for a 'come in' but I just used to walk in. I think he quite liked that, the cheekiness, but Mr. and Mrs. (Linda) Ochiltree were always very good to me.

"I remember he once said to me: 'Look, Alun, let me tell you now, if I want to buy Bobby Schwartz, I will buy Bobby Schwartz'. This was when Bobby Schwartz was one of the kingpins. 'If you want to ride for Coventry, you will ride for Coventry'. That was it, simple as that.

"There were some big names at Coventry, people like Rick Miller – I got on great with Rick – and Tommy Knudsen. There was Kelvin (Tatum), David Bargh and David Clarke, and it was one of the

Swindon Robins 1987. Left to right: Jimmy Nilsen, Rosco, Brian Karger, Ron Byford (team manager), Richard Hellsen, Conny Ivarsson, Mitch Shirra, Stephen Rose.

A year after his season with Coventry, Alun (left) is back at Brandon tussling with England stars Kelvin Tatum (inside) and Jeremy Doncaster in the 1987 British Final.

**A Poole Pirate and first league title in 1989.**

best times of my career.

"There were lots of bonuses and incentives for the riders and I always remember the late, great Bernard Crapper saying that one of my biggest mistakes was leaving Coventry at the end of '86. But by then, the glare of the home-town team had taken over again and I was back at Swindon in 1987."

# Rosco calls time

**THROUGHOUT his career, the lure of the Robins kept dragging him back to Blunsdon and, in all, he had five different stints with the club. He also donned the colours of King's Lynn, Peterborough, Oxford and Wolverhampton and even had an eight-match cameo for Premier League Trelawny in the summer of 2002.**

That season, however, was to be his last as a racer. A crash at Poole on August Bank Holiday Monday in 2002 condemned him to the injury list, from where he never returned. "It was probably the low point of my career," he says now. "I was riding for Oxford that year but guested for Poole in a double-header against King's Lynn.

"In the first meeting, I got nothing, I had an absolute shocker (Rossiter failed to score from five starts) but in the second meeting, I made the start in Heat 2 and me and Henka (Gustafsson) were on a 5-1. But then (Jernej) Kolenko picked up in the middle of the corner, t-boned Henka and Henka's bike clipped my back wheel and sent me into the pit gate. "I actually walked back to the pits but I was in agony. Gary Havelock had got injured in the first meeting, so Matt Ford's going: 'Havvy's broken his arm, we're in trouble here, do some star jumps, jump about a bit, don't let it seize up'.

"So there I am, jumping up and down and doing star jumps! I'd had trouble with my first bike

**129**

Friends and rivals: Rosco and Middlo, opposing team managers for Swindon and Poole in the 2002 Elite League Grand Final.

in the first meeting, so I jumped on my second bike but it was obviously in a bit of a mess, so Lars Gunnestad lent me his machine. I made the start but when I went to go into the pits turn, it was just like a thousand volts going through my leg. I just rolled onto the centre green and keeled over.

"That was it. I was in hospital for about three months. I'd ruptured all of the major ligaments in my knee and it's still not brilliant, even today.

"That was my last-ever meeting. I never came back from it. I'd not long had my daughter, Grace. We'd struggled because we paid out of my testimonial money for IVF and we had two failed attempts at it. In those days, it was quite expensive and all my money went on that. "At the end of it, I thought, 'no, it's time to call it a day now, I'm 37 and I've come out of it relatively unscathed'. I'd just got my first daughter and we'd struggled to have kids, so I thought, 'time's time' and that meeting at Poole was my last one."

As he reflects on his 20-year racing career, Rossiter can look back with a degree of

Proud to wear his country's colours in 1987.

satisfaction at the level he reached. OK, he didn't exactly tear any trees up at World Championship level but he still attained a standard that many riders can only aspire to. "Every young rider wants to be World Champion when they start, I think you all have that idea," he said. "I was never a constant world beater but I had quite a good career. I suppose if I'd knuckled down a little bit more, I could have gone a bit further than I did. But I beat the best on my day. I beat Greg Hancock when he was World Champion and I beat Billy Hamill when he was World Champion. I knew I could beat people like that on my day but it was not on a consistent enough basis.

"It's easy to say it's different for riders nowadays but, in all fairness, in the time when I was racing, the other countries would only allow their clubs to have one foreigner and it was always a top one. Now, you can be a second string in the Premier League and get a ride over in Poland. In our day, it was the top riders only, so that was always a bit difficult and very frustrating.

"Things are very different now. The problem today is that the riders expect everything. In our day, if you wanted to get a van or a mechanic, you had to go out and earn it.

"Mechanics nowadays, they're charging £300, £400, £500 a week, yet in our day, it would have been your mate doing it. It was, 'look, come and give us a hand and I'll shout your dinner in the chippy on the way home and I'll shout you a couple of pints after the meeting'. "We had bikes on a trailer or the rack on the back of the car. But I guess you can't stand in the way of progress and the whole thing has moved forward. You've got to go with the times.

"Maybe I wasn't consistently good enough but I still had some highlights I'm proud of."

## On 2 Minutes With...
## ROB TILBURY

**How did your career progress?**

I got into the team at Canterbury in 1982 and worked my way up to No 1. I was pretty eager and I remember Wally Mawdsley would always say to me: "Gently, gently catchee monkey." I was a racer! I'd been winning things since I was seven but this speedway was a different game altogether – completely different. I was coming third and I hated it! I was going well but I decided I needed to go to a small track because I wasn't so good on small tracks. So (when Canterbury closed) I joined Arena-Essex in 1988 and it was so much better. I really enjoyed it there. But the Arena fans hated me before I'd even joined their club!

**Rob and his brother Terry had a big punch-up on the track with Mark and Gary Chessell during an Arena v Crusaders match the previous season:**

I was fined £100 and the police came looking for Terry because he'd knocked one of them out. He was hiding in the back of my van – and they didn't find him. I won the fans over and in the end – they absolutely loved me. I got to No.1 there as well. There was one year I got an amazing amount of points because Martin Goodwin was injured and I took a lot of his rides.

I went to Rye House after that (in 1991) and then on to Long Eaton but I had a bad crash there and that was pretty much the end of me.

**Which team-mate did you most enjoy partnering on the track?**

Malcolm Simmons at Arena-Essex (1989), even though it wasn't for long. He was 43 at the time and I was about 26 and I remember one race I went underneath him going into the corner and, even though he was my team-mate, I took my hand of the handlebar and waved at him. When I saw him years later at the WSRA dinner in the Midlands, he said: "I'll never forget that. You're a lunatic!"

**What was your worst crash or injuries?**

The one I had at Long Eaton in 1991. My chain snapped going into the corner and I went into the fence – and the fences were pretty hard in those days. That's all I remembered of the crash until I saw the video of it – I just crumpled. I broke both collarbones – the bone was sticking out of my wrist – and I did my back in. I did have another go after that but, I don't know, maybe my bottle had gone.

**131**

By Tony McDonald ● Issue 49 (2012)

# CLASSY CHRISTER

From Hammers hero to prince of the Pirates, Swedish stylist Christer Lofqvist shot to the top in spectacular style. But as *Backtrack* recalls, his career and life ended all too soon . . .

**C**HRISTER **Lofqvist came from nowhere and lit up the London speedway scene in 1970. He was the best thing to happen to West Ham since their historic treble-winning feat five years earlier and went on to become an equally big crowd favourite at Poole.**

His British League career fizzled out unhappily at Hackney in 1975 and within three years he had died of a brain tumour at the age of just 33.

But no-one fortunate enough to see Christer race at his brilliant best will ever forget him.

Before he arrived in England, Swedish veteran Olle Nygren had been holding Hammers together by a thread and due to injuries to several key riders, the East London side were languishing joint-bottom of the British League. They had lost eight of their first nine matches and were badly in need of a boost when 'Varg Olle' recommended his fellow countryman to West Ham's general manager Gordon Parkins.

It's clear from looking through the programme of Christer's debut, their BL1 London derby clash with Wimbledon at Custom House on Tuesday, May 12, that West Ham didn't quite know what they were getting. Before Parkins had seen his new signing in action, he actually compared his riding style to Ivan Mauger's, which was rapidly dispelled within seconds of him dropping the clutch. And every mention of the mystery newcomer in the West Ham programme referred to him as 'THRISTER'! Honestly, how difficult can it be to ask your new signing to clearly write his name on a piece of paper before you start raving about him!

Born on June 4, 1944, Christer was a former car salesman who played ice hockey, handball and football near his home at Visby on the island of Gotland, off the Baltic coast. Aged 21, he was a late starter in speedway in 1965.

He rode for his local team Bysarna throughout his career but his early ambitions were met with some resistance from his mother who feared that the death of Christer's father Frits, in a long-track meeting in Stockholm, might be repeated.

The then teenage Nygren rode with Christer's father and was at the meeting in which Lofqvist senior was killed. Olle, the first Swede to finish on the rostrum in a World Final in 1954, says: "Frits was older than me and rode before the war. He was good at both speedway and long-track. We rode in the same meeting at the 1,000-metre Sulvalla trotting track in 1947 or '48. He was using one of the big 500c bikes while I rode a 350cc junior bike.

"There were 15,000 people watching but it was a foggy day and you could hardly see from one end of the track to the other.

"I was ready and waiting to go out for my next ride when, all of a sudden, the stadium went quiet. We didn't know what had happened at first but then eventually we heard there had been a bad accident. Frits had gone wide on the straight and his throttle stuck open. He hit the wooden boards, the fence split and I think he died instantly when the broken board pierced his neck.

"So having known his dad and what the family must have gone through, it brought me and Christer

Stylish Swede, Christer in Test match action at Wimbledon in 1971.

Fans' favourite at West Ham.

a bit closer when I brought him over to West Ham."

Apparently undeterred by the horrific circumstances surrounding his father's death, Christer won the Swedish Junior Championship in 1967. Yet no-one outside Sweden had heard of him until Nygren brought him to England for the first time.

Christer made his West Ham bow just before his 26th birthday, which meant he was a latecomer to the British scene. Riding in the No.4 body colour and partnered with fellow new signing Stan Stevens, he seemed to cover every inch of the large 415-yard Docklands track. How he managed to stay in contact with his two-valve Jawa for the full four laps of his debut ride, as he appeared to hang on for dear life, remains a mystery to open-mouthed onlookers.

After a hair-raising, though pointless, first outing, he calmed down enough to win his next two rides (beating Reg Luckhurst and Trevor Hedge), then grabbed a third place to finish with seven points that earned West Ham an unlikely 39-39 draw – the first points league-leaders Wimbledon had dropped at that stage of the '70 season. With the unlucky Sverre Harrfeldt (broken arm) injured again that night, Hammers' fans had discovered a new overnight sensation.

Martin Rogers, a prolific *Speedway Star* contributor at the time, recalls: "The instant impact he made was as exciting as any debut I can recall in the 70s. Fast, fearless and seemingly out of control half the time, yet in reality very much in control."

A month after his spectacular debut, Lofqvist visited Wembley for the first time but the national stadium inspired, rather than intimidated, him and he stormed to a 15-point maximum. Not only did he see off Lions' legendary Swede Ove Fundin, he set the fastest time of the night and accounted for almost half of Hammers' losing 31 points tally.

It was no coincidence that following Christer's dynamic arrival, Hammers won five of their next six home matches and completed a home-and-away league double over East End rivals Hackney, which was always a feat for the Custom House fans to savour.

How they needed his spark in the horrendous weeks and months that followed.

Two of Christer's team-mates in the famous red and blue racejacket on his debut night were Martyn Piddock and Peter Bradshaw, while Gary Everett lined up at reserve for Wimbledon. As the speedway world knows, in the early hours of July 14 they were among six killed in a road accident at Lokeren in Belgium. West Ham team manager Phil Bishop also perished, along with Aussie second-half prospect Mal Carmichael and the Dutch minibus driver, in what remains speedway's worst tragedy.

Hammers' Stan Stevens and Gary Hay, as well as Cradley Heath's Colin Pratt and mechanic Roy Sullivan, were lucky to survive the crash but suffered multiple injuries. Stevens was unable to resume riding until the following year, Pratt never raced again, while Hay recovered well but, with cruel irony, has been confined to a wheelchair since crashing in Sydney in the Aussie season that followed Lokeren.

The heart and soul had been ripped out of West Ham Speedway. They never did recover but at least their new boy, Christer Lofqvist, eased some of the pain and briefly breathed new life into an

Spectacular and always good to watch, Chris in full flight around Custom House.

A shining light through Hammers' darkest days.

Christer and Steina on their wedding day with young Dennis.

ailing club.

Voted Hammer of the Year at the end of a first season that yielded an impressive 7.82 average from 27 official appearances, Christer retained the award in 1971, having overhauled Nygren by an average of half-a-point a match, to top West Ham's scorechart with an improved CMA of 8.73.

By '71 he was an established member of the Sweden Test team and although West Ham had sunk to rock bottom of the BL at the end of that year, there was cause for celebration for Christer back in his homeland. Bysarna were crowned Swedish first division champions for the first time, while he and Newport's Tommy Johansson added the Swedish Pairs title to complete a memorable year for the islanders.

A proud Christer enthused about Bysarna's success in his *Speedway Express* (Jan 1972) magazine column (ghosted by Martin Rogers): "Visby is the first town on the island of Gotland," he wrote. "Although there are fewer than 20,000 people in the town, we have the biggest crowds at any track in Sweden and the support is really something. This year was our first in the first division and only our fifth in league racing, during which time we have come up by winning the third division and then the second division.

"The most famous rider from the island has been Torbjorn Harrysson and his success in reaching the World Final at Ullevi in 1966 was probably the start of this great interest in speedway in Gotland."

Christer was almost a carbon copy of Harrysson – a pocket dynamo who hung off the back of the bike and trailed his left leg. Both were a spectacular sight to behold. When Harrysson's career was effectively ended by a compound fracture of his leg sustained in the 1969 World Final, Lofqvist was left to carry the world title hopes of the strong-minded folk of Visby.

He admitted: "Island people like to keep very much to themselves," and he was true to his word.

At the end of 1971 Christer married Steina Olsson, the mother of his young son Dennis, in a private church ceremony. Displaying a trait of fierce Gotland independence, the couple told very few about their matrimonial plans.

Martin Rogers recalls: "Christer didn't open up to too many people but as a regular scribe around the tracks I found him engaging and friendly, even to the extent that when he and his long-time

**136**

Deep in thought before his first ride in the 1972 World Final.

Golden Helmet holder at Poole in 1973.

girlfriend got married in London, photographer Mike Patrick and I were the only two speedway people invited in a total guest list of 11! We felt very honoured."

Dennis Lofqvist, who went on to emulate his father as a Swedish international and rode for King's Lynn for four seasons at the end of the 80s and early 90s, told *Backtrack:* "I still remember my parents' wedding even though I was only four at the time.

"His Best Man was a guy called Ron – I can't remember his surname – who was a West Ham supporter and his best friend in England at the time. The vicar who conducted the church service was a Swede.

"I have happy memories of being with my father at West Ham and Poole. I would go in the pits with him at West Ham and at Poole the riders had to walk across the football pitch to get to the dressing room, which had a big bath.

"My Dad was a skillful rider, I know that, and the supporters liked him very much."

Dennis and his family have lived near Visby all their lives and he agrees that the islanders can be "a bit hard-headed" and independent compared to those on the Swedish mainland.

West Ham withdrew from the BL at the end of '71 and it was somewhat appropriate that Christer went down in history as the last rider to win a first division race at Custom House – where speedway had first been staged in 1928 – before their licence was transferred to Ipswich the following winter. You would have thought there would have been a queue of promoters eager to snap him up but while Nygren, Alan Sage and Alan Bellham joined the new-look Witches up the A12, it was Poole who landed West Ham's best asset for 1972.

And just as he'd been the darling of the Cockney crowd, so his popularity soared on the Dorset coast, where he was a ready-made No.1 replacement for moody Norwegian Reidar Eide, who left to continue his nomadic career with Sheffield.

Christer and fellow Swede Bo Wirebrand lived in Harry Davis' caravan park at Winterbourne Whitechurch, where the new Poole favourite would often have Harry's teenage son, John, and his mate Neil Middleditch for company.

John says: "Christer and Bo stayed at Dad's place during the season and their families would visit

**137**

them occasionally in the summer holidays. As a kid of about 14 or 15, I used to idolise Christer and as well as me and Neil, lots of other kids from our local village would come up to the park to see him work on his bikes. Later on, when I was riding for Peterborough, we shared a workshop. I have a photo somewhere of us posing together when he'd won the Golden Helmet and I held the Silver Helmet at the same time.

"As a teenager, I'd take days off school and travel with him to away meetings and he was always a light-hearted, fun character – not the serious, introverted type that some have portrayed him as. I can remember having water fights with him at the park – he was always doing crazy things."

Middlo recalls: "JD and myself used to ride around in woods behind the caravan park on our pushbikes pretending to be speedway riders and when Christer arrived there in '72 we got to know him well. Around that time, I started practicing on a speedway bike and John's career had only just begun at Peterborough.

"Before home meetings at Poole, Christer used to pick me up from my parents' place. About a quarter-of-a-mile up the road was a humpback bridge, where he would always go airborne in his big Mercedes that had his bike strapped on the back. He landed so hard one day that the sump fell out of the engine!"

As well as topping the Poole averages with figures a shade under nine points a match in 1972, Lofqvist also qualified for his first World Final and again showed his liking for Wembley. He won Heat 4 – the race that killed Ole Olsen's hopes of retaining the title when the Dane slid off in a desperate attempt to pass Christer on the outside – and despite being surprisingly beaten by Russian Alexander Pavlov in his second ride, he bounced back with another win and was joint leader with

Leading Ivan Mauger in Heat 1 of the 1974 World Final aboard the ERM.

fellow Swede Bernt Persson on eight points after they had taken three each.

But his title chances were extinguished in Heat 16, when he trailed  eventual champion Ivan Mauger, fellow Swede Anders Michanek and Russia's Viktor Kalmykov. Looking back, two points behind Mauger in that fourth ride would have earned him a run-off shot for the title against the Kiwi and Bernie Persson, although Olsen, more than anyone, would classify this as one that got away.

As it happened, not even 11 points courtesy of a third victory in his final ride could lift Christer above fourth place on the night, behind Mauger, Persson and Olsen. Still, it ranked as one of the most impressive World Final debuts with promise of much more to come.

Eight days after Wembley, Lofqvist reinforced his world class credentials by top-scoring for his country on his World Team Cup Final debut at Olching, Germany, where he notched six points as Mauger led Great Britain in their defence of the title.

Wembley was a heartbreaker but it wasn't the first time in 1972 that one unexpected blip proved costly for Christer. Earlier in the season he had soundly beaten Mauger and John Louis in his first ride at Hackney's Superama meeting and appeared to have the individual title in the bag. But he threw away overall victory in bizarre fashion.

In between his first and second rides, he decided to leave the pits area and find a quiet place to gather his thoughts and ease the pressure that was building. Unfortunately, he made himself so inconspicuous, not even his mechanic could find him in time. When a frantic search outside the stadium finally located Christer, his second heat was about to start . . . and so he was excluded under the two-minute time allowance!

He won his three other rides in effortless style but had to settle for the minor runners-up placing, behind a grateful Mauger and Barry Briggs, who didn't look too many gift horses in the mouth.

Christer didn't let Sweden down in the Inter-Nations series staged on BL tracks that summer, though. He was their top rider in three of their four matches – against England (12 points at Coventry), the combined Norway/Denmark (13 at Reading) and New Zealand (12 at Swindon), while seven in the draw with Australia at Hackney was no disgrace.

On the domestic front, his near nine-point average was the main factor behind Poole moving four places up the BL table, to seventh, at the end of 1972. Back home, Bysarna retained their league championship.

But things started to go wrong the following year.

In June he fell in a run-off with Gote Nordin to determine the last qualifier from the Nordic Final at Norkopping, Sweden, which ended hopes of a second World Final appearance.

In the expanded International Tournament, Christer began slowly with low scores of five against England (at Sheffield) and the USSR (Hackney), before top-scoring against New Zealand (Swindon). He notched nine against Norway/Denmark (Cradley Heath) and 10 versus Poland (Halifax). Perhaps the most eye-catching performance was his top-score of 10 at Newport, a bumpy, awkward-shaped track few visitors relished, although it didn't stop the Swedes losing 40-38 to Australia in the qualifying stages.

At least they did enough to make it to the big final in July at Wembley, where Lofqvist scored 10 points – bettered only by 11 from Anders Michanek, who was famously excluded in that run-off with Peter Collins. Christer would have returned to the Twin Towers for the World Team Cup Final had he not been ruled out by an ankle ligament injury sustained while riding in his homeland at the start of September, which also restricted his contribution at Poole to just 20 official league and cup matches.

However, the lack of meetings did not conceal the fact that he again improved his average, to 9.90 – the highest any Poole No.1 had achieved since Gote Nordin in 1967. Ironically, when Nordin left Poole after just one match in '68, he had recommended Christer as his replacement but the promoting Knott family opted to bring Norwegian Odd Fossengen to Wimborne Road instead.

# ERM, an engine failure

**THE BSPA's blanket ban on commuting foreigners in 1974 meant Christer was unable to continue his progress in the skull and crossbones racejacket. Not that the lack of weekly cut and thrust racing in what was then the world's toughest league appeared to hamper his World Championship chances.**

He battled through the Swedish rounds to the World Final at Gothenburg, where he chose the biggest night of all to unveil a piece of mechanical history – his 'special' new ERM engine was the first four-valve motor used in a World Final and made its public debut a few months before Phil Crump unleashed his Jawa-Street conversion in Australia. The upside to being banished from British league racing was the extra time Lofqvist had to develop the new Swedish-built power unit in domestic league meetings.

The ERM (which stands for Endfors Racing Motor) was a chain-driven, double overhead camshaft modified Jawa, designed specifically for long-track racing. Ullevi's long straights seemed tailor-made for it and when Christer beat Ivan Mauger in Heat 1 in a new track record time, there was a sense that 1974 could be his year.

But that promising opening race win couldn't be repeated and he had to settle for eight points and joint seventh place – the lowest of the five Swedish contingent, spearheaded by the unstoppable Anders Michanek. A win from Heat 20 would have put him in the run-off to decide the silver and bronze medals but Christer's conventional two-valve Jawa – which he reverted to for his last two rides – didn't complete the race. Once again, one bad ride had cost him a rostrum place.

In the World Team Cup Final, he was the Swedes' lowest scorer with five points. What the bare statistics don't reveal is that he played his part in one of the greatest races of the 70s, eventually having to settle for third, inches behind Dave Jessup and Zenon Plech. Thankfully, the ITV cameras were there to capture what commentator Dave Lanning rightly described as "four laps of sensational speedway".

Christer hadn't given up on the ERM's potential, though, much to Hackney boss Len Silver's irritation.

When the British authorities lifted their ban and commuting foreigners were re-admitted to the BL from the start of 1975, rider control allocated him to Hackney. In theory, a move back to the heart of East London, where he'd been such a huge favourite a few years earlier, made perfect sense. Hawks' fans certainly welcomed him with open arms after their No.1 Dag Lovaas requested a move to Oxford. Promoter Len Silver must have hoped that Christer's presence at The Wick would entice at least some West Ham fans along on Friday nights – if only to cheer one man wearing the check racejacket of their former arch rivals.

Instead, the move proved an unmitigated disaster for all concerned. Although he top scored with an impressive 10 points on his home debut against Newport, there was a foretaste of problems to come when he lost power in one of his races and it cost him a maximum.

Christer's persistent experimentation with the new engine irritated both the Hackney management and fans and whatever future promise the ERM may have had when it first came on the scene in 1974, it rarely reflected in his points scoring and, in fact, the motor failed to seriously challenge the Weslake and Jawa and soon disappeared from the sport.

A hand injury, sustained at King's Lynn and aggravated when he was forced to withdraw from his World Championship round at Visby in early May, must have also sapped his enthusiasm in the early weeks of the '75 campaign.

With Hackney, his last British club, in a troubled 1975.    Dennis Lofqvist with his father's racejacket.

A dozen league and cup appearances for Hackney produced an average of 7.6 – almost two-and-a-half points a match down on his previous Poole high and nearly three points a match adrift of Lovaas' supreme contribution the previous season.

Unsettled at Hackney from almost the word go, the unrest came to a head in June when he missed a couple of Hawks' matches without explanation. There were reports that he and Len Silver had patched up their differences but the truce lasted just days before Christer went missing again after being urged to abandon his new four-valve 'baby'.

A top-scoring 11-point haul for Sweden against England in the Test at Hackney on July 11 was no more than a fleeting glimmer of former glories. He contributed three points and nought in the last two Tests, at King's Lynn and Belle Vue respectively, and didn't even turn up for Sweden's Daily Mirror International Tournament clash with the Rest of the World at Hackney on July 22.

Was the tumour that led to his untimely death already growing inside his head? Was Christer suffering in silence? His unexplained absences and poor form were certainly puzzling at the time.

Writing in the Hackney programme after Christer had severed his ties with Hawks, Len Silver said: "The weary episode of Lofqvist has caused me more pain than any previous experience of promoting I can remember. For what seemed no apparent reason, he took a personal dislike to me and, frankly, I was pleased when he finally told me, at Belle Vue, that not only did he not wish to ride for Hackney, he no longer wished to ride in the British League.

"He let us down very badly, refusing offers of mechanical assistance and continually using and testing untried equipment during our important league and cup matches."

It was a great pity that the mechanical experiments he pursued without reward during his unhappy spell with Hackney in '75 meant he was unable to recapture the glory days of West Ham and Poole, where he had blossomed into a stylish world class performer.

Wimbledon hoped Christer would join them in 1976 and forge a new twin Swedish spearhead with their rising young star Tommy Jansson. Rider Control had allocated Lofqvist to the Dons in January but, despite a series of talks with the south London club's management, he was unable to agree terms and never rode for them or any other British team again.

It wasn't a totally wasted trip. In the first week of April, Christer hung around a few days to guest for Vetlanda-based Swedish tourists Njudungarna in their last two club challenge matches, at National League Peterborough, where he scored a maximum 12 points, and Rye House, where only Ted Hubbard's final heat victory denied him a paid 15-point max. It wasn't quite the last we saw of Lofqvist.

His last competitive track appearance in Britain was in the 1976 World Team Cup Final at White City on Sunday, September 19. By now, Swedish speedway was on its knees. Michanek (who had quit the BL at the end of the previous year), Bernie Persson and 'Benga' Jansson were also a fading force and there were precious few good youngsters emerging from the land of the lakes. By far their best hope for future world glory, Tommy Jansson, had been killed racing in Stockholm the previous May.

The '76 WTC final, Britain's supposed showpiece event of the season, was treated with great indifference by the British public. Without England, who had been sensationally eliminated earlier that summer by Australia on a rare off day at Ipswich, few showed any interest in the meeting featuring the Aussies, Sweden, Poland and the USSR. *Speedway Star* didn't even bother to preview it.

And so it was that in front of a sparse west London crowd, Lofqvist was called up as a reserve and given just one ride. He came in to replace Bengt Jansson in Heat 10, where he finished behind Marek Cieslak and Gregori Chlinovsky and just ahead of John Boulger.

To add insult to injury, *Speedway Star* failed to even notice Christer's appearance and credited Jansson with the third place point in their published heat-by-heat details!

It wasn't the ignominious way an otherwise good career was meant to end.

Sadly, his demise from world star to also-ran became irrelevant in the months that followed his low-key departure from British speedway.

# Christer dead at 33

**CHRISTER'S many supporters were shocked when they heard that he had died of a brain tumour on February 1, 1978, aged just 33.**

Recalling his father's sad passing, Dennis says: "I was only 11-years-old when he died. He had suffered very severe headaches for about two years and had to take strong pills to get him through each day. At that time there wasn't really good care for that kind of cancer available, so his death was expected. He lay in bed for the last half-year of his life. It was very tough for the family."

John Davis said: "My whole family was devastated by the loss of Christer. For me it was like losing an older brother. We were very close."

"I remembered how, a couple of years earlier, I'd beaten him in a run-off to win the Acroma Open title at Vetlanda. It was a very wet night and I borrowed Bo Wirebrand's bike to race against Christer. After he died, I wished that I hadn't beaten him.

"It was around that time that I became aware that he was suffering very bad headaches a lot of the time. He'd talk to me about it but he wasn't the sort of person to go to his doctor about a headache.

"He looked very ill and had clearly lost a lot of weight. It was one of life's great tragedies – like Simon Wigg, who suffered the same thing when he was only 40."

When Christer first came to England, he stayed with his West Ham team-mate and mentor Olle

Nygren at his home in Taverham, near Norwich. Nygren remembers: "He was miserable a lot of the time and when I asked him why, he said he had a headache, although I never saw him take any tablets. I told him to go to the doctor but he wouldn't. I don't know if they could have done something if he'd gone for treatment earlier . . .

"My wife Ann suffered with a lot of migraines, so she understood a bit about what he was going through at that time and we tried to help."

Davis says: "After he died, I was proud to win the first Christer Lofqvist Memorial Meeting at Visby. Young Dennis presented me with the trophy – it was the first one his dad had won at West Ham, which I still have today – and there were tears pouring down my face.

Both Davis and Neil Middleditch went on to star for Poole Pirates after Christer's death but neither will ever forget the little blond Swedish ace with the moustache whose skill captured their imagination as starry-eyed kids who dreamed of following in their hero's tyre tracks. In his role as first a Poole rider and now the club's trophy-laden team manager, Middlo has seen many Pirates legends come, and go and he agrees that Christer is right up there with all their other heroes.

"He more or less broke the mould with his riding style in the early 70s," Neil continued. "So good to watch as he hung off the bike. If he made the gate he was away and gone but he won many of his points from the back, too.

"He used to pull some ridiculous gearings round Poole. While most of the guys were using a 18:61 set-up, Christer would be pulling a ratio of 18:55 or 18:56 – as if he was riding a big track like Belle Vue or Sheffield. It was all down to his size and lightness."

Davis added: "Christer was seriously talented and could do things on a bike that none of us had ever seen before. I helped out as his mechanic at Poole one night. He was drinking from a bottle of water and suddenly he said to me: 'Watch this'. He then proceeded to pour a cupful of water into his fuel tank before his next race. The track was slick on this particularly night and he'd worked out that if he diluted his high octane methanol, his bike would gain more grip – and it worked for him."

The last word on Christer Lofqvist goes to Middlo: "He's still very fondly remembered down here in Poole. He is in the club's Hall of Fame and rightly so. He was a lovely bloke."

No way to go: Christer's last ride in Britain. On the inside, he picked up a point in his one and only outing against (left to right) Marek Cieslak, Gregori Chlinovsky and John Boulger in the 1976 World Team Cup Final at a sparse White City.

# DENZIL
# **KENT**

**D**ENZIL Kent had his first speedway rides a year sooner than he should have, according to South African rules.

"It was 1976 and I was still only 15,"explained the former Canterbury star. "The authorities found out how young I was after my second meeting and they banned me from racing for a year.

"In South Africa at that time you needed a full driving licence before you could ride speedway competitively and I was still too young to take my road test."

Although Denzil's first full season of British team racing was with Canterbury in 1980, he had spent a tough learning season here the previous year, second-halving at Cradley Heath and Oxford under the Dan McCormick promotion.

"My dad (Ted) knew Alex Hughson, the former Edinburgh rider, and it was him who got in touch with Dan to get me over there. I rode regularly in the second-half at both of his tracks but it was tough. I would win one race and crash in the next.

"I lived with Peter Prinsloo and would go and watch him race at Exeter, a track that looked very daunting to me."

With his two official match appearances in 1979 yielding only one point from six rides, it was hardly surprising that McCormick was in no hurry to offer Kent a second bite at the cherry the following year. But his loss was certainly Canterbury's gain.

Denzil leading Canter bury Crusaders in 1983, his last season at Kingsmead. Left to right: Maurice Morley (general manager), Ian Clark, Barney Kennett, Daryl Simpson, Denzil, Keith Pritchard, Mark Martin, Nigel Couzens, Reg Luckhurst (team manager).

Kent in Kent . . . Denzil wearing Canterbury colours with team-mates Rob Dolman (left) and Mike Ferreira.

"I went home that winter and practiced as often as I could, riding for up to two hours every day on the track around the football pitch in Johannesburg. I rode there with an ex-rider, Scotsman Ronnie Ferguson, and was determined to get back to the UK."

In the winter of 1979-80 Kent rapidly emerged as South Africa's most outstanding prospect. He impressed to such an extent against British tourists Pete Smith, Steve Wilcock and his best pairs-winning partner John Barker that Canterbury boss Wally Mawdsley moved in and made the appropriately named Kent his major pre-season signing. Canterbury already had South Africa's top rider, Mike Ferreira, as their No.1 and they were about to reap the benefit of another star from the Republic. Although Denzil was born in Bulawayo, Zimbabwe in October 1961, his parents and two elder sisters returned to their Johannesburg roots in the early 70s.

"I think Mike Ferreira had something to do with me signing for Canterbury but I wouldn't say we were big mates," says Denzil. "He helped me in some ways but after a while he was more worried about his own job.

"By then I was lodging with a couple called Bob and Brenda, friends of my sister, in Dartford. Bob allowed me to drive around in his Austin Marina.

"Dad handled all the arrangements for me to return to England and Canterbury general manager Maurice Morley came down to Dartford to sign me on," Denzil recalled.

Having never seen Kent ride before signing him, Morley decided to leave him out of Crusaders' opening meeting of the 1980 season, an international challenge against the Italy touring side, but the 18-year-old didn't have to wait long for his big chance. Appearing from the reserve berth, he won his first race for Crusaders and went on to score nine (paid 10) from four rides against Crayford in the Kent Cup at Kingsmead on Saturday, April 5.

"I'd never even seen the track before I rode on it," says the diminutive racer with the big heart who finished his first National League season with a creditable 6.64 average from 42 matches.

The Crusaders' heat leaders were Mike Ferreira, Barney Kennett and Ted Hubbard but they were

**Doubling-up with British League Swindon.**

pushed hard by the young newcomer with the dark hair and boyish good looks whom the fans soon took to their hearts. "It was sink or swim when I came back to England and joined Canterbury and I loved being there," Denzil confirmed.

"Wally (Mawdsley) had a word with Invicta Motors and I was soon driving one of their Cortinas. And then I moved to Canterbury and lived in the city with Paul and Vi Loram for a few years."

Denzil's tenacious riding, friendly demeanour and showmanship qualities made a big impression on the starry-eyed son of Paul and Vi. On his recently released DVD, *The People's Champion,* former World No.1 Mark Loram pays tribute to the one Canterbury rider, above all others, who inspired him to want to race on the shale after first shining in junior grass-track.

Loram, Crusaders' schoolboy mascot in the early 80s, says: "The first 500cc speedway bike I rode was Denzil's four-valve overhead cam Jawa that he let me use to practice on at Iwade after he'd returned to South Africa at the end of one season."

When Loramski recently heard *Backtrack* was about to interview his boyhood hero Kent, he enthused: "Denzil was my first favourite speedway rider. There was something different about him. When he came out for a race, he didn't seem to bother to make practice starts. He virtually did a wheelie from the pits all the way to the starting gate and the supporters loved him for it. He was a great character and I hope he's doing OK now."

Kent repays the compliment, saying: "Mark was 11 going on 17, He was a brilliant, little grass-track rider and he just had to make it in speedway, too, because he had the passion and will to become successful.

"As for the wheelies, the supporters pay the riders' wages and if they like it, then play to the crowd. Part of the fight I had with Wally later was that I knew I was popular with the fans and deserved to be paid more."

After acquitting himself well in his first full season, Kent upped his average by more than a point in 1981 to leapfrog Barney Kennett and become the No.2 to fellow countryman Ferreira. And the South African duo brought Canterbury their first silverware since the 1978 championship season when they won the NL Pairs at Halifax. "I wish I could have contributed more on the night, though," says a modest Denzil, reflecting on the semi-final win over Wolverhampton and the final victory against Berwick in which he trailed in last in both races but the title still went to the Canterbury pair courtesy of Ferreira's race wins.

"My bike broke down in the last race but, fortunately, Mike won the race anyway, so we were the overall winners."

After treading water in 1982, when Ferreira moved up into the British League with parent club Swindon, where Mawdsley also held the reins, Kent succeeded Kennett as Crusaders' No.1 in the early part of 1983. But his elevation proved a double-edged sword for rider and management alike.

"I enjoyed the team camaraderie when we travelled together to and from away matches in a bus and I had an absolutely phenomenal time, on and off the track, but I was always drinking and enjoying life too much."

The death of his father during his first season with Canterbury did nothing to sharpen Denzil's focus on racing.

"My dad was very strict and he would have given me a couple of swipes across the face if he'd still been there with me. But when the cat's away, the mice play.

"Wally and Barney Kennett were very good to me. Barney would sit and talk to me for ages and he understood a lot more than he may have realised. He did try to keep me in line but after Dad died I was my own boss."

Kent's relationship with his promoter deteriorated when the youngster began to feel undervalued.

He says: "Basically, Wally and I had a massive bust-up over money. As the BSPA delegate responsible for dealing with the Czech authorities, he did help me out with Jawas but he was adamant that he wouldn't pay me more than the standard rate. He'd been round the block a few times in speedway. I'm not quite sure what happened but in the end I refused to ride. I sat at home for about half-a-season, just going along to Crayford and Rye House to watch. I didn't think I was asking for too much – especially when I discovered our two reserves at the time were on better deals than me. It was a bit of a shock."

The *impasse* was broken when Bob Dugard, boss of senior league Eastbourne, moved in to snap up the disenchanted Kent. Denzil rode in nine matches (3.65 CMA) for the Eagles in the latter part of 1983 before spending a full season with the Sussex club the following year.

Dugard had gambled before on a young partygoer who liked a drink or six between meetings when he signed Kelly Moran in 1981, so maybe he viewed Kent as another risk worth taking. In some ways, Denzil was South Africa's version of Kelly Moran.

**Looking for the opposition at Eastbourne in 1984.**

At home in Johannesburg with his pet dog Bozo.

He says: "I remember going to Eastbourne to watch a three team tournament when Bob saw me entering the pits and asked: 'Have you been drinking?' I told him I hadn't, so he said: 'Good, you're riding today'. I was a reserve for one of the teams, although didn't get a ride on that particular day."

In listing small tracks Crayford, Rye House and Edinburgh's former Powderhall home as his favourites, the tight and tricky Arlington bowl held no fears but he admits the step up in class proved difficult.

"I was happy to join Eastbourne but it was a really tough year for me," he says. "Colin Richardson and Paul Woods were always helpful to me but there was semi-animosity between the riders. They weren't looking to help with advice and it was a case of 'my pocket or your pocket'.

"Having said that, we did mix socially and we'd all go to Deansland bar/restaurant and disco, in the nearby caravan park, for a drink and a laugh after home meetings. I stayed with my team-mate John Eskildsen in Eastbourne at first and then lodged with George Gray, who sponsored us with tyres, at his place in Hastings."

Kent now readily admits that he burned too many candles at both ends and didn't apply himself enough to fulfil his undoubted potential in the top flight.

He says: "I wasn't putting 100 per cent into the racing and was too worried about having fun. I found it very tough in the British League but I should have persevered and put more energy into my speedway.

"I can't blame Bob Dugard. He treated me well, I can't fault him."

As a work permit rider, Kent was unable to remain with Eastbourne for 1985, when Dugard decided the Eagles would be better off financially operating back in the second tier.

"So I decided to leave British speedway for a year and come home, with the idea of returning to England in 1986," Denzil explains. But for one reason or another, he never raced in Britain again.

Morag, his Zambian-born wife of Scottish descent, fell pregnant with their first son and then the military finally caught up with him.

"I was called into the South African army at the age of 28. They had been serving me my call-up papers for years but I kept ignoring them, hoping they would eventually forget about me. After all, I was married with a young child and had started my own engineering shop in Edenvale, a town on the eastern side of Johannesburg.

"Then one day two military police officers turned up at my house in a van and arrested me. 'Are you Denzil William Kent?' they asked before I was handcuffed, driven away and sent to the Potchefstroom military training camp."

Despite his reluctance to join the army and the frustration he felt because it was the last year of conscription in his homeland, Kent admits his two-year service was no real hardship.

"Actually, I quite enjoyed the discipline of it, although not their 'hurry up and wait' attitude. I was older than all of my senior officers, so they gave me a lot of latitude," recalls Denzil, a corporal in the artillery division of airborne gunners.

Having been skilled at throwing his 500cc Jawa and Godden machines into narrow bends with no brakes, the prospect of army life was never going to intimidate him.

"I went on patrol duty in the townships but there was no reason for me to be afraid because I was driving an enclosed armoured vehicle.

"Army life wasn't too bad at all. I'd work hard there for two days but was allowed to return home on Wednesday mornings and didn't have to report back to base until the following Monday morning."

When Kent returned to civvy street full-time, he set about building up his engineering company and for a time he was doing well. "I never really made money out of speedway," he says, "so I had

Denzil at 50, on his visit to England in 2011.

to find work when I went back home.

"I started my own business and we were building chassis for Volvo, around 200-odd a month for a few years. At one stage I employed 14 people. But my earning power was cut when the Volvo contract came to an end. The business suffered and so I closed the production shop and for a while became an independent contractor.

"I became a bit of a recluse. I still worked hard but I also played too hard."

As well as business setbacks, Denzil has struggled to cope with anguish in his personal life. The death of his mother, Thurza, in 1998 came as a huge blow and his marriage to Morag – or 'Rusty' as Denzil and everyone else knew her – also fell apart.

The couple, who eventually divorced in 2007, have two sons – Kieran, now 24, and Tristan, 21 – but they now live with their mother in Scotland and Denzil has no contact with them.

With admirable candour, Denzil admits: "I wasn't a very good husband or father. I know it takes two to tango but if one person in the marriage is not putting in enough time and effort to make it work, then it will usually fail. The factory was growing quite big by then and I was spending too many hours away from my family. We had no quality time together."

At his lowest ebb, Denzil admits he was drinking a case of beer and a bottle of rum most days.

"That was about two-and-a-half to three years ago but I realised something had to change and I'm glad I changed that side of me. I asked myself, 'why be at the bottom of the barrel?' I knew I shouldn't be there and it was down to one person – me – to get myself straight.

"It's been a long, uphill battle but drinking doesn't bother me anymore. I don't think about sitting in the garden drinking beer all day.

"I still enjoy having fun, though, but I seldom drink until the weekend, when I'll probably have a crate of 12 beers. I know now that there is a limit and that limit is not the floor."

Denzil now works as a cook for a small food business in Edenvale, Johannesburg from Sunday to Thursday, which also provides a roof over his head.

"My day begins at around six-ish, when I begin cooking and making all the fillings for the rolls that the owner sells during the day. I also do all the cleaning at the house I share with him and another man. My working day usually ends at 7.30pm.

"On Fridays I go to Shane Horn's place. Shane rides speedway occasionally and I help to maintain the 12 bikes that he has in his collection – there's a Wessie, two GMs, a Jawa and three or four laydowns. I also look after a couple of moto-cross bikes at weekends. I'm a general dogsbody really but at least it keeps me out of the pubs and what I get paid keeps the wolf from the door.

"Another person I'd like to thank is Bob Bulmer, who has a house at Smith Street in nearby Edenglen, where I met a lot of nice people, including the Wain family, who have gone out of their way to be a great help to me in tough times."

## BRIEF ENCOUNTERS WITH… Steve Payne

**How did your move (back) to the UK come about?**

My dad, Ted, was a former rider. By his own admission, he was nothing special but he had promoted a couple of tracks in the UK, at Chiswick and Aldershot, before I was born. Because of his interest, when we emigrated to Australia he used to take the family to meetings at the old Liverpool track and Sydney Showground.

I started riding speedway after racing moto-cross and dirt track and got involved with Tom Shirra (Mitch's dad). He was training another young guy Robbie McGregor, helping with engines, etc, and he was keen to get us to the UK to continue our development.

By this time my parents had come to the UK, so we went to the *Speedway Star* office to get details of tracks and started to ring around trying to get second half rides. We went all the way to Workington for one second half opportunity and it was snowed-off! The van I had bought broke down as well, so that was a harsh introduction to British speedway.

I ended up getting a chance at Milton Keynes and, fortunately, because I had a British passport I was allowed to ride in the Junior League, although I didn't quite kick on like Tai Woffinden!

**Did you have an 'English dad' or did you have to fend for yourself?**

I'd met Gary Guglielmi prior to going to the UK through a bike shop I was working in. I can't remember how it came about but while I was there he suggested I move up to the more central Midlands, where he and Mitch (Shirra) were based. I stayed at 'The Farm' in Coventry with Eric (Hallam) and Mrs H, who became my de-facto parents.

**What was the highlight of your British speedway career?**

Scoring an 18-point maximum at MK, when we were league leaders, which was great for our long-suffering supporters, was a thrill. Probably the best of all was getting a British League contract with Coventry.

**And the low points?**

The low point was undoubtedly getting injured at MK when I'd started to ride really well. I somehow managed to hook my hand into the late Robbie Ashton's throttle cable, we tangled and both careered into the fence. I broke my pelvis and, from memory, Robbie broke a rib. That was the end of my season, which was personally devastating as well as missing the opportunity of winning the league with MK.

**When did you realise it was time to go back home?**

I was progressing in speedway reasonably well but, deep down, I think I realised I was not going to be a world-beater. I got banned as a result of a misdemeanour and feel I was made a scapegoat of on a technicality, even though other higher profile riders had got away with similar situations, so I didn't really have a say. Although, who knows, if I'd kept riding whether I may have had another accident?

# JOHN
# JACKSON

**W**HEN reviewing the lengthy career of a former No.1 rider who only once posted an average under seven and who produced countless double-figure returns, the last subject you would expect to discuss with him is a lack of confidence.

John Jackson was arguably the first major British League Division Two/National League star not to progress into the top league despite dominating racing at two separate tracks.

The big question will always be: why?

The 60s speedway revival hit the Cheshire town of Crewe in 1969 when Allied Presentations unveiled the 'Kings' to the expectant public of the famous railway town. Among the many who came to see the new spectacle was a local teenager by the name of John Jackson, who, as the initial season wore on, decided it was time to try it for himself.

On the night of the 1972 Division Two Riders' Championship at Wimbledon, Kings' representatives Phil Crump and John Jackson hold the BL2 league trophy, with Dai Evans, Garry Flood, Ken Adams and Dave Morton also in attendance.

Crewe after winning the 1972 KO Cup at Peterborough. Left to right: Dave Parry, Gary Moore, Ken Adams, Jacko, Phil Crump, Garry Flood, Peter Nicholas. Dai Evans and the injured Dave Morton are on the bike.

John had seen his brother Fred do well on the burgeoning north-west grass-track scene and had followed him into racing.

"I didn't do much good on the grass-tracks but I went to watch speedway at Crewe in 1969, then started going to a training school there every Wednesday run by Ken Adams," 'Jacko' told *Backtrack*.

Led by Antipodeans Geoff Curtis and Paul O'Neal, the new Kings earned a comfortable seventh place in their debut season, with their Earle Street home quickly proving to be a 'fortress'.

Their second season, 1970, saw John make it into the team proper and his effect was immediate, racing in 32 matches to gain a remarkable first season average of 7.94. It earned the 18-year-old third heat-leader status behind O'Neal and track curator, New Zealander Colin Tucker.

The fact that Aussies and Kiwis were so dominant around the Earle Street bowl was easily explained. Many speedway tracks here had been built around football or rugby pitches but the former LMS Railway sports ground had housed a cricket pitch and the new track was laid to the stunning length of 470 yards. Tucker had built a monster that soon gained a fearsome reputation. It was similar in length to many tracks Down Under, so most Australians and New Zealanders found it a home-from-home in the UK.

The banked track held no fears for a local teenager, though, as John explains: "I really enjoyed it at Crewe, it was a good track. It's where I started, so I didn't know anything else.

"Many other riders didn't like the track because it was so fast and big, like nowhere else.

"At Crewe you could miss the gate but come from the back. If you were brave enough to go round the fence, then you could pass but a lot of riders didn't like doing that. Many of them didn't have the right gearing – it was so different."

A ready supply of railway sleepers had been tapped to create the wooden board safety fence but that didn't deter the young Jackson. "It was the biggest thrill, so fast that you would go right round the boards and bounce off them if necessary. Jack Millen said it was the biggest buzz he'd known

Jacko and Chris Turner finished in front of Newcastle's Owen brothers, Tom and Joe, in the 1976 NL Pairs Final at Belle Vue.

In the British League colours of Halifax Dukes.

on a bike."

Crewe's wide open spaces enabled Barry Meeks to earn a place in the Guinness Book of Records, by clocking the highest speed ever recorded on a British speedway track, 54.62mph, in his track record ride there on March 27, 1970.

But its uniqueness also had a downside. Kings' away matches were obviously all contested on smaller tracks, some up to 200 yards shorter per lap. The challenge was to adapt and Jackson was equal to it.

"I used to struggle at first on the smaller tracks. It was a heck of shock when you saw some of them, even later on going to somewhere like Rye House. You had to change your style, it was much more about throttle control," he says.

An early influence was veteran Welsh rider Dai Evans, who brought vital experience to the young side. "Dai was really helpful," says John. "We used to get on well and he would tell me what to do. He used to say, 'Don't ride these tracks like Crewe, keep to the inside, take gate one and don't move off that inside line, keep really tight and lay that bike down', so I followed his advice and I can't have managed too badly."

Crewe used their huge home advantage to great effect, finishing a solid seventh in each of their first three seasons. In 1971, John's second term, he pushed his scoring over the eight-point mark to progress to second heat-leader, behind new Aussie sensation Phil Crump. "Phil was OK, I never had a problem with him," John added.

The following year, Kings reigned supreme in British League Division Two, winning 22 out of 32 matches and holding-off strong East Anglian challengers Boston and Peterborough to take their only championship. A solitary home league defeat by Panthers being avenged by a 22-point KO Cup Final aggregate win. With Phil Crump taking the Division Two Riders' Championship, held for the first time at Wimbledon, 1972 was a great year for the Cheshire side. John pushed his average into double figures but it still only earned him the No.2 spot behind the brilliant Crump, who achieved a stunning 11-point average.

The celebrations were muted, though. Popular promoter Maury Littlechild, who had also established King's Lynn as a force in the first division, tragically died of cancer in July. Allied Presentations banded together and Ken Adams steered the team through to its eventual double-winning success.

John recalls: "Losing Maury was so sad, he was such a nice person. My main memory of him is how, in my first year, he was always moaning about my bikes. I did have a few engine failures, so the cry went up: 'You must get this lad's bikes sorted out'."

While Crump tried his luck with King's Lynn in Division One in 1973, the promoters installed experienced Hackney and Rayleigh boss Len Silver to take control at Earle Street. Was Jacko tempted to follow Crumpie up to the next level in '73?

"Maybe I should have done but I think it was a confidence thing. If you rode in the first division and had a few bad meetings, your confidence would go," he says.

Silver altered the track by cutting 40 yards off its length but it really was a case of 'no change' for John. "Len was all right, not a problem, and changing the track had no effect on me. There was nothing like Crewe, it was a one-off. I really missed it later since it gave you such a buzz to go round there at such high speed."

Crewe had peaked, though, and with Stoke Potters re-opening just down the road at Chesterton, the writing was probably already on the wall for Kings. By now established as an outright No.1, despite his average dipping back under 10, John was supported by Geoff Ambrose and the emerging talents of Dave Morton and Keith White, who both went on to senior league stardom with Silver's Hackney Hawks, Crewe held their own but by the end of 1974 the surviving members of Allied Presentations were going their separate ways and the group relinquished control for the final season of racing there in 1975.

John was already on his way out of the club but not because he sensed the track's closure. It all came down to sponsorship.

"Vic Wilding owned a big hotel just outside Ellesmere Port and offered me two new bikes if I would ride for the Gunners," he explains. "I'd also get a supply of tyres, fuel and a helmet, so I couldn't turn it down. It was a big incentive for me to move."

Graham Drury went to Crewe in exchange for Jacko but John says: "Although I didn't know then that Crewe was on its last legs, it was probably a good thing that I moved. I didn't mind Ellesmere Port, it was a good track, so I was happy there."

John had been an early track record holder at Thornton Road back in Gunners' first season, 1972. But despite the circuit being almost as long as Crewe, it presented a different challenge.

"It was a fast track but not quite like Crewe since it didn't have the banking. You couldn't go right round the boards, you needed to trap. It was just about confidence. I had the right bikes and I was really feeling confident.

"To be honest, I didn't think I was going to be beaten. For a few seasons I was top of the heap there and I thought I could go to Ellesmere Port and beat anybody."

The records bear this out. John came to dominate his track like no other rider of his time, leading Gunners from the No.1 berth, topping the averages from 1975 to '78 with figures of over 10.00 for all but that first campaign. Overall, Jacko romped to no less than 64 full maximums home and away during those four seasons as he firmly established himself as a major star of what had by then become the National League.

"Ernie Park, the promoter, was a great bloke and we all gelled pretty well as a team. Pete Ellams and I were very close, as I was with Steve Finch. It was great, we had a good team spirit there with no tensions. It was also a good home track to race on.

"The Gunners' supporters were absolutely brilliant, they used to follow us around everywhere. My best memory is of going to the Riders' Championship at Wimbledon and seeing this sea of Ellesmere Port supporters."

In John's second season at Thornton Road, in 1976, Gunners earned their highest league position to date, finishing runners-up to all-conquering Newcastle, led by Joe and Tom Owen, who won the title by a clear 12 points. Individually, John finished second to Joe in the NLRC but he went close to grabbing the coveted prize.

"I had four wins going into my final race against Joe but ended up falling after making the gate on him," John recalls.

Earlier in '76 Gunners' had seen off Newcastle in the NL Pairs at Belle Vue to claim the club's first major honours. It was especially satisfying for John, who led home the Owen brothers and his

Flat out in practice at Ellesmere Port, where John was so hard to beat.

Jacko and Duncan Meredith warming up their Neil Street-Jawa conversions at Thornton Road in 1977, with Steve Finch and James Moore in the background.

**Jubilant John celebrates with joyous Gunners fans after the 1979 NL Fours final at Peterborough.**

partner Chris Turner in the final race at Hyde Road.

Despite his dominance in league racing the closest John got to achieving individual success again was two years later, in 1978, when he finished second in the NLRC to Canterbury's Steve Koppe, so was John frustrated by another near miss? "No, it didn't really matter, I was a team man. I was an Ellesmere Port man and happy to be there."

By 1979 younger talent was emerging in north Cheshire, with Steve Finch taking over Jacko's mantle of top man that year, helping the club to glory in the Four Team Tournament at Peterborough. Gunners won the final by two points from that year's NL champions, Mildenhall, with John unbeaten.

With Louis Carr coming through the ranks, 'JJ' slipped to third heat leader in 1980. Although he still recorded a highly respectable eight-point-plus average, his years of dominance were over. After dropping to fourth overall in the Gunners' scorechart with a seven-point figure in 1981, he recovered to be an ever-present No.1 in 1982, back over the nine point mark, but this was to be his final year at Thornton Road.

The NL reacted to the national economic recession and falling crowds by trying to impose a riders' pay policy, a plan that ultimately backfired on Gunners. Explaining what led up to the closure of Ellesmere Port at the end of 1983, John said: "It wasn't so much me, I wanted to race because I enjoyed it so much, but there were a few others that were pushing to reject the policy and it was a shock to us when the promoters responded by closing the place down."

An enforced move to Stoke in 1983 turned out to be John's finale in speedway. "I didn't enjoy it any more. I'd just had my final race – I think it was at Boston – and I realised I just wasn't enjoying it anymore. My dad had died and I was struggling with my bikes a bit. I'd had enough, it wasn't the same as Ellesmere Port."

John's frustrations were matched by results. Despite earning a heat leader spot behind Tom Owen and Pete Smith, an average under seven exposed the truth. John hadn't done the job that Stoke had hired him for and it was time for the NL's former star man to quit his beloved sport.

Ellesmere Port were briefly resurrected by Mervyn Porter in 1985 and took their one and only league championship. Was John tempted to be a part of it? "Mervyn did ring me but I'd made my decision to retire and I was going to stick to it," he revealed.

So did John have any regrets from his time in speedway, such as not making it at a higher level?

"I always get asked about the first division. Was it about money? No, it was just confidence. Maybe I should have had a bit more confidence in myself and really gone for it."

Apart from a dozen or so outings with Halifax between 1973 and '75, his longest run in BL1 was 21 matches for Wolverhampton in 1976, which yielded a five-point average.

"I never got passed when I was in front but I was just lacking against the big names," he admits. "Maybe if I'd had a bit more faith in myself I could have probably made it."

Did he need someone to 'psych' him up? "Maybe I did. I used to go to all of these tracks and get really quick times. I once went down to Rye House for the Silver Helmet match-race and I broke the track record, which is pretty good when you're one of the visiting riders. I had the speed, just lacked a bit in confidence once I got among the big names. So much of speedway is in the head.

"Wolverhampton was all right. They were very helpful but I wasn't getting the wins like I was at Ellesmere Port. You'd end up getting thirds or lasts. It was a lot harder.

"When I was at Ellesmere Port there was nobody that I was frightened of. I thought that I could beat them all. That may sound big-headed but it's true. As long as the bikes were okay, so was I."

So, did he have any regrets? "No, I don't, apart from not having someone to give me a kick up the backside and have a proper go at the British League. I look at videos and think that maybe I could have been that good but it's too late now. I was worried about riding with bigger names. It was silly really."

Since retiring John has been running a car body repair business with elder son Stephen. He has another son, Michael, and a daughter, Louise, and lives with wife Susan just outside Chester.

## BRIEF ENCOUNTERS WITH... Tony Primmer

**How did your move to the UK come about?**

I started speedway back in 1985 at Newcastle International Motordrome (Jerilderie Park) after a good friend said: 'If you buy a new speedway chassis you can use my Weslake engine'. I remember having one practice on the Tuesday night before my first meeting on the Saturday. I won the rookie class. I couldn't believe I was racing on the track where I had watched all the greats of the 70s, including my favourite Phil Crump.

After three seasons at home progressing to international meetings and seeing some of the guys I was riding with venture to the UK, I decided to give it a go myself. I saved like mad and flew out in February 1988. I had half my Weslake engine in my Bell Helmet bag as hand luggage and some bloke called Simon Wigg was on the same flight. He knew my dad Greg through his brother Julian from the dirt-track Test matches in the 70s.

I ended up signing for Milton Keynes, thanks to Mark Carlson and their promoter Ted Jarvis.

**How did your career progress?**

I spent 1988 in and out of the Milton Keynes team and

had a loan spell mid-season at Wimbledon to replace Todd Wiltshire, who was injured. The stint with Dons got me going and I secured my team place with MK for the rest of the season, finishing with a four-ride max in the last meeting. In 1989 I was back with MK under new promoters at the new, unfinished Elfield Park. It was nothing like The Groveway, which had nice long straights and tight corners. Elfield Park was almost circular, so no home advantage that year.

In 1990 I moved to Eastbourne. Again, I lacked consistency and funds so it made for a tough but enjoyable year and I scored my first six-ride max.

**What was the highlight of your British career?**

Maximums are easy to remember, as I only scored two. Secondly, it would be partnering Hans Nielsen at Oxford. I remember one wet night when he said: 'Just follow me'. I thought everyone did! Thirdly, winning the BLC with Poole in 2003 and, finally, winning the 2012 Lydd Speedway Veterans Over-30s (modern bikes) Championship at the age of 46.

# GRAHAM
# PLANT

**A**S overnight sensations go, they don't spring up more quickly than Graham Plant. He'd attended just six training sessions and had a handful of second-halves before making his British League Division Two debut for Middlesbrough and had the Second Division Riders' Championship in the bag before his debut season was up.

He ended his second year in the sport as a proven points scorer in the top flight and winner of the British Junior Championship, with England recognition soon following.

He never got close to achieving his ambition of being World Champion but nevertheless enjoyed a long career in the sport which finally ended 15 years after bursting onto the scene as a precocious teenager.

Now 61, Graham doesn't follow speedway closely these days, preferring the thrill of road-racing and formula one, but was among the special guests at the relaunch of Leicester, one of his former clubs, earlier this year and was happy to roll back the years for a *Backtrack* interview.

His current passion for road-racing is no surprise really. For even though his dad, Wilf, had been a speedway rider, Plant Junior had always hoped to race bikes on the tarmac when he was old enough.

Graham in his first season of racing, at Teesside in 1968.

"It all started for me about halfway through the 1967 season," recalled Graham, who still runs the Melton Mowbray motorcycle dealership formerly owned by his father who died 10 years ago.

"My dad took me to the King's Lynn practice sessions on a Sunday where you could blast around all afternoon.

"Dad then spoke to Long Eaton and asked if I could have some second-halves there. They agreed, so I went down there with his old JAP which we still had in the garage. I had to alter the back wheel because it had the old big size one on, but I replaced it with an aluminium one.

"At Long Eaton I did second-halves alongside Tom Leadbitter and Ian Champion but before the season was up I broke my left leg. Roger Mills fell in front of me and I went over the handlebars."

While Graham was recovering from his first speedway injury, Archers' promoters Ron Wilson and Reg Fearman announced they would be closing their Station Road operation and transferring Long Eaton's licence to Leicester.

Graham, along with fellow second-halfers

Leicester Lions on parade at Blackbird Road in 1971. Left to right: Ray Wilson, Malcolm Shakespeare, Graham Plant, Alan Cowland, John Boulger, Tom Leadbitter and the non-riding Norman Storer.

Leadbitter and Champion, followed them to Blackbird Road, where the Lions took up residence in the first division from 1968.

Graham's potential had been duly noted by Wilson and Fearman and, although he wasn't ready to be plunged straight into action in the toughest league in the world, the pair were able to offer him a team place – at Middlesbrough.

Wilson and Fearman also reintroduced speedway to Cleveland Park in 1968 to operate in the newly-formed second division, and Graham was tailor-made for a place in the new Teesside Teessiders line-up.

"Ron said he was opening a second division team and he wanted me to be a heat leader," explained Graham, "so that's what I did. It was a fast rise but I picked it up quickly. I was always surrounded by bikes – I'd been keen on them since I was about eight and could slide before I even went to a training school.

"I wanted to do road-racing but it was just so hard to get into, so Dad suggested I tried speedway. I did and it all happened so quickly."

Wilson's belief that Plant could be a heat leader proved spot on and he ended the 1968 season with an 8.5 average, forming part of a spearhead that also featured Leadbitter, his old mate from Long Eaton and Leicester.

"It was about 150 miles from Melton Mowbray, where I lived, to Middlesbrough," recalled Graham, "but it was a nice run. We had a Mini van and I used to take the front wheel off, then put the bike in the back.

"They used cinders from a nearby power station for the track surface, so the track was black and the place always smelled of coal."

He scored five maximums as Teessiders finished third in the first ever BL2 table but the highlight of a stunning debut season was his Division Two Riders' Championship win at Hackney.

He'd gone there as Teesside's No.2 rider but won the title with 23 points from Ken Eyre (12 points) and Graeme Smith (11).

"I'd never even seen Hackney before," said Graham. "Ken Eyre should have won it but his chain snapped in his last ride. It was good to win but it was just another meeting. I think I went home, showed my gran the trophy and that was it."

The season was coming to an end by then and Wilson offered the newly-crowned champ a choice between staying on Teesside or going full-time with Leicester.

He'd already been doubling up with the Lions and his mind was made up – he wanted full-time action in the top flight.

Again it proved the right move. He ended his first full campaign at the top level with an average of 6.2 as Leicester became the first team to go through the season with an unchanged side, using the same seven riders for every one of their 39 league and KO Cup matches.

There were more honours, too – namely the first ever British Under-21 Championship, in which he finished ahead of Geoff Ambrose and Mick Bell.

"It was run as a second-half event at Wimbledon back then, so I only had to win two races," he recalled. "Glasgow were the visitors in the main meeting, which meant Bobby Beaton, who was also in the second-half, had already ridden four races and had time to get used to the track.

"The trophy was fantastic – it was like the one the tennis players get for winning Wimbledon. It was worth £3,000 back then."

Graham spent three years at Blackbird Road, forming a three-pronged spearhead with Ray Wilson and John Boulger in 1970 and 1971 as the Lions finished fourth and second respectively in the Division One table.

But he said: "At times it was like a three-man team. Ray had a near 11-point average, John would get nine or 10, I'd get eight or nine but the next scorer was way behind.

"It used to baffle me. We had a rider called Malcolm Brown whose machinery was mint and he used to drive a Cortina GT. He'd come flying out of the gate in front but within a lap he was at the back.

Leicester co-promoter Ron Wilson offering Graham advice in 1971.

162

A Newport Wasp in 1973.

"The only time I saw him score a maximum was at Newport, which was always a hard place to pass. On this occasion it was raining, too, so you were getting filled in if you were behind. Malcolm got a maximum because no-one could get past him."

Graham's performances in 1971 earned him a call-up for England's Test series against the Soviet Union but he missed out on a place in that winter's Ashes series Down Under after shooting himself in the foot.

"I'd gone out to Rhodesia in 1970 after I saw an advert in *Speedway Star,*" he explained. "It was described as a working holiday – you had to pay your own fare for yourself and your bike on the way out but the promoters would pay it coming back.

"There were three tracks out there and I really enjoyed it. When I came home I had a good season and I was called up into the Test squad.

"The thing was, though, I was No.7 or No.8 (who didn't have a programmed ride under the old Test formula), so I didn't go to Exeter for the first Test. It seemed like a lot of running about just for that.

"By that time I had a letter asking me if I was willing to go to Australia with the Test squad that winter if I was selected.

"I really wanted to go and, after not going to Exeter, Ron Wilson said to me: 'If you want to go to Australia, you'd better get down to Poole for the second Test'.

"Charles Foot ran Poole at the time and told me he wasn't going to let me ride because I hadn't gone to Exeter. But Nigel Boocock fell and knocked himself out, so I was told to go and get changed because I'd be riding after all.

"I didn't get selected for Australia after that. I know I could have gone but I was a bit stubborn then and it cost me."

Graham says he liked to "experiment a bit" during his time as an up and coming rider and admits he used nitro in his fuel before it was banned.

"I used nitro," he said, "because I just wanted to go faster. It was £20 a gallon and you were supposed to mix it with your dope. I remember one night I was beating Anders Michanek when, just as I was coming to the finish line, the bike seized. I only had one bike and I had two rides left, so I couldn't complete the rest of the meeting."

At the end of 1971 Graham decided he wanted a change of track and there was no shortage of interest in him.

He's always gone well at Newport, and the Wasps came in with not only an offer but the guarantee of a signing-on fee.

"Only the top guys like Mauger and Briggo got that," said Graham, "but they wanted to pay me to go there. I told Ron and he offered me the same to stay.

"Wolves then came in with an offer of double the amount to go there, and then Ron tried to do a swap deal to get me to go to Wembley, but I didn't like the track there. I didn't really want to leave Leicester but I thought it best I had a change."

Graham spent two years at Somerton Park, although he wasn't able to maintain his earlier form and promise. His average dropped to 6.4 as the Wasps finished bottom of the table in 1972. It did rise again, though, to 7.39 in 1973, which proved a better year for him and the team.

"Being on the Bristol Channel, there were a lot of rain-offs at Newport," recalled Graham, "and it's frustrating when you've driven 150 miles only to have the meeting called off once you're there. But I liked it at Somerton Park.

"When Ole Olsen was World Champion (the 1972 season) he had the Golden Helmet and no-one could take it off him. Briggo, Mauger, he beat them all – but I was determined to get the better of him when he came to Newport.

"Unfortunately, I had a slow puncture but they put me on two minutes. I tried to change the wheel but the one I borrowed didn't fit, so I just had to pump the tyre up.

"In the race I got him on the first bend and I was in front. But after a lap-and-a-half the bike started snaking. I could feel his front wheel on my calf as he looked to make a move, but I had to pull out because of the slow puncture.

"Two weeks later Terry Betts took the Golden Helmet off him at King's Lynn, who were down at Newport a week later, and I took it off Bettsy. So I got it in the end but it would have been nice to

**Making a winning return to Leicester with Halifax in 1975, Graham leads Lions' Frank Auffret.**

Graham after winning the Dews Trophy at Halifax in 1976.

have beaten Olsen for it."

At the end of 1973 Graham was on the move again after being sold by Newport – quite a surprise since he didn't know he was even up for sale.

"Ron Wilson phoned me and told me I was his rider now," he explained. "He said he'd bought me from Newport. I thought he'd want me to go back to Leicester but his partner Reg Fearman also owned a share of Halifax and that's where he wanted me to ride.

"There was only really Eric Boocock left from the previous year and they were building a new team, bringing in people like Henny Kroeze and Rick France.

"Halifax had special dispensation to use Booey at reserve after he'd hurt his arm really badly the previous year in a crash at Newport, so they put me at No.1."

He spent four years at The Shay, proving a dependable seven-and-a-half point man for the first three of those seasons. In 1976 he won the individual Dews Trophy meeting at the West Yorkshire track but suffered a broken leg – at Leicester of all places – in a GP qualifying round the following month and that brought a half to his season.

"It was a great track," he said, reflecting on his time at Halifax. "You used to go up the banking and shoot down the straight. I saw a rugby match on TV there recently and instead of watching the game, I spent all my time looking at where the track used to be!

"After the match they used to have a disco in the bar and I often didn't leave until about 1.00am, which meant it was three o'clock by the time I got home."

It seems that wasn't the only fun Graham had as a Halifax rider.

"I had the *News of the World* round on one occasion," he says. "They were going to do a story and had some 'sex thing' to ask me about. I was married at the time, so I denied it all and they printed that. But the story they had on me was true."

He declined to reveal any more than that.

Once the 1977 season was over, Graham spent a season out of the sport.

With Halifax promoter Eric Boothroyd at the start of his brief final spell with Dukes in 1979.

Final knight: In his last season with Milton Keynes.

Graham pictured at Leicester's re-opening in 2011.

"I'd got divorced, I was selling the house and trying to get better terms," he said, "so I sat out 1978. There was no end of tracks ringing me – mainly second division clubs but some first division tracks, too – but I spent Christmas in Benidorm and didn't ride again until 1979."

When he did come back it was at Halifax, but his stay lasted just one official meeting.

The team had been rejigged with Kenny Carter and Tormod Langli among the newcomers, and Graham admitted: "I didn't feel part of it. I didn't know what to do. I suggested they gave me some second-halves to get me back in the mood."

In the event it wasn't until the following season that he returned to action – not at Halifax but at National League Milton Keynes, run by his old boss Ron Wilson.

"I'd never seen the track but we did a rough deal on the phone even though I hadn't been on a bike for a year," explained Graham.

The season was a relative success. He established himself as the Knights' second heat leader behind Bob Humphreys, although in truth an average of 6.3 wasn't earth-shattering.

He continued his association with the Knights off and on until 1983, when he finally called time on his speedway career.

Throughout his racing days Graham was never one to shirk a challenge, to the extent that he was often perceived as something of a wild man on the track.

"That's because I gave it a go," he insisted. "I broke both legs, dislocated my shoulder four times and broke my collarbone. But a true racer will get over it and get back out there. With some people, a broken leg will finish them."

Graham recalls a spell when he felt referees had it in for him, and sometimes his opponents took umbrage too. Take Nigel Boocock for example.

"He punched me in the face one night at Leicester," said Graham. "I went under him and he hit the fence but I was already coming out of the corner when he came off.

"I was back in the pits changing the plug when he came over and punched me and gave me a

**166**

nosebleed. I was only 18 at the time.

"Booey apologised in the pages of *Motorcycle News* the following week and said we'd all learned something from the incident.

"For me it didn't matter if I was being paid a fortune or chicken feed to win a race, I'd always go about it the same way. It was the prestige of winning that drove me on.

"I would have liked to have been World Champion, every rider would, but I had some bad luck in the qualifying rounds.

"They were good old days but I don't miss it. It's been and gone and it's not coming back. I don't go to speedway any more and when I went to Leicester it was cold, I didn't know any of the riders and to be honest, I wasn't really interested."

Graham still gets his kicks from bikes, although these days they have brakes and ridden legally on the road.

## On 2 Minutes With...
## GEOFF BOUCHARD

**Who helped you most in the early days?**

I got into the Long Eaton team in 1970 (he stayed there until 1975 when, after rising to No 1, Geoff joined Swindon until his retirement in 1979) and Ivor Brown, who was running the place, was helpful, as was my team-mate Peter Wrathall.

**Best promoter you've ridden for and why?**

I had a lot of respect for Ted Nelson at Swindon. He looked after me well – I think we had a mutual respect. I was a bit disappointed when Wally Mawdsley took over – it just changed. I think he preferred foreigners to home-grown riders – you were OK if you had a Danish or American accent.

**Tracks you never looked forward to visiting?**

I didn't like Sheffield, there was something about it. I had a sort of mental block when I went there and the more I tried, the worse it got. It was always beautifully prepared but I never did any good there.

**Career highlight/proudest moment?**

I scored two full maximums – both of them against Leicester, my home-town club. The first was a five-ride maximum and the other a 12-pointer. I thought to myself, 'I've done this tonight, why can't I do it every week?'

**Worst crash/injuries?**

It was in August 1979 and I was riding in the Midland Cup for Swindon at Leicester. It had been a really hot day and the track had been over-watered because they wanted to keep the dust down. I was out in Heat 1 and there was slurry on top of the track. I was battling for third place, going round the outside, and I got taken past the point of no return, so I knew I had to bail out.

I laid the bike down but, because the track was so wet, it offered no resistance. I hit a lamp standard, which was set in concrete, and suffered a punctured lung. I remember lying there on the track and the next thing I was in intensive care. The doctor looking after me said I was lucky.

After that I retired. It wasn't so much the injury itself as the fact I had a wife and three young children and I thought, 'I can't put them though this again'. I'd had 10 years at it and, to be honest, I wasn't that happy at Swindon at the time and I was struggling for money.

I was in intensive care for five days – and a lot of people don't come out of there.

# SHAWN
# MORAN

**I**T was July 1980 and the pretty 15-year-old German girl serving refreshments in the pits at Pocking Speedway was very distressed. It was the track's traditional eve-of-meeting party for the visiting riders, mechanics and dignitaries, a time of supposed enjoyment for the locals who were looking forward to watching the world's rising young stars who had descended on the small horse-breeding town in Southern Bavaria to contest the final of the European Under-21 Championship the following afternoon.

But some inconsiderate scamp had stolen her distinctive "grandma-style" bicycle and for a while she fretted about how she was going to get home and explain her lateness to her strict parents.

Then, amid the commotion that ensued while they searched the pits for the missing bike, she became aware of some riders larking around on pushbikes and pulling wheelies out on the speedway track. She didn't know who these 'cycle speedway' upstarts were but one was performing tricks on her bright pink bike and, aghast, she demanded its immediate return.

By way of an attempted apology, the American youngster who had borrowed her bike gave the girl a lift home in his transit van. He spoke no German and she was still too annoyed to make an effort to put her English language skills to the test, so very little words were exchanged.

Shawn with Joe Owen and Dennis Sigalos at Hull in 1980.

168

Shawn (inside) and Kelly show their telepathic understanding in their battle with English pair Peter Collins and Dave Jessup in the 1982 Test at Belle Vue.

However, it wasn't until he pulled on his leathers in the pits before the meeting the next day, when the girl was back on refreshments duties, that she heard his name. "At that time, I had no idea who he was," she says.

This is how Shawn Moran and Sabine Neiss firts met.

She saw him again when he returned to race at Pocking a few more times in the 80s and by then he hadn't just nicked her bike, he'd stolen her heart too.

Not that romance was on the agenda for either. She had her life to live in Germany while he continued to travel the world in his quest to set become one of the world's top riders.

Shawn Moran was born in Lakewood, California on November 19, 1961, the son of Tom and Sharon and the brother of Kelly, who had arrived 14 months earlier. Shawn remembers his dad taking the boys to watch speedway for the first time at Costa Mesa in 1972.

The Moran kids were soon skidding around the desert tracks at Saddleback Park and Indian Dunes before taking their first speedway rides at a Barry Briggs training school at Elsinore in Southern California. The boys stood out in their green and white leathers with a shamrock leaf emblem, although Shawn admits he knows nothing of his family's Irish ancestry.

Although he tried various jobs after failing to graduate at high school – school janitor and the local car wash among them, Shawn would more often than not be surfing at Huntington Beach. No doubt this helped him to perfect the balancing skills that would characterise his racing, which began professionally in the 1978 American season. Costa Mesa, San Bernardino, Ventura and the old half-mile circuit at Ascot Park was where he would wow the beer-swilling crowds who appreciated the talented teenager they christened 'The Miracle Worker'.

After Kelly impressed in his first British League season for Hull in 1978, it was no surprise when Vikings' promoter Ian Thomas soon came calling for his new American favourite's younger brother. Thomas had seen Shawn blow away some serious opposition when finishing runner-up to Bruce Penhall in the USA Long-track Final at Ascot in the autumn of that year. The offer was there for Shawn – at 16, the youngest qualifier for the US Nationals final – to join Kelly at Hull from the start of 1979 but he decided he wasn't quite ready and opted for a second full season on home soil.

When he did finally take his first look at the British scene, shortly before the end of the '79 season,

History-maker on the long-track, Shawn after bringing the trophy back to Sheffield in 1983.

he found himself at the centre of the first of several run-ins with authority that would punctuate his career.

Still too young to hold an international racing licence, the Hull management bent the rules by including Shawn in several unofficial meetings under the false name of 'David East' – a pseudonym also used when riding for 'Bruce Penhall's Surfers' in a challenge match at Ipswich.

 "I don't know who came up with that name but Ian thought it was the best way around the problem and it gave him the chance to have a look at me racing in England," recalls Shawn, who copped a 50 dollar fine from the American Motorcycle Association (AMA) for breaking the rules, while Thomas was hit with a £100 fine by the British Speedway Control Board when they found out.

In context, it was a very small price to pay to capture the latest, young Californian discovery who immediately underlined his potential with a near six-and-a-half point average in his 1980 debut season in the BL.

By then, Kelly had moved from Hull to Birmingham and Shawn would soon follow him out of The Boulevard. It was strange timing by Thomas to sell Shawn to Yorkshire rivals Sheffield shortly before the end of his first full season in Britain. To bank a transfer fee of £7,500 for an 18-year-old with promise rather than pedigree could have been viewed at the time as shrewd business on Thomas' part but Sheffield had every reason to believe they had got themselves a bargain. And they did.

"I don't know why Ian sold me to Sheffield, it came out of the blue," says Shawn. "I certainly didn't ask to leave. He just told me one night that Sheffield wanted me, so I went there."

Sheffield boss Ray Glover gambled by shelling out the fully upfront fee that Shawn would repay time and again with his dashing exploits for Tigers over the next eight years. After a subdued start, he quickly established himself as the darling of the Owlerton crowd, a charismatic performer whose flair was matched by results. From 1981 until he was forced to leave the club when it closed seven years later, he was Sheffield's No.1 and talisman.

The '81 season also marked his first major individual success when he progressed unbeaten through the Euro Under-21 qualifier at Pocking (no pedal-powered antics this time) and then again at another German track, Abensberg, before sealing the title with another maximum in the final at rain-soaked Slany in the old Czechoslovakia – the first of numerous major personal successes in that former eastern bloc country where he's still remembered with much affection.

It was also in Czecho, at Marianske Lazne in 1983, that Shawn made history as the first – and so far only – American to win the World Long-track Championship. The fact that he saw off the challenge of the very best at this high speed form of tracksport, including German meisters Muller, Maier, Wiesbock and Hack, 1,000 metre specialists Jiri Stancl, Ales Dryml and Simon Wigg and two former world champions in Ivan Mauger and Ole Olsen, was all the more creditable because he achieved the feat with two pins inserted in the left leg he broke in a bad crash at Hackney just five weeks earlier.

Mere mention of the east London track is usually enough to make former American speedway riders wince – and you can understand why the place left mental as well as physical scars. In 1978, Kelly Moran sustained multiple injuries in an alarming crash there. In 1982, Reading's popular Yank Denny Pyeatt was killed instantly when he was catapulted head-first into one of those unforgiving steel lampposts at Waterden Road. In the same season that Shawn Moran broke his leg in another collision with the metalwork lying in wait on the other side of the wire mesh fence, Bobby Schwartz walked out of his team Reading's match at Hackney after being unable to stomach seeing a series of nasty crashes. And in 1987, Shawn was captain of the USA side that walked out of the Test match against England when rain made track conditions unraceable.

**171**

"The Hackney track itself was fine, it was the fencing that was crap. It was dangerous from that aspect," he said.

When the USA won the World Team Cup Final for the first time, at White City in August 1982, the riders dedicated their victory to their sadly departed buddy Pyeatt. And Shawn, who scored eight points in their victory over Denmark in west London that day, is still proud to have won the Denny Pyeatt Memorial Trophy meeting in the first two years it was staged at Reading's Smallmead raceway.

Throughout his career, Shawn was universally regarded as being an ultra-fair racer and good sport who would never deliberately endanger the well-being of his opponents. But not everyone operated by the same code of ethics.

Recalling his unlucky break at Hackney, he says: "I was already committed on the outside and about to pass Finn Thomsen when he blocked my path and, basically, left me nowhere to go. Yeah, I thought it was deliberate. There was no need for it but you knew who to look out for."

He was prostrate in the notorious Hackney Hospital, his dreams of long-track glory apparently shattered almost as badly as his left leg, when his Sheffield team-mates Reg Wilson and Dave Morton, along with mechanic Norrie Allan, suddenly appeared on the ward and 'kidnapped' him. "I was laid out on the back seat of Reg's Mercedes as he drove me all the way up to Scotland to get treatment from Dr Carlo Biago," Shawn recalls. "Biagi operated on me and gave me a note to hand to the track doctor at Marianske Lazne saying I was fit enough to ride in the long-track final.

"I couldn't bend the leg much – I still can't – but it was enough to convince the doctor that I was OK. That afternoon it was mainly about gating well and I managed to do that on the day and . . . well, 'thanks Ivan!' – he knows he helped me out in one particular race!"

**Work hard, play hard . . . Shawn and Kelly always enjoyed socialising away from the track.**

Shawn's victory helped to put the GR500 Godden engine on the international map, at a time when the rapidly emerging Italian GM was becoming all the rage. Don Godden relished his part in Shawn's biggest individual highlight but his mood changed the following year when he wrote the fun-loving American a terse letter warning him as to his future conduct and instructing him to adopt a more professional image. In his letter, the Kent-based engine and bike manufacturer told Moran he must "be race-fit, train harder and not have sex or drink the night before a meeting."

While Godden may have had a point and his words were no doubt intended to encourage Shawn to give himself the best possible chance of fulfilling his undoubted potential, it was the crass, impersonal method of delivery that took Moran by surprise and meant the underlying point of his message was undermined and ignored. Godden's attempts to force Shawn to adopt a more professional outlook were further ridiculed after the contents of his letter were leaked to the national press.

"It was the sex bit that did it!" jokes Shawn. "It wasn't as if I was a Godden works sponsored rider," he pointed out. "What annoyed Don, and I believe is the real reason why he sent me that letter, is that he didn't like me borrowing bikes from other riders.

"He sent the letter after the 1984 World Long-track Final in which I'd finished last. I was at the back in my first two races and his engine was crap. For my third heat I borrowed Bo Petersen's Godden – and it flew. It was so fast compared to what I had. I tried to explain this to Don but he wouldn't accept it as a reason for my lack of points and, instead, believed it was all down to my lifestyle.

"I never replied to his letter and just thought it was funny," added Shawn, never one to take himself or life itself too seriously.

Shawn and Kelly both reached the 1984 speedway World Final at Gothenburg but a seven-point, mid-field finish on the ultra-slick Ullevi track was just a taster for what would follow in 1985, which turned out to be Shawn's most successful year on the shale. With a match average for Sheffield of 10.65, he finished fourth overall in the BL charts behind the Danish trio of Hans Nielsen, Erik Gundersen and Tommy Knudsen.

He won the Overseas Final round of the World Championship at Bradford, beating local hero Kenny Carter twice in the process, and then won the next qualifier, the Inter-Continental Final at Vetlanda, Sweden. With Carter again pressing the self-destruct button that night, a bad crash ruling him out of the World Final at Odsal, it left Shawn as the biggest threat to Denmark's new stranglehold on the sport.

That's still how it looked after he'd won his first ride at the West Yorkshire bowl well suited to his expressive race style but, in the end, he had to settle for 10 points and fifth place.

"I always went into these meetings simply to race. I didn't think about winning them – the outcome was the outcome. I was never full of confidence. I treated every meeting the same, including the World Final."

Denmark tightened their grip on the sport's major honours a fortnight after Odsal by successfully defending the World Team Cup in California, where Knudsen denied Shawn a maximum at Long Beach. "The Danes were the guys of my time, super-fast and hard to catch once they made the gate," he says.

Kelly Moran was unavailable for the first WTC final to be held States-side but the brothers were reunited in Britain after the elder Moran ended his self-imposed British League exile in 1986, joining Shawn as Sheffield's twin spearhead.

On track, the brothers served up thrills aplenty. Invariably, Kelly would appear on the outside while Shawn, generally regarded as the less spectacular and steadier of the two, would be content to hold a tighter line. In reality, though, they could both go anywhere on the track, interchange in

**World Team Cup round winners at Coventry in 1987. From left: Lance King, John Scott (team manager), Kelly Moran, Sam Ermolenko, Shawn Moran, Rick Miller.**

the blink of an eye and extract speed from different race lines. They shared an almost telepathic understanding and their famous last race surges from the back were a sight to behold.

"You just know," was Shawn's simplistic explanation of their uncanny understanding.

And after racing had finished, they would keep the fun and entertainment going in the bar before ending up back at their rented homes, next door to each other in the Stannington area of the steel city, where they indulged in more revelry. It was hard to say who loved the Morans more – the Sheffield fans or the local breweries, because they did everything pretty much full-on.

"After one England v USA Test match at Sheffield we had some of the English riders and their wives come over to mine and Kelly's place. We made them a Tex-Mex meal, which showed that after racing against each other, we were all friends again.

"The Pine Grove Country Club, which we could walk to from where we lived, was our favourite place to hang out in Sheffield," says Shawn. "We spent a lot of time there – mainly playing snooker – and a lot of money too."

The Morans starred together for Sheffield for three seasons until Tigers' promoter Maurice Ducker, who had bought out Ray Glover in 1984, was in dispute with the stadium owners over a proposed rent increase and pulled the plug on Tigers at the end of 1988.

While Shawn felt sorry for the Sheffield fans at the loss of their Thursday night fix, he admits he wasn't upset personally to be moving on, even though he'd been promised a testimonial in 1989. Some riders can stay too long at one track and he believes this applied to him too.

Even at his peak and earning £35 per point, he had a strong feeling he wasn't being as financially well rewarded as most of his fellow No.1s in the British League at the time. There was a sense that he was being taken for granted.

"The problem for me, and what made it a little difficult to talk finances with Maurice, is that he was my main sponsor (as boss of A&E Transport) before he became the Sheffield promoter, so it was always kind of awkward when it came to doing a deal at the start of each season," explained Shawn.

"I'd thought about asking for a transfer for a couple of years before I eventually had to move on because the track closed. Things had been building up between us, it was minor details."

An indication of his status and true value around that time came with Ray Glover's revelation that he turned down a £40,000 bid from Poole for Shawn shortly before he sold the promoting rights to haulage boss Ducker.

Did Shawn feel undervalued? "Probably, yeah. But I just wanted to race and needed a manager to do my deals," he responded. "When Maurice pulled out, I had no hint from him that it was about to happen. Although I'd been looking to get away, I had good times at Sheffield. Kelly and I both did."

Shawn would have relished a switch to Swindon, the track he names as his favourite away venue in the BL, but he and Kelly both joined Tigers' northern neighbours Belle Vue. The good news was that the Aces' management, including Peter Collins, agreed to stage Shawn's testimonial, so he became the first American to be honoured with a benefit meeting when a large crowd turned out for his big day at Kirky Lane on May 28, 1989.

The bad news was that just two weeks earlier, he had turned up late by taxi for the World Long-track Championship quarter-final in Denmark the worse for wear after drinking one too many the previous night. Although he hurriedly pulled on his leathers and won his first ride at Korskro before finishing fourth in his second outing, he failed two subsequent breathalyser tests at the track and was excluded from the rest of the meeting.

He hangs his head as he recalls a day to forget. "Yeah, it was a late night and I had a good time. It shouldn't have happened. I regret it and was embarrassed by it. Lifestyle, huh?

"Some of us like to go on and I got a little overboard that time. It meant I still had alcohol in my blood system at race time. Yeah, I screwed up," he added, "but that was the only time drinking affected my racing. I did my partying *after* meetings."

The FIM were content to let the matter rest there but the AMA came down hard on their national skipper and banned him from all World Championship racing (individual, team and pairs events) for a year.

He appealed against the ban and with the case pending, returned home to finish second in the USA Final of the World Championship (behind Sam Ermolenko) at Long Beach. But after the AMA turned down his appeal, Shawn was withdrawn from the Overseas Final round at Coventry and replaced by Rick Miller.

When I met up with Peter Collins early last year, he recalled a time when Shawn rarely touched alcohol. PC said: "Shawn won an individual meeting we were riding in at Sheffield one night and after the presentation he just gave the case of beer he'd received as his prize to me."

The silver medal that never was. All smiles after the 1990 World Final before the FIM finally acted.

Practicing at Belle Vue before the 1991 season.

In issue 9 of *Backtrack* former Sheffield promoter, the late Ray Glover, recalled his dismay and sadness when he turned up at a local gym and saw that Shawn – described by Ray as the "greatest ever Sheffield rider" – had given up drinking orange juice and was knocking back the beer with his brother. Glover said: "I had the chance to sign Kelly from Birmingham before selling out to Maurice Ducker but I didn't want him and Shawn together in the same team."

The AMA suspension didn't prevent Shawn from leading Belle Vue, though, and the '89 season ended on a high note when he made another slice of USA speedway history by becoming the first American to win the British League Riders' Championship, staged on his home track. The tight and tricky turns at Kirky Lane were in stark contrast to the speeds generated at Sheffield but it was typical of his versatility that Shawn topped Aces' averages in the second season following their move from Hyde Road.

If 1989 brought its problems with officialdom, it got worse for Moran the following year.

# So close, so farce

**IN 1990 Shawn went oh so close to becoming only the third American, after Jack Milne and Bruce Penhall, to win the World Championship. He was just four laps from victory in the final at Bradford but, as the history books prove, he should not even have been there.**

Shawn was subsequently stripped of the silver medal he won fair and square that night and banned by the FIM from international racing for six months.

His crime? He had failed a drugs test undertaken TWO qualifying rounds and more than TWO MONTHS earlier in the competition.

He explained the bizarre chain of events that marred his best ever World Final campaign, brought him to the brink of premature retirement and heaped embarrassment on the FIM, who plumbed new depths of ineptitude in its bungled handling of the case.

"I rode for my Swedish league team Rospiggarna on the Tuesday before the Overseas Final and was crashed into by another rider," recalled Shawn. "I went to hospital and although they found nothing broken, I was in pain and my whole left side felt very sore.

"The doctors in Sweden gave me painkillers called Colproxamol and I took some of the tablets before I left Sweden. I knew the Overseas Final was coming up at Coventry on the Sunday, so on the Friday I phoned Maurice Ducker – my ex-promoter at Sheffield who was by then the BSPA chairman.

"I told him what I'd taken and that it had already entered my system. But he said it was OK to take them and that there was nothing to worry about as far as competing in the Overseas Final was concerned.

"And then about an hour later I got a call back from Maurice, who had spoken to Eric Boocock in the meantime, saying I was not to take the medication. I told him: 'It's too late, I just did!'

"I didn't take any more tablets between then and the meeting two days later. And when I arrived at Coventry for the meeting, I went to the track doctor and told him what I had in my system and I said that, if asked to give a sample, I was likely to prove positive. I even offered to pull out of the meeting there and then to let Kelly, who was standing by as first reserve, take my place.

"Kelly wanted me to ride, though. In fact, it was thanks to him lending me his bike for my last two rides that I managed to get through the meeting and qualify for the next round.

"I was picked to be drug-tested and, after the meeting, gave a urine sample."

There were 49 days between him qualifying for the Overseas Final (staged on June 24) and winning the next stage of the World Championship, the Inter-Continental Final at Fjelsted, Denmark, on August 12.

Even allowing for time to fully analyse the test results, it is inconceivable that the FIM were unaware he had given a positive sample at Coventry. So why was he permitted to take his place in the next round? Apart from allowing Shawn to compete in Denmark, they were also depriving the first reserve from Coventry the chance to take his place in the ICF.

Even more incredibly, the FIM then allowed Shawn – the newly crowned Inter-Continental champion – to proceed to the World Final at Bradford on September 1, with him still blissfully unaware that he had failed the test TWO qualifying rounds back.

Contemporary reports indicated that the FIM's Gunther Sorber was finally informed of Shawn's positive sample during a breakfast meeting with SCB manager John Eglese the day before the World Final. Maybe Sorber decided to gamble that the Belle Vue No.1 wouldn't succeed in front of 26,000 fans the next night rather than spark a major controversy by forcing him to withdraw?

Mercifully for the FIM, they were spared the ultimate embarrassment at Odsal when Shawn was pipped for the world title by Per Jonsson.

But the outcome couldn't have been any closer – it all came down to a run-off between the American and the Swede after they had tied on 13 points.

Shawn's thrilling Heat 16 victory from the back to defeat Jonsson, which effectively set up the dramatic run-off decider, remains one of the classics in the history of the old one-off World Championship. But it just wasn't meant to be for the Californian.

"Michael Lee prepared my engine and did a good job. It was like a little 'grunter' – good for getting out of the start and good on the slick."

There was talk afterwards that Shawn's GM motor was so finely tuned that it was set up to do a maximum of six races (five programmed rides plus a possible run-off) and that it lost compression as the meeting went on. Just how crucial did his second ride win prove to be because, after a false start, the race was inexplicably allowed to go the full four laps by referee Henny Van Den Boomen before the much criticised Dutch official finally ordered a re-start, which meant Moran's engine effectively did seven races?

Typically, he made no excuses. "Per was faster than me in the race where I passed him, so I knew I had to get in front of him in the run-off. I certainly didn't feel over-confident after beating him in our previous race," says Shawn.

"I didn't feel nervous before the run-off. Sure, it was exciting being in the deciding race but it didn't feel much different to any other race. I can't even remember if I won the toss for choice of gate positions – perhaps I did."

Shawn started from gate three, Jonsson off one. The Swede led by a bike's length going into the first turn – an early advantage he never looked like surrendering. "It was chase-time but he was just faster than me," added Shawn.

His disappointment at being out-gated in the run-off was compounded when he received his silver medal. Someone later pointed out to him that the back had been incorrectly inscribed 'World Team Cup Second Place'.

"It didn't matter to me – I gave it away," he says.

Moran suspects that the FIM deliberately gave him the wrong medal knowing what fate had in store for him at their Autumn Congress. They would also have noted that he produced a positive sample under similar circumstances at the 1988 BLRC that went unpunished. If they did know of his guilt, the bureaucrats in Geneva were still keeping schtum beyond the individual World Final.

Worse, they allowed the farce to drag on until October before making any public announcement that Shawn could have breached their regulations by using medication that was included on their banned list.

**Champions! Shawn holds the British League trophy aloft after Belle Vue's 1993 victory at Wolves.**

In fact, 16 days after Bradford, Shawn won his second World Team Cup gold medal when he skippered the USA to a hard-fought victory in the final at Pardubice. With his leathers lost in transit, he borrowed a set from a local rider and scored 10 points, although it was Kelly who pulled out all the stops by trailing last in his first ride before winning his next four as the Yanks pipped England by three points.

But there was still no mention from the FIM of his failed test at Coventry some THREE MONTHS earlier.

"The first I heard about any problem was when I got a call from the FIM to say I needed to appear at a hearing in Budapest at the end of October. I don't know why it took so long – maybe their phone lines were down! They could have kicked me out before the Inter-Continental. It was crap.

"I didn't want to get caught up in another controversy, which is why I informed the officials at

Coventry before the Overseas Final that I'd been taking painkillers. OK, it would have been a big deal at the time if I'd stepped down from that meeting at such short notice but at least that would have soon passed. Instead, I ended up getting the call to go to Hungary and that's when they banned me."

Shawn was joined at the tribunal by the AMA's representative Bill Boyce but the official was unable to save the US captain from a ban. "Bill told the FIM that I was telling the truth but I wished he'd said a bit more. His batteries were out!"

The BL-based American riders never did get much support from their own governing body that was more interested in mainstream motorcycle sports.

We can only wonder what might have been. Had Shawn got the jump on Jonsson at the start of the run-off or been able to force his way past, as he did in their previous clash, what a huge embarrassment it would have been for the sport had the FIM then taken the action it did in stripping him of his medal and removing his name from the World Final record books.

"If I'd won, that would have been something, huh? But I'm sure they would still have taken the title away from me," says Shawn, whose six-month suspension amounted to missing just the opening weeks of the 1991 BL season.

And when he was cleared to race again for Belle Vue from April 28, he did so using a British ACU licence. The BSPA/SCB wouldn't allow him to contest the World Championship rounds but at least he was spared those inconvenient compulsory return trips to ride in California, which cost the British-based American riders time, energy and money.

"I don't look back now and feel too badly about what happened. I'm fine with it," he says.

"I just wanted to race and could have ridden for nothing. I had a great time racing and loved it all the time. It would have been nice to have had a World Championship medal but it was all good for me anyway."

# 'Frightened' to race

**WHILE the more nomadic Kelly switched to Swindon, his final BL club, in 1993, Shawn belatedly agreed terms with Belle Vue to complete a fifth season in their famous colours under no-nonsense boss John Perrin. And it was some way for 'Shooey' to bow out of the Manchester scene, remaining ever-present as he led Belle Vue to the league title.**

"It was great to win a team honour because that was always more important to me than individual success. To me, that was just a pat on the shoulder. Winning with the team was the main thing and I remember Bobby Ott clinching the title against Wolverhampton."

Shawn's average had dipped to around the 7.5 mark and, little did we know, the writing was already on the wall when he took the decision to drop into the lower league . . . with Sheffield, who had been revived at second division level in 1991 under the promotion of Neil Machin and Tim Lucking.

He hoped a return to his spiritual speedway home would rekindle his fire for racing but it backfired.

Shawn says: "I was scoring bad points in the last couple of years of my career and needed to get rejuvenated. I made a point of not going to ride in Australia that winter, in order to get myself ready for the British season and a fresh start back at Sheffield."

But after just 10 matches in Tigers' colours and scoring 11 points against Oxford in what proved to be his last home match, he suddenly announced his retirement. The team was about to race at Newcastle on Sunday, May 1 (the day Ayrton Senna was killed at Monza) but he didn't go to the North-East. Instead, he made the phone call to Neil Machin that he knew had been coming for some time.

The fearless 'Miracle Worker', scorer of 4,000-plus point for Sheffield, who made it look as if he could perform the most intricate passing manoeuvres blindfold, declared he had lost his bottle.

"I was scared s\*\*\*less, frightened of getting injured, and I don't know why," he admits. "I just had a bad feeling that came over me. It had nothing to do with anybody else crashing or getting seriously hurt. It was just something that had been building up inside me for some time and I now wish that I'd stopped racing after the 1993 season at Belle Vue.

"Bobby Ham (the Bradford co-promoter) called and suggested it might help if I went to see a psychiatrist or talk to some people but it wouldn't have worked. Even taking a few months off wouldn't have made any difference to the way I felt. My mind was made up.

"As I went to the start before a race, I was thinking, 'I don't want to make the gate, I don't want to get tangled up with the other riders'.

Looking strangely unspectacular in faded leathers and fork covers, Shawn riding for Sheffield in 1994, just two weeks before announcing his sudden retirement.

"I felt so embarrassed and bad about the way I quit. I felt very guilty for letting down Neil Machin and the Sheffield fans. I wish I hadn't left the way I did but I just knew I couldn't go on. I'd lost it. I got really scared about racing."

Given all his success in a successful career spanning 16 years and despite not earning as much as many of his contemporaries, Shawn could have retired from speedway at the age of 32 a relatively well off man. Certainly, he should have been able to enjoy a comfortable lifestyle. For all the entertainment he had given fans all over the world, it was the least he deserved.

But he is the first to admit that he lived for today, never planned for tomorrow and was poor at managing his money. There were no property investments either in England or California.

And he soon realised how difficult it would be to start a new career on civvy street with no qualifications or experience of a trade, although a couple of old friends and former USA Test team-mates tried to help.

"After I'd been back in America for a couple of years, Bruce Penhall found me some work, through a friend, in construction," revealed Shawn. "It was indoor work remodelling buildings but I was still a rookie and didn't know what I was doing. Also, I didn't like being told by others what to do, so I only lasted there six months.

"Ron Preston got me a job moving furniture at a big department store. It was fine, I did my term for six weeks but, again, I didn't like people telling me what to do.

"I know you've gotta stick it out and bite the bullet but I didn't like it. At one job, they called me in at 11 o'clock at night. About half-an-hour later the boss came in and told me it was time to go – they had too many people.

"I got so turned around when I retired from racing that I didn't know what to do. And after I'd done my time racing in England I didn't want to hang around over there.

"I had to get speedway out of my brain for a while, so I hardly went to meetings in California either. And no-one tried to tempt me back into racing."

Shawn admits that his drinking had got worse towards the end of his racing career. Booze became an even bigger escape valve for him after he returned to Southern California and began living with his mum, who had divorced the boys' father when they were still at school. Shawn wanted to be there to care for her but, in truth, he needed someone to look after *him*.

"I dumped down in the high desert at Adelanto with my mum. There was no work going where we lived or money to take the bus into town. We didn't have a phone or a television until the state bumped up Mum's money a bit and we could watch a little TV. It was a really hard time."

Describing his depressing existence, he went on: "My routine would be to get up and walk to the recycle to earn a few bucks, which is what poor people from our area did for money.

"I had a friend called Ricky who ran a tyre shop, so I'd hang around there doing odd jobs for him. I'd try and keep my spirits high but drinking was my little escape. Beer gets rid of the bad feelings for the time being – until it wears off.

"I'd say my drinking got really bad from year 2000. I'd mainly stick to beer but every four-to-six months I'd knock back shots – as if to remind myself where NOT to go. I'd wake up some mornings not knowing anything about what had happened the previous night. It was hopeless but became a way of life that I got used to."

It was after knocking back a few that Shawn suffered a serious arm injury that still troubles him.

He explained: "Gary Hicks and a few others we know got together up at El Mirage, which is a flat dry lake about three miles wide. The guys brought some bikes down and there was also an Odyssey car, low to the ground, which I got into this particular afternoon. I made my own 'speedway track' and was driving round when I rolled the car. My arm came out and it snapped."

Shawn rolls up the right sleeve of his t-shirt to reveal scar tissue resulting from the bad break. In fact, he still wears a dressing over the wound to protect it from infection. "They could have stitched it up at hospital but it's called 'not having insurance'," he says.

Shawn had reached the lowest point in his life. "I sunk really low and hit bottom. There wasn't a lot of hope for me job-wise and my confidence slumped. I was just getting by from day to day."

# Everyone loved Kelly

**AT the same time Kelly's health was also deteriorating. After years of drinking and smoking cigarettes, he was admitted to hospital in Los Angeles at the start of last year and eventually died of respiratory failure in April 2010, aged 49.**

"I didn't know his situation until he was committed to the hospital," said Shawn. "He'd lived with Mum and me for two years but then he moved out and went somewhere else. While he was still with us, there were times when we'd go visit friends or maybe walk to the store and every so often he'd want to stop and take a little breather. It seemed no big deal at the time – I thought it was because he hadn't been getting any exercise," recalls Shawn.

"He went back down to where he was living and after a couple of years I started hearing different things. Then I got a call from Ronnie Preston to say that Kelly was in the hospital and it was looking real bad.

"Bobby Tocco and his girlfriend Alison gave us a lift to the hospital and it was tough seeing Kelly. He seemed OK but then it was a case of finding out what the deal was. Could he recover? If not, how long did he have left? I guess his lungs were filled up past the point of recovery, so then it was a case of making the best of the time he had left.

"It's sad, man."

Mike Donaldson created a Facebook page in Kelly's name, which rapidly snowballed to attract thousands of members from all corners of the globe as news of his terminal condition spread. At least Kelly died knowing that thousands in the 'speedway family' loved him.

"That was neat, a very fine thing. It was great that so many people said so many nice things about Kelly. Facebook brought a lot of people closer together and it was good for me too," agreed Shawn, who became a Facebook user himself.

"I don't know anybody who didn't like Kelly and I miss him so much. We were so close. I can't do anything about it, he's in a better place now, but every day I still say 'hello' to him.

"What I loved so much about him as a brother is that whenever I asked him a question, he always came back to me with something. He was knowledgeable, always had the right thing to say and he had a good memory too. Yeah, we'd fight at times just like all brothers do, but he was a little-big brother to me and we were good together."

No-one epitomised the natural team spirit the Americans exuded at meetings better than Shawn and Kelly. But captaincy was never their forte. Reflecting on his time as USA skipper, Shawn admits: "I don't think I got the answers the other boys were looking for and I didn't like telling a rider he was dropped from the team, as I had to when Ronnie Correy was left out of the '90 World Team Cup Final in favour of Billy Hamill.

"I wasn't a spokesman like Bobby Schwartz, who had a good way of saying things. I didn't like being USA captain at all. I just wanted to race."

Their selfless approach to their sport rubbed off on team-mates, who could always count on the Morans for the loan of a bike, a helping hand or just simple words of encouragement.

"Some people had to have the inside gate or the outside. But me and Kelly . . . we were like, 'let it go'. It didn't matter to us which gate we had," says Shawn.

Shawn and Sabine in March 2011.

Shawn at 50, chilling out at home in Pocking.

Had they been in any way selfish and ruthless, like many champions, they would undoubtedly have won more titles. But that wasn't their way, and it's a big part of why they remained so universally popular throughout their careers. They were more interested in pleasing the fans and enjoying themselves, on an off the track, than winning for the sake of it. And who can really argue with that?

The general perception among the speedway fraternity who marvelled at what the Morans did on a speedway bike in their prime, even when they were well past their best, is that they wasted their talent, failed to fulfil their immense potential and natural skill.

Shawn points out: "We did what we wanted to do and had a great time doing it. Titles and trophies are great to have but they are just things on the wall. To have won more, even the World Championship, wouldn't have changed us as people in any way. We enjoyed our sport, big-time. It was all good."

Shawn will be remembered as a terrific racer who cared more about his teams than himself. He saw it as his duty to entertain and race with a smile on his face. Approachable at all times and personable, he was idolised by so many supporters who appreciated the time he gave them.

"I'd like people to remember me as they saw me – any way they want. When I go, I don't even want a headstone," he says with typical self-effacement.

Shawn Moran's worldwide legion of supporters will be hoping that he will not be joining his sadly departed brother any time soon! He will be 50 later this year and I'm happy to report that there appears to be a welcome new sense of purpose about him these days.

You see, the 15-year-old girl whose bicycle went missing from the Pocking pits more than 30 years ago is now his girlfriend, soul-mate and, most importantly, his rock.

"Sabine saved me from my hole when she came out to California to see Kelly and myself at the start of last year," says Shawn, relaxing in the spacious detached house (with outdoor pool), where they live with her two teenage daughters and six cats in the small German town.

"She tried to contact me when Kelly became ill and it was Mike Donaldson who put us in touch.

**184**

I was a bit nervous about meeting Sabine again after all these years when I picked her up from LAX airport but we soon clicked. We flew to the Dominican Republic, where she has a holiday home, and I've been living here in Pocking with her full-time since last October.

Sabine, who runs her own shop supplying breeders and pet lovers with food and grooming services from purpose-built premises adjacent to the family house, is fully aware of Shawn's colourful past. She is a strong-minded woman and has clearly brought much needed discipline and stability to his life. A little latitude goes a long way, though, and they do both smoke, while Shawn is not completely teetotal. He is making a big effort to turn his life around, though. As Keith Richards would say, he has learned the difference between scratching his backside and ripping it to shreds.

"I still like a couple of beers but that's all I have now – usually no more than two per day and Sabine makes sure that's my limit," he says. "She's got me under control. I can't say that I exactly wanted it but I guess I needed it!

"This is the start of part two of my life. Let's see what happens . . . "

### On 2 Minutes With...
### MIKE CAROLINE

**Who helped you most in the early days?**

Alan Murray helped me a lot and so did Mike Fullerton and Roger Wright in the Berwick team – they'd seen it all before. All speedway riders are the same – if they can pass on a bit of their knowledge, they will. Dave Gifford was another one – he used to give me lessons on how to start because I was so bad at it and he was so bloody good! And Rob Grant's dad, Alec, used to tell you how to knock them off, because that's what he'd done in the 40s!

**Who was the best promoter you rode for?**

Mr (Ken) Taylor was one of the nicest people you could ever meet in the world and was very family-orientated. Davie Fairbairn, who replaced him at Berwick, was very good too. He used a pay scale where everyone was on the same rate, so it didn't matter if you were a reserve or No.1 – if you scored the most points, you got the most money. And if we were away we were on double money.

One night we ran Newcastle close and he said he'd pay us treble if we won – so that would have been £30 a point. Rod Hunter was very money-minded and he couldn't believe it when we told him we were on £30 a point! He kept coming over to ask us again how much we were getting – I think it put him right off his stride. And if we got beat, we'd be fined £10 for every point below our average we scored. So there was an incentive to do well.

**What was your favourite track?**

Shielfield Park. In 1980 my home average was phenomenal for a reserve – I was scoring about seven points a match. Of the away tracks, I liked Canterbury, Weymouth and Exeter.

**And ones you never looked forward to visiting?**

The worst was Crayford. My best score ever there was seven from seven rides. I ended up over the fence and face-first in the dog track on one occasion.

**Worst crash or injuries?**

I was knocked out twice. One time was at Newcastle when my helmet came off. The supporters didn't see my head and when they saw my helmet on the track they thought I'd been decapitated!

**Proudest moment or highlight?**

Winning the KO Cup with Berwick in 1980 – one of four KO Cup finals I rode in.

# GRAHAM
# **BROWN**

**A** TAP-DANCING Tony Childs is one of Graham Brown's abiding memories of his time with Boston in the 70s and 80s.

That Childs happened to be standing on top of rival promoter Ian Thomas' Rolls-Royce at the time, and had his steel shoe on, is probably the reason why it remains so fresh in the former Barracudas team manager's mind.

"We'd only just signed Tony Childs from Hull and Newcastle were visiting," explained Brown. "Ian Thomas was promoter of both teams and he wouldn't let him ride for us.

"Tony had already changed into his leathers and was ready to go, so they were ringing the BSPA up before the start of the meeting trying to sort it out.

"While all that was going on, Tony decided he'd do a tap dance on Ian's Rolls-Royce with his steel shoe on! It was funny but Ian obviously didn't think so. He went mad. He got his way, though, because Tony didn't ride in the meeting."

The 1983 Barracudas. Left to right: Billy Burton, Peter Framingham, Phil Alderman, David Gagen (on bike), Graham, David Blackburn, Steve Lomas, Guy Wilson.

Boston legend Carl Glover was an inspirational captain.

Brown, now 67, is living in retirement in the village of Algarkirk, just outside Boston. A local lad born and bred, he was a familiar figure at New Hammond Beck Road, where he held various positions within the club, including clerk of the course and press officer, as well as team manager.

He was heavily involved behind the scenes when the Barracudas swept all before them to win the Division Two league and KO Cup double in 1973 with a team which included the likes of Carl Glover, Arthur Price, Jim Ryman, Russell Osborne, David Gagen and Ray Bales.

He saw Robert Hollingworth and Colin Cook take Pairs glory for Boston at Belle Vue in 1977 and a teenage Michael Lee take his first steps towards global speedway stardom at the Lincolnshire track in 1975.

And he shared the pain of all Boston supporters when the club fell on hard times in the early 80s, ultimately leading to their demise in 1987. By then, though, Brown's connections with the club he had served so well had been severed, the legacy of a painful fall-out with long-time promoter Cyril Crane who had given him his first job in speedway in 1971.

"The first time I ever met Craney was when I went down to the stadium one afternoon in the middle of winter," said Brown. "He was six foot down, digging out a bloody great big trench. I asked him if he could point me in the direction of Mr. Crane. He said: 'I'm Mr. Crane'. I said: 'No, the Mr. Crane' to which he replied: 'I am THE Mr. Crane'. And that's how it all started.

"Boston was originally a greyhound track in the 60s and I used to operate the photo finish. I'd always been into grass-track, which was big in Lincolnshire in those days, so I had some knowledge of what speedway was about.

187

Steve Lomas, Tony Featherstone and Gary Guglielmi.

"I used to supply greyhound reports to the local paper and when speedway started, they wanted somebody to cover it, so I offered to do it. Nobody else wanted to, so basically I won a one-horse race! That was in 1971, so I'd have been in my mid-20s at the time.

"For the first year or so, I was a supporter on the terraces, I didn't go to any away matches. But then in 1973, when they won everything, I was PRO and became assistant team manager to Cyril. It was Cyril in 1973, '74 and '75, followed by Ted Holding and then I took over, so I was there throughout the glory years.

"That 1973 season was phenomenal. Boston just got on a roll, it was a close-knit community and it's entirely different to living in a city. Everyone got behind the speedway. Boston United were big in non-league football in those days and I remember their chairman complaining at the time, after speedway had been going for about a month, because the football crowds had just about halved.

"He also used to run bingo at the Gliderdrome, the football club used to own that, and Sunday night bingo was a big thing. But it just evaporated once the speedway started on a Sunday.

"The speedway crowds would have been in the region of 3,000 every week, which is mind-boggling when you think what they get today.

"The camaraderie in '73 and '74 was terrific but, obviously, riders move on and all that success couldn't continue. Ted had taken over by then because Cyril had become more involved at King's Lynn. I can't quite remember why now, maybe the Littlechilds were getting old, but anyway he took on more responsibility at Lynn, even though he always said he had no affinity with them!

"Boston was his baby. Cyril and Gordon Parkins had started it, along with Maury Littlechild who was part of King's Lynn and Allied Presentations at the time."

In 1975, the prodigious talent that was Michael Lee burst onto the New National League scene, topping Boston's averages with a 9.03 figure.

"That first year, when he was 16, just to see him on a bike was unbelievable," says Brown. "My outstanding memory of Michael was when Boston became the first team to giant-kill in the Inter-League Cup. We beat Hackney at Boston. In the first round, the National League sides got home advantage but in the second round we were drawn away at Belle Vue.

"It's always remained in my memory, the stature of Belle Vue, because if you go back to that era, they were huge. We expected to be tagged on to a British League match as a double-header on a Saturday night but as soon as the draw was made, I can remember the guy from Belle Vue ringing up and saying: 'No, it's a national competition, we'll give Boston all the respect we'd give to anyone else'.

"So they put us on a Monday night, which was bloomin' brilliant. And we went there and scored more points than four British League clubs did that season, even though we only got 24. And my outstanding memory of Michael? Seeing Soren Sjosten and Chris Morton team-riding, only for Michael to go blasting right through the middle of them.

"But things went downhill a bit for Boston after that. The success wasn't maintained but in 1977 we had all local riders from the outlying villages. Crowds were still healthy, even though we never looked like winning anything as a team. Rob Hollingworth and Colin Cook won the Pairs but around that time, it was the start of the decline, if you like.

"Up until then, it had been terrific, watching local riders who you would bump into in the street and seeing them develop. But when it was ailing, we had to get loan riders in. The big one was Gary Guglielmi. For two years, he was tremendous, absolutely terrific.

"But by then, 'Craney' wasn't putting his heart into it and it was fizzling out. Various other promoters took over until it eventually closed but I'd finished by then.

"Various people tried to keep it going but I know one meeting they ran when Kevin Jolly earned more than they took through the turnstiles.

"I felt a bit sorry for the promoters who went in after Craney because he would give them just enough rope to keep their heads above water with the stadium rental, providing the crowds were there, bearing in mind he owned the bar and got the takings. They were on a hiding to nothing."

## Banned from the stadium

**CRANE and Brown's working relationship ended in an acrimonious fall-out, which culminated in Brown being banned from the stadium.**

That didn't prevent him from continuing to supply match reports to *Speedway Star* and *Speedway Mail,* though, as he watched the action from a vantage point outside the venue.

"Basically, my energy went away from the speedway and I was concentrating on the stock-cars, who virtually employed me full-time," he explained.

"It all came to a head because the speedway coverage in the local paper was getting smaller and smaller and coverage of the stocks was getting bigger and bigger. The stock-car crowds were huge and we had a fall-out from that. I got banned from the stadium for being a traitor!

"So I went on the bank behind the first and second bends by the river – you could see the whole stadium from there, no problem at all. Craney kept putting announcements out about me, while I was there waving my programme at the crowd!

"What started with just me and someone else walking their dog up there on the bank soon changed. Within about a month, there were 50 or 60 people up there with me watching the speedway. Once, when we had a Sunday afternoon meeting, we had a barbecue and I think that really did it then – that wound him up big time!

**Robert Hollingworth – Graham was gutted to be banned from attending his testimonial.**

"It's all water under the bridge now, we laugh about it. Cyril always says now, in the cold light of day, that when he and I fell out, it was the worst thing ever. It was the beginning of the end for Boston.

"If the sport's not getting projected in a small town like Boston, it does go under. From having absolutely masses of editorial, content and space, it just got smaller and smaller.

"The saddest bit of it all for me was missing Robert Hollingworth's testimonial. I'd travelled the length and breadth of the country with Robert, I was his unofficial manager before managers were invented, and I did think Craney would relent for that one, but he didn't. That was a big disappointment.

"We had our fall-outs over the years, and certainly at the end. We always argued – sometimes I won, sometimes he did – but it was all for the good.

"He was a real old school promoter and I enjoyed them a lot more – people like Craney and Ian Thomas.

"Craney did a trapeze act, he had professional tuition for a long while and he also wrestled on a professional bill. It was all about putting interest into the speedway.

"I can remember the time Craney and Ron Orchard, who was the team manager at Peterborough, got involved in a little fracas at Boston, which ended up going to Belgrave Square (Speedway Control Board headquarters). There had been fisticuffs but people like Craney and Ian Thomas, they used to put it on because they were showmen. Things like that would be worked out before the meeting.

"One of my favourite stories about Cyril was probably the night he kicked the panther at Peterborough. They had this panther mascot, which they used to put by the start-line, and Cyril went and kicked it over. Oh, it caused havoc! But it was over-the-top havoc. What we didn't know was that someone who was disabled had made it and that's why everybody from Peterborough was so up in arms.

"Cyril didn't know that, though, and it was just a bit of showmanship again. He couldn't have been more apologetic. I think it was a Good Friday and they were back at Boston on the Sunday, so Cyril arranged for this young girl and her family to be treated like VIPs."

Brown looks back at his time in the sport with fondness, saying he "thoroughly enjoyed" himself.

"I met many lovely people in speedway and I got on well with a lot of the team managers, as well as promoters. People like Tony Coupland up at Middlesbrough – we had some titanic battles with them.

"Team managers were team managers then. I loved the tactics of it. One particular meeting sticks out at Barrow – not at Holker Street, but their second track at Park Road. Obviously it was 13 heats in those days, we were using rider replacement and we were six points down with four heats to go, so I shoved Gary Guglielmi out as a tactical. It would have been Heat 10, then he rode in Heat 11, he was r/r in Heat 12 and he was out in 13 as well. I said: 'Come on, Gary, we need 12 points from you here' and he's saying: 'I can't ride four on the trot'.

"I said: 'Gary, I wouldn't even ask anyone else but I'm only asking you because I know you can do it' – so he did, and won all four. Unfortunately, we still lost 41-37!

"I remember one night when we went to Mildenhall and Rob Henry slammed Gary into the fence on the first turn. You would have thought that was him out of the meeting. But he came back and got an 18-point maximum. God, he was so tough.

"Boston always had a good relationship with the Australians. Apart from Guglielmi, there was Jim Ryman in the double-winning era, going through to Steve Regeling and Guy Wilson later on.

"They came over with nothing but didn't expect anything to be given to them. What they earned, they earned.

"Guglielmi was one of the easiest riders I ever had to deal with. The nicest was Rob Hollingworth but the best captain I ever had was Carl Glover, without a shadow of a doubt. He was just so professional, he would always pass on tips and hints to the others.

"David Gagen was probably the most inspirational No.1 we had. If you wanted a big result, Gagen was the man. He was a good lad, David, and we did have some good riders at Boston down the years. Steve Lomas was another. He was the fastest man ever round New Hammond Beck Road. Sixty seconds dead. No-one ever got under the minute, which was a surprise considering how good the track was. It had a beautiful shape. It was 10 yards shorter on the straights than King's Lynn, otherwise it would have been a Lynn replica.

"There were also those riders who had plenty of ability but often didn't show it. Billy Burton was one. He had a tremendous amount of ability but he didn't always put it in.

"He was exasperating, one you would pull your hair out over. There would be others who would always give 110 per cent but probably didn't get the rewards, like Tony Featherstone for instance. He was fighting diabetes but he would give absolutely everything every time he rode."

Brown's stint at the Cudas' helm was at a time when the second division was at its peak, numerically speaking.

The National League in the late 70s often had as many as 20 clubs going to the line, which meant plenty of travelling around the country.

"It was a terrific era to be involved in, with some of the places we had to go to," says Graham. "I can remember the battles we had at Hull, in particular, at the old Boulevard.

They were tremendous and I remember Hull for being a good party town afterwards! I've always liked a drink, they always liked a drink and that's

Showman Cyril Crane in his prime at Boston in 1973, the year Cudas won the league and cup double.

191

Friends again, Cyril Crane and Graham Brown at a recent reunion.

how it was – you'd get the meeting done and go for a drink.

"I always enjoyed going to Peterborough too. It was a derby for us and always tense there. If you won, it was worth winning. The sort of tracks I wasn't so keen on were the likes of Rye House and Eastbourne, because I didn't like the smaller ones.

"After I stopped, I really missed the travelling. I remember one Easter, we were at Edinburgh on Good Friday, that was rained off; then it was all the way down to Canterbury on Easter Saturday, that was rained off; we were at Boston on Sunday and we rode; and on Easter Monday, we were at Exeter . . . for an 11 o'clock start. The logistics of Boston on a Sunday night, finishing at 10 o'clock, and then doing an 11 o'clock start at Exeter the next morning . . . incredible!

"At Edinburgh once, something had gone against us, I forget what now, but I decided I would climb up to the referee's box to protest.

"At Powderhall, you had to climb up a big ladder to get to the box, so I went charging up there to have a go at the ref, got to the top and opened the door . . . only to be confronted by the referee's bloody great big dog. I quickly decided I wasn't interested in taking it any further and shot down the ladder again!

"We were at Newcastle and Steve Lomas was so confident he'd got a third place on the line, but the referee hadn't given it to him. Steve was beside himself. It was only for third place but we stopped the meeting and I wouldn't let them carry on until we'd sorted it out. "They used to show the races on the TV at Newcastle in the bar. The ref was upstairs somewhere but in the end he had to go down to the bar so they could play it back for him. So we all watched the replay and it turned out Steve had been beaten by about a length-and-a-half. It wasn't even close!

"So it made me look a right prat. We'd held the meeting up just for that and they were on a curfew as well."

Nowadays, Graham maintains his interest in the sport through Sky Sports but only attends the occasional meeting.

"I retired through ill health eight years ago and just lead a life of leisure now. I go to the World Cup meeting at King's Lynn but I've only got my pension and I don't have a lot of money, so I can't go regularly. But I'm quite happy watching it on Sky. I don't think the speedway is any better these days but it does come over terrific on TV.

"I still keep involved because Rob Lyon lives quite near me and I speak to him. He started out on the terraces at Boston and I've known Rob since he was eight or nine-years-old. I didn't ever think he would become Team GB manager, so I tell him now that I must have been his inspiration!"

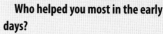

## On 2 Minutes With…
## RICK TIMMO

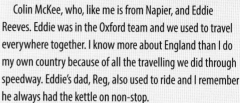

**Who helped you most in the early days?**

Colin McKee, who, like me is from Napier, and Eddie Reeves. Eddie was in the Oxford team and we used to travel everywhere together. I know more about England than I do my own country because of all the travelling we did through speedway. Eddie's dad, Reg, also used to ride and I remember he always had the kettle on non-stop.

**How did your career develop?**

I only ever rode for Oxford when I was in England (from 1967 to 1974). I was happy there. I'm a steady kind of fella and I was happy to stay there. Barry Briggs rang me one day. He was at Swindon and asked if I wanted to go there but I said 'no'. I liked to be true and faithful.

Maybe if I'd gone to Swindon I could have done a bit better. If he'd taken me under his wing perhaps he could have taught me a lot more. We all want to be World Champion but I was young and crazy. You have to have a life as well as dedicate yourself to the sport.

**Best promoter you've ridden for and why?**

Danny Dunton was in charge at Oxford for all but my final two seasons, when Dave Lanning took over. I was close to Danny. He'd been a rider, so he knew what it was all about.

Everything is about money now but when I came over I didn't think much about money, I just wanted to ride a speedway bike. But Danny was good and one of the deals he gave me was that if I got out of reserve and into the main team, he'd help me with my air fare back to New Zealand. Sid Knibbs was the manager at the time and I could never understand him!

**Which team-mate did you most enjoy partnering on the track?**

I didn't really have a favourite. Both Arne Pander and myself had a workshop at the stadium and I remember being partnered with him. He was a brilliant gater and I could never get out of the start before him. One night he looked round to see where I was and he came off. I ran over him – there were tears in my eyes because I thought I'd killed him. Luckily, though, he was OK.

Colin Gooddy was a good team-mate, too. One night when someone wanted to punch me on the nose, he was there with his steel shoe in his hand to defend me!

By Doug Nicolson ● Issue 57 (2013)

# SCOTTISH REFEREES: AN INSIDER'S VIEW

Doug Nicolson recalls his years as announcer at both Blantyre tracks that were home to Glasgow Tigers and the controversies that engulfed some of the referees with whom he shared 'The Box' . . .

**I**WAS intrigued as I drove out to Blantyre for the first night that I was being admitted into the 'Holy of Holies', the official's box. Would it live up to – or perhaps down to – some of the howlers I could remember from the past?

Like the evening at Coatbridge when the referee started a race with the pipe band still on the track. We soon found out what a Scotsman wears (or doesn't) under his kilt on that occasion.

Or the night at the White City, where the referee couldn't decide whether Tigers' Lars Jansson or Cradley's Tommy Berqvist was the cause of the stoppage. The debate went on for close to 20 minutes, with both team managers succeeding in persuading the ref to change his mind. The problem was getting him to stick to a decision. Obviously you can't please everybody.

It was quite an eye-opener.

Jack Cuthbert, the timekeeper, was an interesting character, often given to asking: "Who is out for us in the next heat!" It should be stated, however, that his role was limited to simply recording race times and he had no input to refereeing decisions. One night, he gave the time of 67.0 seconds for FIVE consecutive races. No amount of cajoling could persuade him that this was both unlikely and, indeed, wrong. Perhaps his watch had jammed.

There were no controversial incidents that night but I had already picked up on announcing the words "the decision of ACU appointed referee . . . " as a prelude to a call that was definitely not going to go down well with the home support.

Doug Nicolson on announcing duty at Blantyre 1.

There was the time Crayford arrived on a grey night with rain threatening. The referee was one E. S. (Edward) Chapman, who looked every inch a country gentleman in his tweeds and deerstalker hat. He brought his borzoi dog with him and it lay on a blanket in a corner of the box, oblivious to all going on around him.

Famously, a meeting at Berwick was delayed for about 20 minutes when the dog escaped courtesy of a disgruntled rider's boot.

'Chappie' was quite certain he wasn't going to start the match against Crayford until the stretchers were brought out of the ambulance and sited on the centre green. This caused quite a furore, as this had never previously been the procedure at Blantyre and ambulance staff were reluctant to have their stretchers

Mildenhall's Ian Gledhill gets in trouble but Charlie McKinna was excluded this time.

soaked as the evening progressed. Numerous calls were made to the box before the stretchers were finally brought out to fairly sarcastic applause.

By now it was raining and as well as the stretchers getting wet, the track was beginning to look a bit dodgy too. After a couple of races, it became apparent that Crayford weren't happy. Their team manager Peter Thorogood was gesticulating to the box, pointing at the puddles that were forming.

After Heat 5 was run and Kestrels' captain Laurie Etheridge had trailed in last, he immediately phoned the referee to say it should be abandoned. This obviously influenced Chapman, who rather quaintly declared that Etheridge was "a wise old bird".

Thorogood then came heading up to the box to add his tuppence worth. Timekeeper Jack Cuthbert, a kenspeckled character, wasn't for letting him in and made a suggestion involving sex and travel. However, the visiting team boss did gain admittance and pretty soon Glasgow promoter Jimmy Beaton had also joined us. He was firmly of the opinion we should continue.

A fairly full and frank discussion took place before Heat 6 was run but with rain continuing to fall, the referee then asked me to announce the meeting was being abandoned. It was the correct decision and the promotion were probably relieved that because the sixth race had been run, no readmission tickets were required.

# Mildenhall melees

**MEETINGS with Mildenhall were always 'interesting', with some generating more feeling than local derby clashes. The Fen Tigers were used to slick tracks and never hid their dislike of the deeper Blantyre surface. They did a good line that they had turned a ploughed field into a speedway track at West Row, while at Blantyre the process had been reversed. How droll.**

This perception rebounded on them, though, as Blantyre invariably took delivery of shale immediately before their visit. In 1981 Mildenhall were making a concerted early challenge for the National League championship and they rolled up to Blantyre with both teams joint top of the table. This was going to be some meeting – and so it proved.

The match started brightly enough with the pre-meeting introductions seeing Rob Henry, the Mildenhall captain, being teased about never having scored a point at Blantyre. However, Rob made

Laurie Etheridge: Crayford Kestrel and "wise old bird."

Steve Lawson unusually came down on 'his' bend.

us eat our words with a win in Heat 3. I would like to think that I mustered a modicum of sincerity to congratulate him while announcing the result.

However, things heated up after that. Heat 8 saw Richard Knight excluded after falling in a tightly contested first bend. Mildenhall weren't best pleased by this but their protest to the referee fell on deaf ears.

Then the start of Heat 9 was delayed while the visiting team manager gesticulated that a Tigers rider was encroaching into Ian Gledhill's gate position but to no avail.

When the race did get underway all four riders fell at the first bend. Astonishingly, from the home point of view at least, referee Smith excluded Charlie McKinna. The photo shows quite clearly that Gledhill had locked up in front of him.

But it was Gledhill that came off worse and while he was taken to the ambulance room for treatment, reserve Carl Blackbird was brought in as a reserve replacement. Both Mildenhall riders were at the starting gate but it seemed Fen Tigers' management wanted them to swap helmet covers for no good reason, other than in the vain hope that Gledhill would recover in time to resume his place.

Feelings were running high as I apologised to the crowd for the shameful lack of cooperation from the visitors for delaying the meeting. All good stuff.

Referee Smith seemed to agree with my comments by excluding both away riders for delaying the start. Mildenhall later sought to explain their actions by claiming there was a shortage of white helmet covers – Gledhill had one with him in the ambulance room.

After Heat 11, the meeting was finely balanced with Glasgow ahead by three points. Rob Henry took an early lead but Steve Lawson went diving under him going into the third bend and fell off, much to the surprise of us all in the box.

At this point I should point out that the box was of a fair size and it was standard practice for the referee to bring friends with him, as it afforded the best view of the racing by far. Off duty referees would also pop in.

**196**

Someone commented that Steve would never have fallen on that bend, his favourite, unless he had been 'fouled'. Surprisingly, referee Smith agreed with this rather unusual reading of the situation. Exactly how Henry had pulled Lawson off from the outside was never clear but no-one in the box was going to persuade him otherwise, that was for sure. In any case, it evened out the Heat 9 'boob'.

The resulting Glasgow 5-1 clinched the league points for the homesters, so Mildenhall finished the meeting under protest, a common occurrence in the coming years. Fen Tigers claimed that senior referee Arthur Humphreys had been present at the meeting and had been seen shaking his head at the things that went on. He may well have been there but I certainly don't remember him coming up to the box prior to the meeting, which was surely something that could have been expected.

Mildenhall were never backward at coming forward and put in a protest to the Control Board to have the result declared void and the meeting rerun. Unsurprisingly, they were unsuccessful in this quest.

The following year saw Mildenhall travel north again when well placed near the top of the league. On a fine summer's night, when the track was certainly well watered, they were again protesting about anything and everything. They were upset that the sun was shining and causing problems to their riders when motoring down the back straight. Strange that we'd had a good summer that year and in the preceding weeks neither home nor visiting riders had raised this issue. (It would later be announced that sunglasses were available at the track shop.)

Apparently, reserve Carl Baldwin had been sick in the pits after taking his first ride and the Mildenhall management wanted the doctor to rule him unfit to continue. This would allow him to be replaced by his fellow, and decidedly higher scoring, reserve partner. The doctor was unimpressed and ruled him fit to race on.

If my reporting of this outcome is a tad unsympathetic, it was nothing compared with some Glasgow fans standing just outside the box. They felt if Mildenhall's claim had been accepted, off-form riders would be throwing up in the pits with some regularity.

Like I say, feelings certainly ran high when the Fen men were in town. Baldwin never rode again that night and as a consequence, Mildenhall were obliged to track only one rider in the last heat.

Once again they were beaten in a meeting they expected to win. And once again they returned home with the huff. Mildenhall were sponsored by FSO Cars and the company had planned to present a trophy for the rider-of-the-meeting but reneged on this and took it home with them.

Yes, visits from Mildenhall were always warmly anticipated up here in the north.

# New track, new box

**BY the start of 1982 Glasgow had moved across the lane to Blantyre Celtic FC's ground. In a stadium that could only be best described as basic, the referee's box was a garden shed perched at the top of the terracing. Unlike the previous box at the dog track, it had only two windows – located on the front. These windows were always opened and the referee would often put his head out to get a better view.**

The timekeeper had commandeered the second window, which meant the announcer had to stand about four feet behind him. This meant I now had the worst view in the stadium. In fact, I couldn't really see bends one and four at all, which led to a few sketchy announcements. Well, that's my excuse and I'm sticking to it!

The referee's box was padlocked after every meeting but during racing there was no means of securing the door from the inside. One night referee William Freeland was having a tricky time, with most marginal calls – mainly false starts – going against the home side.

Aggrieved locals were 'growling' and after yet another upsetting decision, one disgruntled fan

**Simon Wigg encouraged his Weymouth team-mates to ride on.**

decided to come into the box and give us his view of the world. An unruffled Freeland very patiently answered his points and he was ushered out.

However, the following races brought more controversy and additional box visitors. By now the ref's patience was wearing thin and he demanded that the Glasgow promotion made the box secure. Promoter Jimmy Beaton did this by nailing a huge plank of wood over the door, which precluded any entrance . . . but also any exit, too. We had to climb out the windows that night.

Late in the 1982 season, Weymouth arrived at Blantyre amid heavy rain and it looked like the meeting would have to be postponed until the following week. But Simon Wigg, the Weymouth No.1 and captain, had a lucrative grass-track booking then and was instrumental in persuading his team-mates that they should ride. Jimmy Beaton, too, was quite keen to get the meeting raced, as it was going to be costly to bring Wildcats back from England's south coast.

Referee Bill Easton was quite prepared to order a postponement but, with both sides insistent that it went ahead, he agreed to start the meeting. He came close to abandoning it on two occasions, though, for rather unusual reasons.

The first was that he couldn't see the first bend due to spectators' umbrellas obscuring his view – Jimmy Beaton soon remedied that by moving the offending spectators. The referee's box was a glorified garden shed and the roof was leaking badly, with rain dripping on to the electric control box, which was sizzling. It seemed pretty unsafe and, again, the meeting was in jeopardy.

But, in these pre-Health and Safety days, a couple of polythene bags and some duck tape were all that was needed to save the day. I think everyone was relieved when the meeting was finished.

# Different views

A GOOD refereeing performance is one that you don't really remember after a meeting, so reflecting on officials from the past can depend largely on a few isolated incidents which upset you.

Starting procedures were invariably a bone of contention, with team managers from 'down south' often getting a bit hot under the collar about 'Tartan Startin' – which, if the complainants were to be believed, featured a rather quick release of the tapes, akin to 'green-lighting'.

But I never felt the starts at Blantyre were particularly dubious and would point out that the official on the button may well have come from middle England himself.

In his excellent *Confessions of a Speedway Promoter,* former *Backtrack* columnist, the late John Berry, was fairly scathing about a couple of referees with whom I'd shared the box on many occasions, Gus McLeod and Will Hunter. Both were regular guys, who would happily say 'hello' to you if you met them away from the speedway.

I was amazed to read that Gus had suggested that he and Berry "go outside with their jackets off" – a Scottish invitation to fisticuffs. Gus was always a calm and measured individual who made his point in a reasoned way. I can remember him phoning the Glasgow team manager, telling him to get his rider to sit still at the start, "otherwise he'll miss the gate", which got his point over without any real confrontation or threat.

Will Hunter apparently threatened to fine Berry for dissent if he shook his head at a decision. I would have thought John Berry would have been a real pussycat when compared to a volatile character like Glasgow promoter James Beaton.

Like I say, isolated incidents tend to colour your opinion of referees. In eight seasons doing the announcing at both Blantyre tracks, I shared the box with many referees. A few were aloof and occasionally officious. Most were pretty sociable and a few were decidedly helpful in telling me in advance that they were shortly going to sound the two-minute warning. This ensured the siren didn't sound while I was halfway through announcing some message.

All of them, however, were completely impartial, and I never doubted their sincerity even when coming to a questionable decision. I don't know what referees got paid in my time, but it certainly wasn't nearly enough. Every tight decision usually upsets someone and your good calls are never remembered.

Me? I wouldn't touch the referee's job with a bargepole!

## BRIEF ENCOUNTERS WITH… Keith Chrisco

**Which club(s) did you ride for over here?**

Birmingham in 1981. It came about after I'd ridden at Ventura one night, which was longer than other tracks over here in the States, and I did fairly well. Bruce Penhall asked me afterwards if I'd thought about riding in England and I said I'd love to, so he set it up. Barry Briggs told me not to go. He said it was too soon. I believe he was right. I had a few good meetings but minimal success.

**What were your first impressions of the UK?**

It was a little bit of a culture shock. I'm a bit of a beach bum and here I was living in Sutton Coldfield. I was used to the sunshine but in England it seemed to be overcast all the time. There were a few changes I wasn't ready for but Erik Gundersen helped me out technically, even though he rode for Cradley and I was at Birmingham, and Ari Koponen became a good friend. Without them it would have been a lot harder.

**What did you miss most about home?**

The food. I was used to tacos and burgers back home and there was nothing like that in England.

**How did you find the tracks in the UK?**

Birmingham suited me really well and I loved Belle Vue. I was happy on the bigger tracks – I guess that's why Bruce suggested I go to England.

**What was the highlight of your British speedway career?**

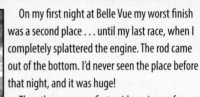

On my first night at Belle Vue my worst finish was a second place . . . until my last race, when I completely splattered the engine. The rod came out of the bottom. I'd never seen the place before that night, and it was huge!

Then there was my first paid maximum for Birmingham against Sheffield. Hans Nielsen was captain but he wasn't riding that night. Erik Gundersen came in as a guest, so I was paired with him. I even got an extra ride.

**And the low point?**

At Eastbourne, another rider – I don't remember who – took a dislike to me and took me off. He was bragging about taking me off. I broke my collarbone and I was out for five or six weeks. It was the first time I had ever been hurt.

**When did you realise it was time to go back home?**

At the end of my first season they wanted to sell me to Sheffield but it didn't happen and I just never got asked back. I struggled to keep my six-point average which I needed to be able to return the following year (it was 5.13 at the season's close) but I think the Control Board would have allowed me back because I had been injured.

**Any regrets?**

I think I should have gotten a little more experience in California before I came over. Maybe then I'd have done better. I'd only been riding for three years and that wasn't enough.

# PETER
# **ADAMS**

**T**WO empty seats in a Chinese restaurant changed the life of Peter Adams forever and led to him becoming the most successful team manager in speedway history.

It was 1970 and Adams' enthusiasm for the sport had just been rekindled by the buzz surrounding his local club's capture of Ole Olsen from Newcastle.

"I remember sitting in my back garden and revising for my university exams when I heard the bikes from the speedway track. I then read in our local paper about this new Danish bloke the Wolves had signed who was going to do big things," Peter explains. "I went along to Monmore Green to see him in action and, sure enough, he did live up to all the hype.

"At that time, Paula, my missus, and I used to go for a Chinese meal at a restaurant in Wolverhampton called The Good Sea after every home meeting. One Friday night we arrived there and the place was so packed that there was only one table for four available.

"The owner said we were welcome to take it but on the proviso that if another couple came in, we'd have to let them share our table.

"Ole and his wife Ulla were next through the door. They joined us at our table, we got chatting and it went from there.

"Over dinner, Ole told me that he wanted to build a large extension at their home in Holmes Chapel. Being a civil engineer, I said I could help by designing the building, producing the drawings for it and organising all that entailed.

"I believe in fate and that's what brought Ole and I together."

The Olsen-Adams partnership flourished from that day on. The Great Dane won the first of his three World Championship titles the following year and by the time he regained the crown at Wembley in 1975, Adams was well established as his full-time business manager.

"You could see Ole was going to be a very big force in the sport but he never seemed to offload much until he got himself a full-time mechanic in England to take care of his bikes and then I did everything else.

"I dealt with his contracts, travel arrangements, administration and even things like making sure his phone bill was paid on time, as well as taking care of other domestic stuff. My office was based at his house and I'd travel up from where I lived at Winchester to work from there at least twice a week."

At that time Adams was still combining his role as Olsen's guru with his engineering work at Tarmac (they later changed their name to Carillion) and it was a job relocation that had sent him from his native West Midlands to Hampshire's capital city. But when Ole left Wolves to sign for Coventry in 1976, he persuaded Peter to give up his day job to manage his affairs full-time.

"Ole was a great bloke to work for and be around – very firm, but very fair too," says Adams. "We never had a cross word in all the time we spent together, although I don't recall falling out with any riders I've worked with."

Olsen took advantage of his manager's civil engineering skills in 1975, when he opened the

Peter Adams with the Coventry Bees of 1977, his first season in team management. Next to him are Jiri Stancl and Mick Bell and in front (left to right) Gary Guglielmi, Alf Busk, Mitch Shirra, Ole Olsen, Alan Molyneux.

purpose-built Vojens track not far from his home in southern Denmark. It was Adams who helped him design the world famous circuit by providing all the technical spec and drawings.

His introduction to speedway came in 1962, when his father was pressured into taking him to Monmore Green. "He wasn't very interested in the sport and was soon bored by it but I badgered him to take me one night. I remember sitting on the barrier on the fourth bend and being mesmerised, completely intoxicated, by the racing and general atmosphere," recalls Adams.

"After the interval, they had handicap races in which the better riders started from behind the others. This enthralled me even more. I soon started going every week with my school mates – we stood on the second bend. It's funny the things that stick in your mind . . . they always seemed to play the Frank Ifield hit, *I Remember You,* between every race!

"My favourite rider as a kid was Pete Jarman, who was a snail out of the start but entertained us by scoring most of his points from the back."

Dudley-born Adams was destined to play a key role in West Midlands sport since he was a young boy and football, as well as speedway, consumed his passion. He was born on September 15, 1949, just before the great Wolverhampton Wanderers teams of the 50s became a dominant force in England and famously made their mark against elite continental teams, too.

"I was brought up in Sedgley," continued Adams, "which meant you either supported Wolves or West Bromwich Albion. We lived on the Wolverhampton side of town, so there was only one choice for me. That's also the reason why I went to Wolverhampton Speedway, instead of Cradley Heath, as a boy,."

The football Wolves were managed by the legendary Stan Cullis when young Peter, a budding inside-forward or winger, was offered an apprenticeship at Molineux. But hopes of pulling on the Old Gold shirt as a professional never materialised. "I thought I was a fantastic player but, unfortunately, the people who mattered didn't!" Peter laughs.

With his dreams of football stardom in tatters, Adams' parents persuaded him to pursue an academic career. He took their advice and went to Wolverhampton University, where he gained an Honours Degree in civil engineering.

"I lost touch with speedway for a few years while I was studying," he says. "For instance, I never saw Hasse Holmqvist ride for Wolves."

Then came that chance meeting with Olsen in 1970. And the rest is history.

Their partnership developed to the extent where, less than two years into his stint as skipper of Coventry, the influential Dane put his mentor forward as Bees' next team manager.

Adams recalls: "At the end of 1977 I received a call out of the blue from Coventry promoter Charles Ochiltree asking if I could meet up with him on a business trip to London. I thought it was something to do with Ole – who had joined Bees from Wolves in 1976 – but he said he was going to sack Mick Blackburn as team manager and asked if I fancied taking over.

"I studied the rulebook, although I already knew most of the regulations anyway because Ole was by then a riders' delegate on the FIM and, between us, we'd worked on rule changes that the governing body had introduced.

"I was nervous at first. Managing one rider is one thing but seven is a bit different and I was only 29-years-old at the time I took the job at Coventry."

He admits, however, that having close friends in high places helped smooth his introduction to team management.

"I never had a problem with any of the Coventry riders. They all idolised Ole and, in a way, they were frightened of him, so they all co-operated with me. As I was his 'henchman' and we were virtually an item, this probably made my job as team manager easier."

Coventry obviously responded well to the new manager's motivational skills, because they won the British League championship in 1978, Adams' first season in charge. And to cap a great year for the pair, Ole returned to Wembley to comfortably secure his third individual world title, led Denmark to their first World Team Cup win at Landshut in Germany and won the British League Riders' Championship for good measure.

It was Coventry's first BL title victory in 10 years, although Adams perhaps savoured his second title success with them, the following term, even more.

"In 1979 it all came down to the last match of the season, against Hull at Brandon, and when we won it to retain the title I felt particularly pleased for Ole. It wasn't only about Coventry beating Hull, it was him against Ivan Mauger. When Ole beat Ivan in the first race, it set the tone for a memorable night."

Coventry were unable to complete the hat-trick in 1980, slipping to fourth place, and with that uncanny sense of timing that has rarely deserted him, Adams sensed he should move on. While he had great respect for the CO and never suffered an ounce of interference from him, he couldn't resist when arch Midland rivals Cradley came calling.

"It was Bruce Penhall who first approached me out of the blue in the middle of 1980 about going to Cradley the following year," Adams reveals. "Dan McCormick and Cradley owner Derek Pugh were about to amicably part company and Bruce, having seen what we'd achieved at Coventry, wanted me to join them.

"Charles understood my reasons for wanting to move. Let's face it, no-one else was ever going to become the promoter at Brandon while Charles was alive.

A match made in Heaven. Peter has some words of advice for Ole Olsen before a race at Eastbourne in 1977.

"Ole was all for me going to Cradley, too, because he was coming to the end of his racing career and, having persuaded me to give up my day job to work full-time for him, he was worried that I might be left in limbo when he retired and disappeared off into the Danish sunset."

As it happened, Olsen went on to spend another three seasons with Coventry before finally hanging up his leathers at the end of 1983 without having added any further major domestic team silverware to his trophy cabinet. By then, Cradley Heath had succeeded Bees as the dominant force in British speedway.

"Derek Pugh didn't want to have anything to do with the running of speedway at Cradley, so it was an opportunity for me to become the promoter as well as team manager," Adams explained. "The Coventry fans didn't like it, though, when word got out that I was lined up to join Cradley. On two occasions my car was damaged in the Brandon car park and it got pretty nasty before I finally left there at the end of '80.

"Cradley fans didn't exactly welcome me with open arms, either. At first, I think they viewed me as a bit of a disciplinarian and wondered what they were getting. But they soon calmed down when we won the league championship!"

The flamboyant McCormick and the dour, deadpan Adams (or at least that's the public persona that has followed him throughout his career in speedway) were chalk and cheese. And unlike the ebullient Scot with the big personality and even bigger mouth, the much more measured and circumspect Adams delivered silverware by the barrow load over the next three seasons of an unprecedented trophy-laden spell at Dudley Wood.

"I wasn't the slightest bit surprised that we won the league in '81. I could see from the start of the year that we had the potential to win it," Adams says. "Bruce was flying, Erik Gundersen was advancing rapidly and it was just a question of focusing the talents of Phil Collins and Alan Grahame."

Adams had fans and pundits scratching their heads in bemusement when he recruited Aussie John McNeill and lower-ranked Dane Bent Rasmussen, who had done little to impress with King's Lynn, to fill two of the bottom end team places. They didn't pull up any trees in the Black Country either but their inclusion gave the new team boss the scope to track two superstars at the top end and a very solid middle order. "Besides, both John and Bent were good workhorses for us that year," acknowledged the man who made history by becoming the first team manager to win the championship with two different teams.

Cradley gained their first BL title by finishing an emphatic seven points clear of Ipswich but hopes of retaining the crown in 1982 suffered a setback at the start of the season when Adams found himself in a "stand-off" with his No.1 rider and captain, Bruce Penhall.

The popular American was by now firmly established as the best rider in the world, underpinned by his brilliant victory in the last Wembley World Final the previous September, and was the darling of the Dudley Wood crowd. Understandably, speedway's 'golden boy' wanted to cash in on his new found status as the sport's top draw but the recession of the early 80s had hit the West Midlands as hard as anywhere and money was getting tight.

Adams recalls the first big test of his authority as the man at the helm, saying: "Bruce and I crossed swords at the beginning of the '82 season. He came back from the States in March with his new American manager in tow – I can't recall his name – and they were asking for twice as much money as we'd paid Bruce the year before.

"We were adamant that what we were offering him was all we could afford, so I went to the BSPA and was granted a guest facility to cover his absence.

"Two days later Bruce tapped on my office door at the stadium and said: 'Where do I sign?' To be fair, he still rode brilliantly for us that season."

In fact, Penhall retained his World Championship at the Los Angeles Coliseum at the end of

Cradley Heath's first BL title winners in 1981. Left to right: Alan Grahame, Erik Gundersen, Phil Collins, Peter, Bruce Penhall, Bent Rasmussen, David Shields, Arnold Haley.

**Erik Gundersen wouldn't be lured away from Cradley Heath for arch rivals Wolves.**

August. It should have been another great celebration night for Heathens' fans to savour but, instead, it quickly became clear that Bruce had already ridden his last race.

There had been reports earlier in the year that he was taking acting lessons in Hollywood but when he announced on the podium in LA that he was quitting speedway, there and then, to take up a lead role in the US TV cop series CHiPS, Adams insists it came as a bolt from the blue to all concerned at Cradley.

"I didn't expect it and had no warning that he was going to retire like that," he says. "We had some meetings to try and persuade him to see out the rest of the season with us but he was at pains to point out that it was a huge opportunity that was too good to turn down.

"We were very angry about it and, without doubt, would have won the league again that season had Bruce completed his commitments."

History records that Belle Vue overhauled Heathens to snatch the BL title, while a revenge victory over the Aces in the KO Cup Final was hardly compensation for season-long endeavours that had turned sour in a most abrupt manner.

"We did consider suing Bruce for breaking his contract," says Adams, "but it would have been a messy business and there was no guarantee at the end of it that we would succeed in court, so we dropped it, rolled our sleeves up and got on with life."

Adams was faced with the unenviable task of trying to replace the irreplaceable, the sport's top rider and biggest personality – and so he did.

Instead of signing another superstar, he promoted Simon Wigg full-time from second division Weymouth, saw Gundersen slip effortlessly into the spearhead role, nurtured Californian youngster Lance King further towards world class status and, as well as relying on the ever-dependable Phil Collins and Alan Grahame, he signed the two best reserves in the land in Danes Peter Ravn and newcomer Jan O. Pedersen.

Without Penhall to lead Cradley, Adams confirms he took far more satisfaction from building what is still regarded as the strongest-ever British League team in 1983. "Bruce left a big hole to fill but we did it," he added.

Cradley, who had faded and finished six points behind Belle Vue the previous season, galloped seven clear of Ipswich in the race for the '83 title. They set a record by dropping only four BL points in the entire season – defeats at Coventry and Ipswich – and runaway victories were the norm, home and away.

As it turned out, the expensively assembled Heathens (Derek Pugh confirmed his track ran at a financial loss in its greatest ever season) were too powerful for their own good. They exceeded the maximum points limit to such an extent that they were forced to release two riders to rival teams at the start of the following season.

But by then Adams was long gone . . . just a few miles up the road to take charge of their fierce Black Country rivals Wolverhampton, where his love of speedway began and where his heart has always belonged.

There are cynics who still suggest that the shrewd Adams deliberately encouraged and manipulated his Cradley team to steamroller the opposition, knowing (as he did in August 1983) that he would not be staying on at Dudley Wood beyond the end of that season. I put this accusation to him and he responded: "There was no intent at all on my part to sabotage what was a juggernaut of a team that demolished almost everyone. I've never heard such a ridiculous notion.

"Derek Pugh was happy to pay the riders' cheques at the time and the way the team was set up that year, there was no stopping us."

Perhaps reminding us all that it was the rules, and not him, that ultimately caused the break-up of the all-conquering '83 Cradley side, Adams continued: "I couldn't exactly tell my riders to deliberately throw races towards the end of the season in order to reduce their averages. This accusation has recently been levelled at Poole promoter Matt Ford, so it's nothing new."

So after guiding Coventry and Cradley to two league titles each in the previous six seasons, not to mention KO Cup victories in his last two years at Dudley Wood, Adams sought another big challenge when he reopened Wolverhampton as sole promoter at the start of 1984.

Monmore Green had not reverberated to the sound of the bikes since the ill-fated 1981 season, when Dan McCormick failed to make a success of National League racing there on Sunday afternoons. Could Adams pull off a successful revival with his own money, instead of succeeding while Charles Ochiltree and Derek Pugh were paying all the bills? He was certainly going to give it his best shot – but with no help from any of his double-winning Cradley riders.

Adams reveals: "I often confided in Erik Gundersen because we were very, very close in those days. He and his wife Helle would often dine with Paula and myself at our favourite English restaurant in the Worcestershire village of Clows Top. We were there one Saturday afternoon in August '83 when I told Erik that I'd be looking elsewhere at the end of the season.

"I said I was going to knock on Ladbrokes' door at Wolverhampton Stadium to see if there was any possibility that I could bring speedway back there. I think he was pretty devastated and saddened by the news at first, especially as we'd won two league titles in three years – it would have been three if Bruce hadn't quit when he did.

"But I explained to him that I needed a new challenge. This may sound churlish, but winning all the time at Cradley had become a bore. I felt similar when I became a little stale in my third year at Coventry."

Adams further revealed that he'd hoped to tempt Gundersen away from Cradley to join him in his new challenge at their near-neighbours but the Danish ace decided to stay put and spend the rest of

**Before the wheels came off, Peter soon after taking control at Wolverhampton in 1984.**

his career at Dudley Wood. "I think he got cold feet in the end, although I don't blame him for that," says Adams. "He would have been hung, drawn and quartered if he'd left Cradley for Wolves but sometimes you have to make big decisions in life.

"I did phone Ladbrokes, though, and because they were having a tough time with greyhound racing, they welcomed speedway back at Wolverhampton with open arms. In fact, they let me use their stadium rent-free in my first season, and then at a reduced rate in 1985. "

Instead of Gundersen, the new-look Wolves of '84 were led by American star Dennis Sigalos, probably the best rider in the world at the time, who was signed from Ipswich in a complex deal that also saw Preben Eriksen leave Foxhall Heath for Monmore Green.

Adams now confirms what many inside speedway at the time already knew or suspected that Belle Vue boss Stuart Bamforth was oiling the financial wheels in favour of the new Wolves promoter.

"I was starting from absolute scratch," says Adams, "and I was grateful for Stuart's help. The stadium was like a bomb site when I arrived and we spent between £20,000-30,000 putting in new dressing rooms, relaying the track and tidying the place up generally.

"John Berry was in the process of selling Ipswich Speedway to Chris Shears before emigrating to Australia, so I approached Stuart about helping me to broker an agreement that ensured we got Sigalos and Eriksen at no cost.

"The plan was that Berry would sell Ipswich to Bamforth, who would in turn immediately sell the club on to Shears . . . but Sigalos and Eriksen weren't to be included in that deal, because they would be coming to Wolves for nothing.

"But the plan collapsed at the 11th hour when Shears couldn't find the money."

The bottom line is that Adams went into his first season as sole promoter trying desperately to cover a large shortfall of between £50,000 and £60,000 that he had expected from the original deal, via his agreement with Bammy.

"We went into the season very under-capitalised and to compound matters, we suffered about 17 rain-offs in my first season there. The damage this caused in financial terms was irreparable,"

With Dennis Sigalos at Wolves before his serious ankle injury in 1984.

recalled Adams, who had already been forced to compromise over choice of regular race-days. Wolves' traditional Friday night had to be conceded to Midlands neighbours Birmingham and so they opted for a new Monday race-day as the lesser of several evils.

The club suffered another massive blow early in the season, when Sigalos sustained a badly broken ankle. He'd ridden for Wolves in only 17 official matches before this season, and virtually his career, was over.

"The weather didn't improve much in my second year either," says Adams, who turned to another American Test star, Bobby Schwartz, to replace former world No.3 Sigalos at the top end. It couldn't stop the rot, though, and after finishing 10th (of 16 teams) in '84, the same position in '85 left Wolves just one place above wooden spoonists King's Lynn in the diminishing BL.

Adams was slowly drowning in previously unchartered waters, down among the basement boys, and his luck didn't change in 1986 as spectator interest in a top flight of just 11 teams continued to dwindle.

"The Royal Bank of Scotland in Worcester had supported me well in the first two seasons but because things hadn't improved, we continued to eat deeper into the overdraft and it became difficult."

Adams' mounting financial struggle – Wolves riders were owed their wages – came to a head in July '86, when he suffered an "awful personal blow" that would cause him to pull the plug at Monmore Green.

Peter has been nothing but candid throughout this interview and credit to him again for explaining the full extent of his problems during this very harrowing period in his life.

He says: "We had Sam Ermolenko (his third American big-name signing in three seasons) and his wife Shelley living with us and I can still remember driving home from the office one sunny Sunday afternoon in July.

"I got home and was surprised to find that my wife Paula wasn't there. When I asked Sam if he knew where she was, he just pointed to a letter on the table. She had left a note saying that she was leaving me. I didn't see it coming at all.

"I asked Sam and Shelley to leave as soon as they could and, great credit to them, they packed up all their belongings there and then and moved out straight away.

"I met up with Paula to see if she really meant what she'd written in her letter and when it became obvious that there was no going back, we obviously had to discuss what was going to happen with our two boys, Christopher and Thomas, who were just seven and five-years-old at the time.

"They both wanted to stay and live with me, so I virtually became a house-husband, cooking their meals and taking them to and from school and helping with their homework, that sort of thing.

"But as far as Wolverhampton was concerned, the break-up of my marriage was one problem too many for me to handle. I just couldn't face the task of promoting speedway anymore, so I had a business decision to make. Either try and struggle on until the end of the season, or close up there and then in the hope that the BSPA would collectively throw their hands up and say: 'We can't have this happening to a big club like Wolves in the middle of the season'.

"Luckily, my judgement proved correct, because that's when Chris Van Straaten and his consortium came in and kept Wolverhampton Speedway going. Who knows, if they hadn't saved it then, the track would have closed in July '86 and might never have reopened."

Adams can't recall the identity of every member of Van Straaten's promoting company that rescued Wolves 24 years ago but Tony Mole, who, like CVS, is still going strong in speedway today, was also a prominent figure in the takeover.

"I remember the moment when the takeover was announced. I'd phoned BBC Teletext to break the news and when I read it on my television screen I had a feeling of absolute relief," says Adams, who returned to Wolves as team manager under Van Straaten three years later and the successful partnership has happily endured to this day.

By liquidating his limited company, Adams was at least spared any further financial turmoil – "I didn't lose my house over it or anything bad like that," he points out – but the trauma of simultaneously losing his speedway club and his wife of 10 years was a devastating blow that left him reeling for some time afterwards.

He says he didn't suffer a nervous breakdown or have to visit his doctor for anti-depressants but there was certainly a period of anxiety before he got his life back on track.

"I had the local press turn up on my doorstep for several days after what happened to me at Wolves," he recalls. "My mother would phone up and ask: 'What is your picture doing on the front page of the *Express & Star*?' While I was finding out the name of the reporter and what he wanted to know from me, a photographer would be up a tree with a long lens and taking my picture!

"I didn't mention then about my having split from Paula – that information only dribbled out over time – but this was definitely the lowest point in my life."

# Back on track

**PETER had no inclination to attend a speedway meeting between his traumas of 1986 and his return as Wolves team manager three years later. Not because he felt any bitterness towards the sport, his priority was clearly to get his life back on track. He brought up Christopher and Thomas alone after Paula left and started a new career path that has led to handsome financial rewards in the world of finance and property.**

"I answered a job advert in the local paper but it was a bizarre interview procedure. Even after my first interview, I still didn't know what the actual job was. But I liked the people who were doing the recruiting and they liked me and soon it transpired that I'd applied for a financial advisory role," explains Adams.

The Class of '91, Wolverhampton's first senior league champions. Standing, left to right: Wayne Carter, Charles Ermolenko, Sam Ermolenko, Graham Jones, Ronnie Correy. Front: Scott Norman, Andy Phillips.

He used his sharp brain and his contacts to build up a strong portfolio of clients and his career away from speedway continues to flourish to this day. Adams is now employed by AFH, providing specialist corporate financial advice, but he also owns two companies himself.

"One is a company that owns and lets luxury apartments in central Birmingham, while the other has seen us build and sell a new housing development, from which I've made a lot of money," he says.

It was during his employment at his first financial services firm that he met his partner Liz. "She came to work at the same place as me in Wolverhampton as a financial services advisor herself and we've been together since 1990." The couple have a daughter, Olivia, while Liz has a son, Daniel, from her first marriage.

Of his own sons, proud Peter says: "Thomas is still successful with the Carphone Warehouse, while Christopher is a full-time truck mechanic by trade. He has been most closely involved in speedway through working as a mechanic for first Peter Karlsson and then Mikael Max. He's also helped David Howe and Nikolai Klint."

It wasn't until Adams received a call out of the blue from Van Straaten in the winter of 1988-89 that he returned to speedway as Wolves' team manager without the burden of running the show. "I'd had a complete break from the sport and genuinely thought my career in speedway had finished. I had no intention of going back, because I'm not a good watcher and feel I have to be involved in the thick of the action to enjoy it.

"But I was delighted to accept Chris' offer," he recalls. "It was easy to integrate again, as if the place had been in mothballs while I was away, and Sam Ermolenko greased the wheels for me with the riders."

Adams and the inspirational American star would forge a formidable partnership that brought the previously unfashionable Black Country team unprecedented success. "Wolverhampton has never been a moneybags club, so whatever we have achieved here has been done through hard graft and skill," says Adams.

"Chris and I are very close and on the same wavelength and we do everything together in terms of team-planning. There's not a day goes by when we don't talk. We bounce ideas off each other and rarely disagree. If we ever did, then obviously the final call would be his, and rightly so because he's the man with the money."

After his bitter and costly experience in the mid-80s, when he boldly resurrected Wolves after a three-year absence, Adams confirms he has no desire to promote again. His strength is his rapport with his riders, organising and motivating them, often to scale heights even they hadn't considered possible.

"It was fantastic to win the league in 1991 (Wolves' first senior league title, which they repeated in 1996, 2002 and 2009)," says the man once described as the Sir Alex Ferguson of speedway. Given his trophy haul, it's a not unreasonable comparison. But 'Fergie' built his long period of sustained success at Manchester United on a reputation as a hard-nosed dressing room dictator who ruled his players by fear. I prefer to see Pete Adams as more Arsene Wenger, the sophisticated French coach of Arsenal who goes about his work in a more calculating and measured way and who isn't prone to throwing tea cups around the dressing room if things aren't going his way.

Ferguson was a rugged centre-forward in his playing days with Glasgow Rangers while Wenger's modest playing career never extended beyond the foothills of the French third division. It matters not. The most successful team managers in British speedway have never slung a leg over a bike.

"I've never ridden a speedway bike. I have far too many brain cells to do that!" Peter quips, before quickly adding with diplomacy. "I must say that I admire tremendously what speedway riders do for a living. It might look easy but I know it isn't."

So what are the secrets to his unrivalled success as a team manager?

He's not shy in blowing his own trumpet at times, so I was surprised when he responded: "I'm no svengali. I can't turn oily rags into mechanics. The riders have to have something in them in the first place for me to be able to motivate them to succeed by more subtle means, to bring the best out of them and get them to think positively.

"If Tony Rickardsson was our team manager the riders would hang on to his every word because he's been there, done that and got the t-shirt. He would command instant respect from them, whereas I have a glittering history in team management and I try and make that experience work best for us.

"It's all about professionalism and organisation. Some teams turn up at a meeting, walk the track and that's it. We walk the track, too, but what people don't realise is that we've previously met up somewhere away from the stadium to discuss what is required. Before certain key meetings, for instance, we get the riders together at the Belfry golf club and talk about what we need to do over coffee and scones."

Adams also attributes much of his success to a close working relationship with his captain. And for years he had the perfect partner in Sam Ermolenko, the 1993 World Champion and Wolves legend.

"If you've not ridden a bike yourself, then I've always said that it's important to see management as a two-man job, which means my captain is always important.

"If, say, Freddie Lindgren has made a mistake on the track, I can see what the problem is but there's no way I can tell him how he should be riding the bike, so I'll say what I need to through our skipper, Peter Karlsson."

In terms of captains, Adams has had the luxury of working with the very best: Ole Olsen, Bruce Penhall, Erik Gundersen and then Ermolenko at Wolves since 1986. Which of them does he rate most highly?

"Ole was the best captain I ever had, although Bruce was perhaps a better rider than Ole. But in terms of that bit extra needed to get the result, then Ole had it.

"Overall, though, if you're talking about a captain who could motivate, had great riding skill and team-riding ability, you would have to go a long way to beat Sam. He is the one who had it all in his pomp.

"People forget how good he was at his best and perhaps you had to be as close to him as I was to fully see it. And for him to come back after the terrible injuries he suffered at Herxheim in '89 and win a world title makes his many achievements all the more astonishing. I was there in Germany that day to witness his crash and I really thought he would be finished as a force at world level.

"When Freddie Lindgren went about 40-odd races unbeaten at Wolverhampton in 2009, they started checking the record books to see if it had ever been done before. What people discovered is that Sam had gone something like 70 consecutive races undefeated at home years earlier."

If Ermolenko was the best all-round rider he has worked with, who did Adams regard as the top team manager besides himself?

He doesn't hesitate to say: "John Berry, without a doubt. He might now make the occasional snipe from the security of Western Australia but he and I got on well as two intellectual fellows and I liked him. He was a very good team manager. We've over-achieved in the past 20 years at Wolverhampton but John over-achieved for the same period at Ipswich in the 70s and 80s.

"And he gained his success without ever resorting to the use of guests. In fact, he was the only person to win a match by using double rider replacement for TWO absent riders! He turned up one night with only five riders but still won the meeting. It had never been done before and it won't ever happen again, because the rules as they stand now won't allow it.

"Cradley won four times in one season at Ipswich. On the last occasion, it was a fluke because one of their riders was winning the last race when his bike broke down. They had been desperate to beat us and when I think about it now, I can still see John trudging back to the pits."

We touched on some of the rules now governing speedway and how much has changed, for better or worse, since Olsen talked him into becoming involved on the inside at Coventry in '78. "You could always run a third part to this interview!" he suggests with a wry smile that tells you he has seen it all in this sometimes mad sport of ours. In a nutshell, and without getting into the politics that have cast dark clouds over British speedway throughout this winter break, he remains an advocate of the end of season play-offs as the best way of determining the overall Elite League champions.

"It's about entertainment and trying to throw a blanket over as many teams as possible at the end of every season. The situation needs to be addressed when a team like Poole can finish 50 points ahead of Ipswich and the net result is that Ipswich don't want to be in the league anymore."

Adams recalls the days, after he became a promoter for the first time at Cradley in 1981, when he served as a very influential member of the BSPA management committee. He doesn't miss that level of involvement now and, besides, he still attends many promoters' gatherings, even if he no longer has the power to vote.

"I chaired a 'rules committee' back then and many of the regulations I couched were adopted and are still in use today. The tape-touching rule introduced in 1984 was my brainchild. And the current points system adopted at the end of matches, which give greater rewards and incentive for the away team, was also my idea."

But as a shrewd operator who has always prided himself on knowing the rule book inside out and the best way to exploit it, he remains "miffed" that today's regs have largely diluted the influence of the most capable team managers. "What with fixed gate positions and the eight-point tac sub rule, our hands are largely tied but there is still some scope for team managers to make a mark. It's no coincidence that the same teams with management stability keep finishing at or near the top of the table at the end of each season."

And being at the top is still what drives the 61-year-old Adams on today. "My enthusiasm for speedway is undiminished," he insists, "and I have no thoughts at all of retirement. I'm still as ambitious as ever and it would mean a lot to me to win 10 league titles. I've won eight but two got away from me – firstly, when Bruce Penhall retired and Cradley missed out on the title in '82, and again in 1993, when Bobby Ott won Heat 15 for Belle Vue at Monmore Green to stop us winning the league. My team has finished second eight times, so those two extra league championships are well overdue."

*\* Some five years after this interview was recorded, Peter won his ninth league title, when Wolverhampton beat Belle Vue in the 2016 Elite League Grand Play-Off Final.*

*\* In the three previous seasons he mentored Britain's top rider Tai Woffinden and played a very influential behind-the-scenes role in his two Speedway GP World Championship victories, in 2013 and 2015.*

# Grand masterplan

**THE Speedway Grand Prix didn't replace the traditional one-off World Final until 1995 but the concept of an international series was conceived, tried and tested by Peter Adams and Ole Olsen long before then. Way back in 1978, in fact.**

That's when they launched their innovative Master of Speedway series, which saw the world's best riders compete at different European tracks for lucrative prize money – Belle Vue's Peter Collins pocketed around £10,000 for winning the inaugural series.

Adams recalls: "I had the idea in 1977 after I saw how Kerry Packer had revolutionised cricket, by assembling all the game's top players and taking them to play with and against each other in various top venues like a travelling circus.

"I remember Ole and I driving down the M6 one afternoon when I told him about Packer and what he'd done and I said: 'You know what, Ole, we should seriously think about doing something similar in speedway'.

"But I had no vision at the time that the World Championship would ultimately be run along similar GP lines."

Adams and Olsen took their show to Germany, Sweden and Denmark but their efforts to establish it on the international

Brains trust . . . Pete Adams and Ole Olsen planning for success.

calendar were seriously undermined by their failure to stage a round in Britain, then still the sport's nerve centre, where all the world's best rode every week.

"The downside to the Masters was that the BSPA would never agree to let us stage a round here," he recalls. "I attended an interview with the management committee at the Sinah Warren Hotel, near Portsmouth. I said to Charles Ochiltree: 'It's not quite the end of the earth but I think I can see it from here!'

"Reg Fearman was chairman at the time and I can still remember his exact words to me when we sat down to discuss the possibility of Britain staging a round of the Masters. He said: 'So how much money is there in it for us?'."

With Ochiltree's blessing, Adams and Olsen – his team manager and No.1 rider and skipper – hoped to stage a round at Coventry. "We offered the BSPA a flat fee – I think it was £10,000 – for full use of the Brandon facilities but they turned it down. I think they saw it as a threat to their own major individual shared events, although I still believe they were short-sighted in denying us the chance," says Peter.

Adams revealed, though, that he and Olsen changed the deal they offered staging tracks after the first year. "It worked the same way the SGP operates today. We took a set fee from staging promoters – it was around £12,000 per meeting – in return for delivering them all 16 riders. If the promoters made more than that figure through the turnstiles, then they kept the extra cash."

After Collins' lucrative win in '78, Bruce Penhall and Hans Nielsen won the next two MoS series but the Masters was scrapped and never staged again after a difficult 1980 summer. There was a costly abandonment at Linkopping, Sweden, which reduced the series to just two rounds (half the number held in the first year), and four riders failed to turn up for the last-ever round at Vojens.

# Britain's loss

**IT'S generally accepted that Peter Adams is the best team manager England never had. Since Adams entered management at Coventry in 1978, at least a dozen different men have managed England (or Great Britain) but only twice, in 1980 and '89, have the toothless Lions won the World Cup.**

So why has the man many regard as the ideal choice for the job always dodged the ultimate challenge?

"I've taken an entirely selfish view of it," he admits. "I've never wanted to manage England because I thought taking the job would damage my reputation as a team manager."

It was during the glorious spell in which he guided Coventry and then Cradley Heath to four BL championships in the space of his first six seasons as a team boss, between 1978-1983, that the clamour for Adams to be given the national job intensified.

"I didn't want the job because I simply couldn't see any prospect of England winning anything," Peter continued. "They did have one or two World Cup wins in the 80s but, by and large, it would have taken something extra special for England to succeed. The Danes held all the aces at that time and since then the Swedes and now the Poles have been on top. And even the Americans enjoyed a period of success."

Adams admits he was also put off by the dubious attitude of English riders in general.

"I'll not name names but I was involved in the Master of Speedway series and in the international meetings at Vojens and I wasn't impressed with the attitude of some of the British riders. I'm virtually tee-total myself but they were amateurish compared to the professionalism shown by their foreign rivals."

Adams certainly has no interest in a belated attempt to add some international plaudits to the many he has earned in domestic speedway.

"My life is already too full to even consider being Great Britain team manager," he says. "I'm out of the house at 7.30 each morning and don't return home from the business until 9.00-10.00pm, five days a week. And at weekends I'm busy dealing with paperwork. I have to fit my commitments with Wolves around that schedule.

"If it was a case of just turning up and filling in the programme, then perhaps I could take it on. But I would want to do the job 100 times more efficiently and effectively than that."

Peter telling jokes as after-dinner speaker at the World Speedway Riders' Association Dinner in 2014.

## Sweet-talking guy

**WHAT have Sherbet Fountains, chocolate eclairs and other assorted confectionary delights got to do with running a successful speedway team? Quite a lot according to Peter Adams.**

You see the Wolverhampton team boss is in the habit of dishing out sweets to his riders before every home match. "I'm deeply superstitious, as is Chris Van Straaten, and if we find something that works well for us, we tend to stick to the same routine.

"At the start of the season, I say to myself: 'If I wear a certain pair of socks or underpants on race day and we win the match, then I'll keep wearing the same things until we lose'. One year we went about 16 matches unbeaten with me still wearing the same pair of unwashed pants, so even I was grateful when we eventually lost – and so were the riders, because they weren't coming anywhere near me by then!

"These days we're into Rowntree's Fruit Pastilles – I'm even thinking of approaching them for sponsorship! – and it's got to the stage where the riders choose their own favourite coloured sweets depending on how well they rode the previous week. So there's a superstition within a superstition. For instance, Tai Woffinden won't ride until he's eaten some Butterkist Toffee Popcorn!

"We've tried all sorts of things over the years. We once won an away match after I'd bought a packet of wine gums on the way to the meeting, so we kept giving them out to the boys before each subsequent match until that particular winning streak ended. Since then we've tried chocolate eclairs, Sherbert Fountains, you name it."

Who is anyone to question Adams' smooth, sweet-talking approach? After all, he's by far the most successful team manager in speedway history, the only person to manage three different teams, Coventry, Cradley Heath and his beloved Wolverhampton, to the senior league title.

# RETRO SPEEDWAY SHOP

*Great nostalgic gifts for you, a friend or loved one*

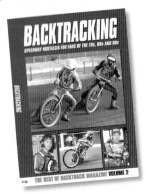

## BOOKS

### BACKTRACKING VOL. 2

**£16.00 (post-free in UK)**

IF you've enjoyed this book, then the follow-up Volume 2 is a must-have for your collection. Includes in-depth interviews with: TERRY BETTS, GORDON KENNETT, KELLY MORAN, OLE OLSEN, TONY DAVEY, MARTIN DUGARD, SOREN SJOSTEN, ALLAN EMMETT, JAMIE LUCKHURST, DAVE PERKS, STEVE FINCH, TONY CLARKE, BERWICK AWAY DAYS, HAMPDEN HORRORS, JOHN BERRY, etc.

## MAGAZINES

### BACKTRACK

Now in its 15th year, the bi-monthly retro magazine for fans of the 70s and 80s. Every 48-page full colour issue is crammed with new, exclusive and candid interviews and evocative photos from speedway's last golden era.
**Subscriptions (6 issues):**
UK £22, Europe & Ireland £29, ROW £37.

### CLASSIC SPEEDWAY

Our quarterly 48-page full-colour magazine, launched in 2008, with interviews and features on the post-war boom period and the two-valve upright pre-70s era.
**Subscriptions (4 issues):**
UK £16, Europe & Ireland £19, ROW £22.

## DVDs

Choose from our ever-expanding range of more than 40 DVDs recording the great names, races and moments from the 70s and 80s.

'Track Memories' series featuring: BELLE VUE, HALIFAX, IPSWICH, KING'S LYNN, WIMBLEDON, WEMBLEY, WEST HAM, HACKNEY, RAYLEIGH, CANTERBURY, SWINDON, BERWICK, NORWICH.

Plus: WORLD FINALS OF THE 70s, WORLD FINALS OF THE 80s, SPEEDWAY IN THE 70s, SPEEDWAY IN THE 80s, BRITISH FINALS, HISTORY OF THE WORLD TEAM CUP, NATIONAL LEAGUE HEROES, DEFUNCT TRACKS, etc.

Our series of pure 'Racing' DVDs features: PETER COLLINS, KENNY CARTER, KELLY MORAN, BRUCE PENHALL, MICHAEL LEE, CHRIS MORTON, OLE OLSEN, BILLY SANDERS and AMERICANS IN BRITAIN.

Individual rider DVDs on: IVAN MAUGER, MALCOLM SIMMONS, SHAWN MORAN, CHRIS MORTON, NIGEL BOOCOCK, MARK LORAM, etc.

**Check out all our various products by phoning 01708 734 502
Or go online at www.retro-speedway.com**

## RETRO SPEEDWAY . . . keeping great memories alive!